Cover ~~Photographs~~ *Is*

Left - ***Shapur I's victory relief at Naqsh-e-Rustam*** - This famous rock carving depicts Roman Emperor Valerian kneeling to ask for mercy from Shapur the Great, the second emperor of the Sasanian dynasty (224-651 AD). Following the destruction of the Roman army at the Battle of Edessa, this was the first and only time a Roman emperor had been taken prisoner. The unprecedented defeat was one of the greatest shocks and disasters in Roman history.

Middle - ***Imam Mosque of Isfahan*** - This early 17th century mosque is a national icon and UNESCO heritage site. It is famed for the beauty of its seven-color mosaic tiles and calligraphy. Prior to the revolution it was called Shah Mosque.

Right - ***Demonstration following the assassination of Qasem Soleimani*** - The major general in the Islamic Revolutionary Guards Corps and leader of the Quds (Jerusalem) Force had become a global anti-terror hero for directing the victorious campaign against Western-backed ISIL/Daesh extremists. He was illegally murdered by a US drone in Baghdad on January 3, 2020, sparking global condemnation for Washington's latest assassination.

Dedication

To the countless, countless millions of unsung and
ignored leftists.

Special Thanks

Special thanks to two websites: The Saker and The Greanville Post.

These articles first appeared in a serialised form on those two admirable websites, and without their help and support this book would not have been published. I extend my sincere thanks to all of their staff.

www.thesaker.is

www.greanvillepost.com

By the same author

I'll Ruin Everything You Are: Ending Western Propaganda on Red China

Contents

Foreword

Iran and its unique socialist system is one of the greatest untold, even hidden, stories of our era. Ramin Mazaheri's book "Socialism's Ignored Success: Iranian Islamic Socialism" is a detailed and very serious compilation of the author's analyses, published by various progressive outlets in the West and now re-edited into this powerful and thought-provoking volume.

Mazaheri is smashing to pieces our perceptions about Iran - one of the deepest, most fascinating and original cultures on Earth. Many foreigners thought that Iran can be labelled and boxed into established categories. "No!" writes Mazaheri. Iran can be socialist and religious at the same time. And it can be, and in fact is, on the vanguard of many modern achievements of our humanity. It is a proud, brilliant country which should be listened to, and respected, by all of us.

Mazaheri is an internationalist, living and working (for PressTV) in Paris. Part of his family is in Chicago and the other is in Tehran. He is at home in Iran, as he is in Cuba, or in the West. He clearly understands Iran as an insider, but he is also able to explain it to those who are geographically and culturally far away from it. He understand what points are missed by outsiders.

The book is passionate and angry, full of facts and unexpected revelations - precisely what a great book is and should be. It is perhaps the most fascinating work I have recently read about Iran. And it is a "socialist book", about a great socialist nation. It teaches and gives hope. It shames those who are trying to belittle and harm one of the most important countries on Earth - Iran.

Andre Vltchek
Author of many revolutionary books, including "Exposing Lies of the Empire" and "Revolutionary Optimism, Western Nihilism".

Introduction

In February 2018 the World Socialist Web Site (www.wsws.org) published a three-part series, and then a for-sale pamphlet, in response to my published criticism of their coverage of the December 2017/January 2018 protests in Iran. However, they went much further than complaining about my critique: their second goal was clearly to try to rebut a concept I did not invent but do often discuss - "Iranian Islamic Socialism". Their third and final goal was to revise the history of the 1979 Iranian Islamic Revolution to try and award all the credit to the Iranian Communist Party, which is something absolutely no Iranian – regardless of political affiliation – would consider remotely credible.

This book first appeared as an 11-part series, published by www.thesaker.is and www.greanvillepost.com, in order to: explain the undeniably socialist-inspired nature of Iran's economy, give the first leftist examination in the West of the Basij, and to explain how the religious-cultural roots of revolutionary Shi'ism ultimately created Iranian Islamic Socialism.

The series began to be published in June 2018, after I had returned from an inspiring stint in Cuba covering their presidential elections and the election of Miguel Diaz-Canel. Diaz-Canel was truly greeted with open arms by almost everyone I spoke with while reporting for PressTV, Iran's English-language television news station…of course he was not welcomed by the capitalist-imperialist West, nor in their many Latin American satellites.

But the main reason I waited to issue the series – which is full of facts, figures and analyses I would imagine nearly every Iranian is aware of, but which are totally censored, ignored and even unreasonably denied in the West – was to see what Washington would do with the Joint Comprehensive Plan of Action (JCOPA) agreement on Iran's nuclear energy program, as that would dramatically affect any discussion on Iran.

Unsurprisingly, the US maintained their centuries-old policy of not keeping their policies – they unilaterally and illegally withdrew in May 2018. Their European allies and satellites have not kept their word either: the unveiling of the special purpose financial vehicle the Instrument In Support Of Trade Exchanges (INSTEX) only facilitates trade between small- and medium-companies and, at the time of publication of this book, it would be perhaps not even be successful in its secondary, modest goal of breaking the blockade on humanitarian, medical and farm products. It will not, crucially, facilitate oil sales. Therefore, INSTEX does not to constitute a sovereign break with Washington's inhumane and deadly anti-Iran policy

The obvious injustice of Washington's decision has – I hope – increased receptivity towards new ideas which analyze Iran sympathetically, instead of so very, very antagonistically.

Some quarters are so reactionary as to be almost without hope. For example, National Public Radio (NPR), operated by the US state: In January 2019 Iranian-American PressTV anchorwoman Marzieh Hashemi was inexplicably arrested at the St. Louis airport and illegally detained for ten days. NPR used a very common and subtle propaganda technique Western media employs to cast doubt on anything Iran says or does: their headline read, "*Iran Says U.S. Has Detained 'Press TV' Journalist*

And Calls For Her Release". "Iran says", "Iran claims", etc. – that is not new, but putting "PressTV" in quotation marks – as if NPR was not even sure PressTV existed - that was a record low! If NPR was just far too busy interviewing US generals about foreign policy choices and diplomatic relations they could have just asked me: I promise – PressTV is undoubtedly a real, tangible thing!

The WSWS, however, is not at all in this same league of fake-leftist, fake-news. I was not at all surprised when the WSWS publicly denounced the US government and called for Marzieh's immediate release.

In the first two articles which set off our (sadly, no longer that typical) journalistic point-counterpoint (*"WSWS on Iran protests: Good leftists going bad at the worst time, again"* and then *"Iran protests: Reply to the WSWS response to my critique"*) I praised the WSWS for being on the right side of very many Iranian issues in a very brave and admirable fashion, and they were right again regarding the unjust incarceration of my colleague Marzieh.

Media like the WSWS and those who read such websites are my intended audience with this book - I feel that their opposition to modern Iran is due to their lack of the most basic facts about the socialist-inspired policies and practices of Iran. This lack should not be surprising: there is a Western media blackout on all things positive about Iran; there is also a Western media blackout on all things positive about socialism. This double whammy thus creates exponential ignorance regarding Iran since 1979.

I think that if open-minded leftists would simply become aware of these facts and these modern socialist interpretations of Iran's policies – many of which I'm sure are being presented in English for the first time - I'm sure that they would not be waiting breathlessly for the collapse of the Middle East's greatest bulwark against imperialism and capitalism, as the WSWS appeared to be.

It is urgent that Western leftists understand that the reversal of Iran's popular, democratic revolution would have incredibly negative ramifications for the anti-imperialist movement in the Middle East, and thus the global anti-imperialist movement, and it certainly would be the cruelest loss for Islamic Socialism, which is taken quite seriously in the Muslim world even if atheistic Trotskyism cannot even discuss the concept without resorting to insults.

And, of course, a counter-revolution in Iran would be a major blow for global democracy, as there is no doubt that the Iranian People support their revolution, constitution and unique system in a democratic majority.

Therefore, this series aims to include four things: a response to the WSWS and their contention that *"Islamic Socialism is a sham"*; a historical and structural analysis of the Iranian economy, from its unique never-colonised era of the Shahs to the modern era, with its totally unique (revolutionary) economic aspects; an analysis of a cultural phenomenon and institution which cannot be ignored, but about which there is almost total Western ignorance – the Basij; and finally an explanation of the religious, philosophical and cultural roots of revolutionary Shi'ism, the dominant popular ideology of the 1979 Islamic Revolution and the modern Islamic Republic of Iran.

This book seeks to bridge the tremendous gap between leftists in the Muslim and Western Worlds: The former has been oppressed, occupied and ruined by Western capitalist-imperialists for two centuries; the latter is often full of (not merely Islamophobia since 9/11) resentment towards any religion in governance, to the point that they believe Muslim leftists have nothing whatsoever to teach Western leftists.

The lessons of socialism cannot flow in such a one-sided manner; socialism certainly cannot succeed that way.

We in the Iranian government are in good company: they are unsupported by the WSWS...along with everyone else

4

who is not openly Trotskyist! Iran is thus alongside the vast majority of socialists today, and also all the socialist countries which have ever been in existence.

I do not seek to uproot Trotskyism from the WSWS or any person. Socialism is similar to Islam – it is perfectly logical, but it is requires faith: the Koran says over and over that faith cannot be forced on someone (this is why Islamic missionaries have been so much more gentle and so much less active than Christian ones, historically).

A common question is: if Iran is socialist, why is it not openly trumpeting it? Why isn't it the "Islamic Socialist Republic of Iran" instead of just the "Islamic Republic of Iran"?

The answer to this is contained throughout this book, but to summarize: socialism's forced atheism - which was the single biggest tactical mistake they made from a political point of view (putting aside the obvious human rights violation of the right to freedom of religious belief) - almost universally undermined the desire to carry the banner of socialism in Iran.

But this was not just in Iran – all over the world it is usually the case that the vast majority of a nation's population is religious; even in the 21st century, there is not a one country where committed atheists are the majority. The refusal to accept this reality meant that all over the world socialists wound up fighting against lower class people who should have been socialists but were not, due to early socialism's brutal, intolerant, deadly, fanatical rejection of religion. Indeed, the Nazis came to power in Germany in large part because they defended religion – socialism's radical "scientific atheism" earned them the enmity of not just the capitalists, imperialists, racists, sexists and other reactionary forces, but the enmity of many in the working classes. That is a problem which living socialists must remedy.

Socialism's atheism has not endured: as I will describe later, from China to Cuba to Iran to Vietnam modern socialists have rejected the failed, radical, intolerant war on religion. Religion be a positive political force. Iran proves this (to say nothing of religious forces in Cuba, Vietnam, etc.). Khomeini famously said that he could hear the bones of Communism break – indeed, for many people the lack of any sort of holy spirit produces a feeling of tremendous tension. Modern socialism must differ from early socialism and their anti-democratic failure as regards religion.

Furthermore, many in the Iranian government are obviously quite predisposed to crediting Islam for all of its successes; they repeatedly say things which are from the first page of socialism's texts – that Western Liberal Democracy is a failure, for example – but they do not follow that up with how Socialist Democratic structures in Iran are more modern, more democratic, etc. Stressing the Islamic influence in Iranian structures is not incorrect, but it is also not the complete story.

However, Iran's lack of trumpeting of the socialist inspiration does not change the fact that myriad of their policies *are socialist in conception, application and outcome*. Talk to any Iranian about, for example, the fact that the Iranian government controls (but does not own) essentially 100% of the economy which is not *petit bazaari*, carpets and the Black Market and they usually respond: "*Well, that's true, but....*"

"*But*" nuthin' - Iranians who deny their own "Islamic Socialism" only show their lack of understanding of socialism.

Socialism is not merely mouthing the "right" words but actually implementing policies which serve the ideology's twin pillars: redistribution (democratization) of wealth, and redistribution (democratization) of power down to the individual level as much as possible.

This book lays out many of Iran's policies regarding these two pillars for the very first time: I leave it up to the reader to decide the question of "Iranian Islamic Socialism" for themselves.

I will make this prediction: only the ultra-dogmatic will finish this book without acknowledging that Iran is incredibly socialist in many ways.

Maybe Iran is not "100%" socialist, but that is not my concern at all: such claims are evidence of an ivory tower perfectionism and idealism which has no place in journalism, politics, the real world, the lives of the average worker/citizen and many other places besides. If I wanted to hear that Iran is a failure because their streets are not paved with gold and their houses are not made of diamonds – I would have to talked to a disgruntled member of the Iranian diaspora! Such Iranians play no real part in Iranian politics precisely because they refuse to make real-world, real-time decisions; such non-Iranians likely choose to abstain from any serious role in the domestic politics of whatever nation they inhabit.

The reality is that many in Iran are perhaps not well-schooled in the ideology of socialism but they are in *the practice* of socialism. Thus they have much to teach Western leftists – socialism is an incredibly new process in the human experience, after all.

Therefore, this book can be an aid to both Iranians as well as Westerners: this is a book about "socialism in Iran", and not a book simply "about Iran". Indeed, this book is also about the West – their ignorance of post-1979 Iran. In these pages readers can, I hope, learn about Iran, the West and the practices of modern socialism.

The Trotskyists won't like that last part: after all, they reject the basis, innovation and success of Stalinism – "socialism in one country". This desire to insist that Trotskyism is the only "true" socialism is the exact reason why the WSWS wrote a whole pamphlet dedicated to the idea that "*Islamic socialism is a sham*" – they want to limit what socialism is to only their view.

Obviously, this is why they also reject China's "Socialism with Chinese characteristics", Cuban-style socialism, Vietamese socialism, etc.; they seek to downplay the socialist *bona fides* of any non-Trotskyist, no matter how great the successes which result from what are undoubtedly socialist-inspired policies. Trotskyism is thus not only totally unsuccessful but intolerant: Muslims have every right to build an "Islamic socialism" – to deny that is to show one's rejection of democracy in favor of replacing a bourgeois elite with a Trotskyist elite.

Western socialists will never win in their own nations if they refuse to learn from those socialists who have won.

Western socialists will retard the victory over capitalism-imperialism if they continue to not support the countries which truly do have a socialist economic and political basis.

This book aims to end the tremendous macro-level confusion regarding Iran by making its key socialist components crystal clear. Iran, I will prove, is the ignored success story of socialism. All that nonbelievers need to accept this reality are the basic facts of modern Iran, which are never relayed due to capitalist-imperialist aggression, and I humbly present them here.

Chapter 1
Only among non-Iranians could credit for 1979 be awarded to the Communists...

*W*hen it comes to differences we must start at the end and work backwards, reverse-engineering ourselves into mutual comprehension and cooperation.

At the end of all their objections, the problem is that no revolution exists or has ever existed which was good enough for the World Socialist Web Site to support, excepting only the very early years of the Russian Revolution. In many years of reading the WSWS I have never seen them express genuine support for the actual policies Iran, Cuba, China, Eritrea, North Korea, etc. So Iran is not alone to be a leftist country which is left hanging at the time of Western "soft war", as Iran certainly was in the winter of 2017/18.

However, what the WSWS does with incredibly admirable consistency is condemn the policies produced by capitalism and imperialism. They do it very well, and I'm certainly glad they do it. But we all surely see how such an ivory-tower, impossible-to-please approach produces imbalances, and thus a host of subsequent errors.

The WSWS also is politically partisan – they champion the Socialist Equality Party. Iran must be an original sinner to the WSWS, having had their revolution 30 years before this party's inception. I don't know what their plans are for starting an Iranian Socialist Equality Party, but they should definitely read this book – and not only WSWS tracts - before launching any recruitment efforts.

(And they should be aware that calling for the downfall of the nation is unacceptable and undemocratic sedition which will not be tolerated, much less accepted and then elected. This crass democratic concern – compromise in order to get elected in order to at least prevent capitalist-imperialist gains – has never been a strength of the proudly never-elected/unelectable Trotskyists.)

This chapter is the only one which liberally quotes from the WSWS's pamphlet – The Struggle against Imperialism and For Workers' Power in Iran: A reply to a proponent of "Iranian Islamic Socialism, available online for $3.50 (I appreciate the socialist pricing!) – all the rest focus on the unsaid truths, the unrelated facts and the never-heard leftist analyses of modern Iran.

Among their many other examples of ignorance regarding Iran, the Western left is under the false impression that leftist and socialist ideas are something which have not existed in Iran for nearly as long as in the West.

> *"The task of revolutionary socialists is to politically arm the working class in Iran with a socialist and internationalist strategy."*

Daste shoma dard nakoneh – thank you for your troubles! (Literally: May your hand not hurt.) But Iranian revolutionaries in the working class – and religious class, and lower class, and other classes – have already shown how very well-armed they are with socialist and international strategies.

By starting with a view point that Iran does not have ideas which are socialist and internationalist already, it is not surprising that the WSWS does not understand modern Iran – and since they can't understand it, how can they defend it or even praise it? This lack of understanding explains why so many Western leftists pile on Iran alongside the capitalist-imperialists whom they swear are not their allies. Never their allies…except when it comes to Iran?

The narcissism of small differences is seemingly the biggest obstacle leftists have to overcome, and a similar tone would also be proof of divisive narcissism on my part. What the WSWS may not realize is that Iranian Islamic Socialism is something which was created entirely without any help from me, but sprang from the Iranian working class. (Or the Iranian 99%, or the Iranian 99% minus the so-called "talented 10th", or the Iranian People, or the "Iranian proletariat plus their housewives" – choose your preferred term, but my meaning should be clear.)

What the WSWS series has primarily achieved done is: it helped educate people about the rarely-discussed role of Iranian communists in the 1979 Islamic Revolution. That is something…and it is positive. However, this series hopes to educate people about the uniquely Iranian concepts, structures and facets of history which were greater motivating forces in the 1979 Islamic Revolution than the communist Tudeh Party.

Let's return to the 2017/18 winter protests in Iran:

The reason for the first article in their series was to, "…reject their (the Iranian government's) attempts to blackguard opposition to rampant social inequality and capitalist austerity as imperialist subversion."

The WSWS has taken the reason for opposing the protests which Iran broadcasted to other nations as if it were the same reason which they broadcast within Iran. That is not the case.

This is just one of innumerable examples I could give which indicate to me that the WSWS wrote their series with seemingly zero input from any Iranian person – that is a huge, huge problem in journalism. The author is listed as Keith Jones, a member of the WSWS International Editorial Board. It doesn't totally discredit the efforts of Mr. Jones – people have the right to publish intellectual statements on countries they have never set foot in, and the outside perspective is often beneficial – but it is obviously a huge handicap. Again, the idea that the Tudeh Party was the primary force behind 1979 is totally ludicrous to any Iranian – no Iranian would even attempt to defend such a statement, much less write an entire pamphlet seemingly dedicated to the idea…but here we are. However, this book would be quite boring if I listed all the examples which indicate this apparent lack of involvement of any actual Iranian, and so I will drop the matter here; what is of far more interest is to discuss the intellectual ideas presented.

Yes, the government talked about the obvious foreign involvement – these forces, so incredibly (and immorally) well-funded by Western nations and their allies, are paid expressly to spring into action and co-opt any social movement for the aims of counter-revolution – but within Iran they acknowledged repeatedly and loudly that the economic reasons for the protests were justified. Few Westerners imagine that Iran has a vibrant media, but I can assure everyone that many journalists and politicians had a field day over the protests, raking parts of the government over the coals. The economic basis was so obvious and so well-broadcast that the government couldn't have denied it if they tried.

But Iran has been subject to an economic blockade for decades, and thus has been forced to tolerate economic protests since at least way back to 1992. Iran is not like Cuba which (likely due to their closeness to the United States) truly tolerates no protests at all, excepting the Ladies in White - the wives and other female relatives of jailed dissidents who silently march to Sunday Mass. I suspect that the WSWS convinced itself that the government actually attempted to pin all the blame on "imperialist subversion" because this was the main theme of the Western coverage of the protests. Not only does that ignore, once again, the point of view of Iranians, but it reveals a very typical Western self-centeredness ("we, the West, are the reason for every happening").

Too much Tudeh from the Trotskyists

The stated reason for their 2nd article was to remedy my failure to apply class perspective to my already-faulty historical analysis – faulty, because I do not give enough credit to the communist Tudeh Party for their role in the revolution, of course.

Well, I know a little bit about the Tudeh – my uncle was jailed by the Shah in 1954 for protesting on their side!

The bulk of their three-part series is devoted to describing Tudeh's involvement, and all I can say is... they have a right to focus on what they wish. I thank them for giving time to present Iran's history from a sympathetic perspective, even if limited in perspective.

But I am not much interested in retelling the history of the Tudeh Party, and this book does not do that.

Every Iranian knows the role Tudeh played; every Iranian sees the impact they made in government policy, even if they lost; and every Iranian knows why they absolutely deserved to lose, democratically, and despite the many decades of efforts of people like my Amoo (uncle on the father's side).

After World War II, the communists were always confined to two small groups – the students and the intellectuals. I think I can quite easily hang the WSWS with their own words:

"(Other Stalinist and Maoist parties in Iran) Like the Tudeh Party, they were taken unawares by the explosion of mass opposition to the Shah's rule in 1978..."

How could the communists be so unaware if they were truly a grassroots, embedded, mass movement in Iran? How democratic can a party be if they were not aware of the huge opposition to the establishment? This quote admits and illustrates just how out of touch with the average Iranian the Iranian communists were, and why democracy would necessarily forbid their victory.

To compare Tudeh to the communists in 1917 Russia or 1949 China is absurd – even at the height of the revolution Tudeh had perhaps only 5,000 members. Tudeh's main influence was informal – by influencing discussion for decades – and not in a real, grassroots, tangible, organisation-driven – and thus truly revolutionary – way.

As far as those students, it is critical to know that there were not many universities in Iran until after 1979. Therefore, the idea that the students came from a broad cross-section of society, as they do now, is simply not true: middle- and upper-class families were privileged in university selection… again, this is clearly not enough to win or deserve the democratic support of a nation.

We should not ignore the influence intellectuals have in shaping the talking points and water-cooler discussions of a culture, but during the Iranian Islamic Revolution Tudeh was a party for the intellectuals and not the People. That is not stating an opinion - it's stating a fact.

Now let's compare all of this with the mass grassroots presence of Islam and it should be clear how and why Islam was – and continues to be – democratically chosen to be Iran's primary revolutionary force.

It was the mosque which was the grassroots centre of revolutionary activity, and not the Tudeh Party's local headquarters. This is something so basic that to deny it would only produce eye-rolls from Iranians. Unfortunately, the very idea that "a mosque can be the grassroots centre of revolutionary activity" produces eye-rolls in Western leftists.

However, considering their much larger post-WWII role, their decades of political presence, and how they helped advance the political modernity of Iranians, it is commendable and natural that the WSWS should want to tell their history. But the facts show that it is easy to exaggerate their influence among the average Iranian who, polls repeatedly show, overwhelmingly reject atheism to the tune of 95%. Of course, most of the communists in Iran were also devoted Muslims – this is another reality many Westerners cannot handle intellectually, to their own consternation and discredit.

The communists obviously did not win – Iranian Islamic Socialism emphatically & democratically did

Given this fact of the Tudeh Party's lack of grassroots presence and support, it makes the WSWS's standard Trotskyist explanation of "when in doubt, blame Stalinism" seem woefully inadequate when discussing Iran:

"It was the vacuum of working class political leadership created by the decades of betrayals by the Stalinist Tudeh party that enabled Khomeini to cast himself as the Shah's most indefatigable opponent, and for he and his clerical followers to develop a mass following, extending from the bazaar to the urban and rural poor, between 1975 and 1979."

This falsely implies that Khomeini came out of nowhere in 1975 and co-opted the revolution like some sort of political opportunist. That is terribly, terribly inaccurate.

Apart from actually being implanted for decades among the working class, many in Iran's clergy had long ago abandoned the inherently pro-status quo quietism which is what the clergy – especially in Western Europe - practices today. This difference requires Westerners to use their imagination – Iranian clergy did not choose to absent themselves from their political process. The two are simply not comparable; the Western tendency to assume a sort of "Western universality" is not at all applicable, especially here.

Politically-progressive clergy in Iran were exiled,

imprisoned and killed pre-1979, and the failure of Western leftists to acknowledge that the clergy can play a positive role in political liberation dooms, I believe, their chance to successfully implement any of their policies which have nothing to do with religion.

And this is perhaps the ultimate irony, which Iranian Muslims have repeatedly claimed: it is actually possible to be Muslim and socialist! In their pamphlet the WSWS even cites the open marriage between socialism, the Tudeh Party and Islam…and yet they also deny that it happened:

> *"Caught unawares by the revolutionary upsurge of 1978-79, the Tudeh Party emerged, in the aftermath of the February 1979 overthrow of the Shah's regime, as the staunchest supporters of Khomeini, anointing him the leader of the "national-democratic revolution." Kianuri, now the Tudeh General Secretary, hailed Shiism as 'a revolutionary and progressive ideology which we shall never encounter blocking our road to socialism….'"*

Strong stuff from Kianuri, but the WSWS apparently imagines that the Tudeh's alliance with revolutionary Shi'ism was also one of political opportunism. In reality, it was the loving marriage of socialism and Shi'ism after decades of courtship. This ideological marriage – while foreign to Western experience and preference - obviously formed the basis of the entire 1979 Revolution.

Such concepts break the rigid brains of Western leftists, but if they will not take it straight from the mouth of the head of the Iranian Communist Party then they are truly not listening to anyone but themselves….

Iranian Islamic Socialism, unlike Tudeh, is not out of touch with the working class

Why are my assertions largely not new? Well, it's because Iranians think about God, and they also think about socialism, and the human brain does not explode by holding these two ideas in one's head at the same time. Combining these two ideas does not make Iranians hypocritical, nor doctrinally unsound, nor bad Muslims – in our context (open-minded people) we even pass for normal!

Iranians for decades had been discussing how to marry socialism with Islam via intense political involvement of the type which was the same as in pre-1917 Russia. Both revolutions were nearly bloodless at their triumphant ends, and the reason for that is because the anti-reactionary forces in both countries (and also the religious faithful in Iran) had worked hard for decades to win over the People. Neither of these were "10 days that shook that world" – mere explosions of violence – both were "many decades of struggle which finally shook the world".

Therefore, it should be easy to see why Iranian Islamic Socialism has taken such firm root, and why 40 years of near-total global opposition has been unable to dislodge it – it was preceded by decades of grassroots preparation. That is the only way revolutions can succeed and to not backslide into counter-revolution.

Iranian Islamic Socialism, however, does not pass for normal in modern global politics… and I'm very glad for that, considering what does pass for normal in the neoliberal, neo-imperialist age. This is good for Iran, but quite sad for the rest of the world.

What leftist readers need to accept – even if they disagree with the tenets of it – is that Iranian Islamic Socialism is not going anywhere, and that its failure would be a reactionary-inspired human rights disaster no less lamentable than that which befell the people of Russia after the fall of the USSR. The ripple effects on the Middle East and Muslim Worlds would be overwhelmingly negative. And, LOL, it would certainly not pave the way to make Iran

Trotskyism's very long-awaited first victory.

The third part of the WSWS series is mostly dedicated to Trotskyist propaganda against modern Iran, relaying unproven conspiracy theories to accuse Iran of secretly working with imperialists like Washington. That won't play in Peoria nor Palestine, and I already rebutted such nonsense in my reply to their critique of my initial critique. And, in something as regular as Old Faithful, the final part of nearly every WSWS article does (and I admire their ideological discipline) – it trumpets a call for Trotskyist revolution.

This book does not follow a party line, but rather creates a new one by analyzing Iran from a very rarely-heard perspective. We can now dispense with the WSWS.

Why do I use the phrase 'Iranian Islamic Socialism'?

This is not haphazard – it is in this particular order for a reason.

"Iranian": many people have a mistaken idea that Iran aims to follow the Koran to the letter in every instance, and that Iranian society aims to be an exact replication of the time of Prophet Mohammed. That is known as "Salafism". However, Iran is openly and actively fighting against Salafism at home and abroad – there is no doubt about this anti-Salafist stance whatsoever.

Incredibly importantly, what they fail to realize is that Khomeini was unequivocal: the imperatives of the state must take precedence over the needs of Islam.

It was made completely clear: good temporal governance on behalf of the inhabitants of the country must take precedence over Shariah, and may God forgive us. This debate was public and went on for years during and after the

Iranian Cultural Revolution (one of only two state-sponsored Cultural Revolutions ever) and yet it is still not properly understood outside of Iran.

In these public and democratic debates over what the new Iran "should be", what won out was an idea often associated with Abdolkarim Soroush: "religion" and "religious knowledge" are two different things; the former is sacred and immutable, the latter evolves and changes so that societal solutions can be found. Make no mistake: It was democratically decided that the Islamic Republic of Iran would be based on the latter – religious knowledge, which is used to promote democracy, pluralism, equality and Islam.

Many of the more religious did not like making religious injunctions secondary to politics, but the idea of a government designed to promote only Islam simply did not democratically win out, just as the Tudeh did not win out. It does not mean neither of these groups' ideas are not present, however, as Iran is a democracy – religious proponents are well-represented in Iran, obviously, and so are socialist ideas, perhaps less obviously to non-Iranians.

Are there traditionalists who want the former? Yes: some want "Islamic Iranian Socialism", but they have not prevailed.

The 7th century Revolution of Islam was a political revolution in large part because Prophet Mohammad ended tribalism, and by extension nationalism. Thus, many others want just "Islamic Socialism".

But these two groups have a very tough convincing job to do, considering that results of the transparent democratic debate, and the fact that Khomeini and his many supporters opposed them, and because Iran has now had decades of subsequent hardening of this "Iran is based on religious knowledge and not religion" concept. However, they certainly have many supporters among the Iranian people and play a role in the spectrum of political discourse in Iran.

I realize that, on a global level, the idea that some Iranians say that Iran is insufficiently Islamic may seem surprising, but on a domestic cultural level it remains a genuine issue. Complaining about the lack of religious feeling among Iran's public servants is also a guaranteed-acceptable method/safety valve for Iranians to criticise their government whenever they are having a bad day!

Many Westerners have not taken this long-standing reality into account when they talk about Iran's government, but the primacy of "Iranian" should radically reorient anyone who doesn't realize what is the main priority of Iran's Islamic and democratic government: the Iranian nation.

Therefore we see that Iran is definitely "patriotic" above all, like China or Cuba, and the opposite of the formerly independent nations of the European Union and especially the Eurozone. And, of course, we should remember that those who want "Islamic" first are not anti-Iran in the slightest – they just want more religion in Iran.

"Islamic" comes second, because we see that it has clearly and democratically been placed there.

We should now be able to understand why Iran's system is truly not the fundamentalist, everything-is-religion government it is portrayed as – it is a modern system built upon the most modern ideas of governmental structure available in 1979, and all while being hugely inspired by Islam.

"Socialism" is the final term, and the most contentious, mainly because socialism has yet to shake its original association with destructive, undemocratic, state-enforced atheism.

Socialism is clearly based on two fundamental precepts: empowering the lower classes and average person with democratic rights and tools of political influence, and massive state-organised economic redistribution. Thus, socialism is both a structure of government and an economic policy. This book will prove that Iran meets the definitions of a socialist society.

An overview of what is to come in this book

Chapter 2, How Iran Got Economically Socialist, and then Islamic Socialist explains Iran's very atypical economic-historical development.

The reality is that some of the Tudeh Party's socialist ideas were indeed integrated into policy – the proof is quite easily found in the pudding, which is Iran's state-controlled redistribution-and-not-profit-oriented economy.

Iran's economy is something which is rarely appreciated properly and not only because the WSWS and others purposely obscure accepted definitions: it is because Iran has a unique (revolutionary) structure which is just not that easily comprehended. This is the basis of Chapter 3, What privatisation in Iran? or Definitely not THAT privatisation.

I do not believe that Iran – nor China, nor Cuba, nor a few others – can be talked about as "bourgeois" states when they have had and have sustained anti-bourgeois revolutions: new rules regarding discussion of them must therefore apply. I think those nations are revolutionary because they have fundamentally changed their class structures.

This is the reason why I have included something which I think may be unprecedented in a Western language book: an objective analysis of the Basij.

Just as few Westerners know or can explain why or how the 1979 Revolution incredibly put 10-15% of the entire Iranian economy in the obviously anti-capitalist hands of charity (the bonyads, or state charity cooperatives, explained in Chapter 2), I think it is impossible to understand Iran without understanding the 10+ million member organization, the Basij. The WSWS series made no mention of it at all. I devote Chapters 4-7 to them.

The reason I think it's so important to talk about the Basij now is: it could reduce the chances of war. Non-Iranians need to realize that any foreign invasion of Iran implies the mass, grassroots involvement of the Basij. Certainly not all of them, as only a small percentage of this volunteer group are involved daily in security operations (contrary to popular belief), but very certainly foreign invasion would involve a lot of them. I think that if people learned about the solidity of this group – whether one condones or condemns them, and I remain 100% objectively neutral in my examination and refuse to either condone or condemn them – one must simply accept that they are a huge force to be reckoned with in any war.

However, there is quite nearly zero scholarship of the Basij. What little exists is sensationalist nonsense or based on the decades-bygone birth of the Basij during wartime. Hopefully these four chapters clarify and demystify the Basij, and it is certainly the first leftist analysis of the Basij ever available in the West.

However, not everyone wants to understand modern Iran via discussing in detail their economy and their socio-political institutions. Therefore, Chapters 8 and 9 attempt to describe Iranian Islamic Socialism via religion and culture.

Chapter 8 talks about the "Cultural Revolution" of Imam Ali and Chapter 9 talks about the "Permanent Revolution" of Imam Hossein, and makes historical-political examinations of their lives and messages, which came during the context of the Revolution of Islam.

Islam, unlike Christianity, was indeed a sweeping political revolution: therefore, these two religious figures of the early Islamic era can also be viewed in a completely areligious and historico-political fashion; the post-revolutionary culture & era, initiated by Prophet Mohammad, is thus actually (and necessarily) very similar to the post-revolution eras of other massive revolutions such as the Russian & Chinese revolutions.

The ideas represented by Ali and Hossein are so firmly

lodged in Iran's collective unconscious and current political reality that, like the Basij, they simply must be understood in order to understand how Iran arrived at its governmental policies: prioritizing Socialist Democracy over Liberal Democracy and socialist economics over capitalist economics certainly explains a lot, but not all.

Also, Imams Ali and Hossein provide superb revolutionary models for non-Muslims, too, so Western leftists would be quite enriched to learn about them, I am certain.

Chapter 10 explains the Iranian Islamic Revolution via pop culture. I discuss the greatest Iranian movie of all-time – The Death of Yazdgerd – which is also the greatest political movie of all-time.

That is a very bold statement, but merited. If I may say so humbly: Iran is widely considered perhaps the greatest pound-for-pound cinema-producing nation. Therefore, if we also consider that Iran has produced one of the greatest political human dramas since the advent of cinema – and in the last 40 years - is it not quite possible that they also produced the greatest political drama within cinema?

The movie is a relentless moral machine-gunning of the institution of monarchy – something which every society can relate to, adding to its genius – with obvious calls for Socialist Democracy and not bourgeois, Western Liberal Democracy. It is truly unparalleled in film, and it is even available with English subtitles for free on YouTube. For a fascinating and whirlwind two hours – and to see what your ancestors endured (unless you have royal lineage) – I encourage you to watch it.

The final chapter discusses the future of Iranian Islamic Socialism in the context of a post-JCPOA world.

Chapter 2
How Iran got economically socialist, and then Islamic socialist

I am finished with rebutting the WSWS, but I will occasionally refer to them as a springboard to other ideas:

> *"Ramin Mazaheri, a foreign correspondent for Iran's PressTV, posted a blog accusing the World Socialist Web Site of betraying its 'socialist principles' and aiding imperialism, because we welcomed the working-class opposition to Iran's capitalist government..."*

From nearly the beginning of the WSWS's 3-part rebuttal to my criticism of them is the refusal, or inability, to understand that Iran's government cannot accurately qualify as "capitalist". I don't mind when people don't understand the nature of the Iranian republic and its modern democratic structure (which combines Islam with Socialist Democracy, and not Liberal Democracy), as that is theoretical and complicated, but Iran is SO VERY SOCIALIST economically that I am appalled there is such ignorance about it.

Of course, many leftists don't understand economics at all.

Certainly, fake-leftists have absolutely no idea, as they are too timid to openly call for economic redistribution (and in general they appear to often fear the non-relative, non-subjective, logical certainty of mathematics).

Regardless, economic issues are the single most important issue for anyone to understand about Iran because the West's siege has been economic since the end of the Iran-Iraq War in 1988.

Six fatal flaws when it comes to Western leftists' understanding of Iranian economics

- They view Iran's economy in Western terms, which is impossible due to Iran's totally unique (revolutionary) economic structure. Iran was also structurally unusual pre-1979, which few appreciate as well. This chapter will explain these historical and current facts.
- Apart from their obvious lack of data and information on the Iranian economy in general, they also have essentially no data on any of the leftist aspects, because these are never relayed by a Western media which is both anti-Iran and anti-socialist. These facts will be relayed in this chapter and the following chapter.
- They don't understand that the Principlist camp (conserving the principles of the Revolution, often called "conservatives" or "hard-liners" by anti-Iran media. They are also, in an act of true propaganda, called "fundamentalists", which gives the erroneous impression that their primary political attachment is to the fundamentals of Islam (which would make them Salafists), when the primary attachment are the principles of the Revolution.) they love to openly detest are also strongly associated in Iran with promoting

classically leftist economic ideas centered around redistribution. This is the inverse of the West's conservative parties. On the other side of the aisle, the current Reformist (moderate reforms of the principles of the Revolution) government is pursuing economic rapprochement with Europe; for this they are absurdly and inaccurately being called "neoliberal capitalist" when many of them are certainly more committed to economic redistribution and economic justice than most Western leftists. Indeed, when it comes to economics both Iranian mainstream parties are leftists on the global political spectrum because the 1979 Islamic Revolution was decidedly anti-capitalist.

- They are confounded in their understanding of an economy where moral concerns actually play a key role, as this defies secular Western logic, experience and culture. I do not naively say that morality alone guides Iranian economic policy, but it is undeniable that moral and religious concerns are often the best explanation for many aspects of Iranian economic policy.
- They continue to exaggerate the importance of the bazaar: this is as if Iran still has a pre-industrial economy, and as if the Iranian government doesn't own, control and operate the overwhelming majority of the economy in the 21st century. This emphasis on the bazaar's economic dominance is outdated by many decades. The WSWS and others persist with this analysis because they are so out of touch with the facts, structures & ideological motivations of modern Iran, I assume. *Bazaari* do not play the key economic role they used to because Iran does not live in the 19th century. Have you not heard that there was an oil price boom in the 1970s....?

- Some Western leftists, in their dogmatic rigidity, cannot see that Iran - like China, Vietnam, Cuba, North Korea or any other socialist country – essentially practice "socialism at home, mercantilism abroad". This is in order to survive and to care for their People, and it does not make them non-socialists. The only socialist group which decry this would be the "socialist universe NOW" Trotskyists (like at the WSWS), who have made the fewest gains of any socialist school. Many Western leftists refuse to even investigate possible examples of socialism in the Iranian economy, and thus they do not understand it properly today.

Add these six fatal flaws together and it explains why you get *almost total nonsense* when it comes to Westerners and their uninformed economic pronouncements about the nature of the Iranian economy.

Some of these flaws simply will not be remedied, due to willful blindness. However, there are four key mistakes which can be, must be and will be remedied with simple data over Chapters 2 & 3:

- They do not appreciate that an anti-capitalist stance reigned in 20th century Iran even during the time of the shahs.
- They do not realize the enormous extent to which the Iranian economy is state-owned and state-directed, which is the indispensable economic component of socialism – without it, how can adequate economic redistribution occur? Even returning to the 70% tax rates of the 1970s will not (and did not) do it.
- They do not realise how very little privatisation – the transfer of government/public properties to private entities (whether domestic or foreign) - has actually taken place, despite the constant talk of it.

- They have no idea about the *bonyads* (state charity co-operatives) or any the other (poorly-named) "Third Sector" entities, for which there is no Western equivalent, but which play a major part in Iran's economy.

All of this ignorance means that Westerners cannot possibly understand or appreciate the situation of the Iranian economy in 2019. Therefore, we should not be surprised that they cannot appreciate recent Iran's tactical (and decidedly not neoliberal) capitalist overtures to Europe, and that do not support Iran in violation of their own avowedly leftist ideals.

We must remember that capitalism tolerates no competition - "China is not communist" is but one example. But many on the left, especially Trotskyists, tolerate no competition or individualism either -"*Islamic socialism is a sham*". "The Western model is the most advanced - whether of the left or the right," is yet another unsaid but widespread Western belief and message.

This all explains why Westerners have *never had any real interest* in unearthing the actual policies and structures which compose what can only be called "Iranian Islamic Socialism" because they competitively feel it will only undermine them. Westerners are trying to "win" an argument, not see socialism "succeed" or "flourish", sadly – this is a result of their imperialist cultures, most likely.

Many wonder what's the point of trying to sway the dogmatically rigid and the open/latent imperialists?

The truth, which is rarely reported by any of the aforementioned groups, is that economic war has - like for Cuba and North Korea - caused horrific pain, suffering and death to innocent Iranians. By clarifying the obviously hugely socialist nature of Iran's economic structure, I hope to win some timid leftists to the side of Iran and away from the camp of the imperialists, and to provide ammunition for the true leftists to openly defend Iran.

In the 21st century socialism is undoubtedly present in varying forms around the world in every country – I can easily show that Iran is as economically socialist as any of them. If one supports efforts to destabilise Iran, one is supporting the toppling of a socialist-inspired economy and socialist-inspired government.

The 20th century shahs: Terrible, but let's not act like they were neoliberal globalists

Iran is very much like Thailand and Ethiopia in that they have a fair claim to have never been colonized. Iran has almost always been run by Iranians.

(Egyptians, however, were ruled by non-Egyptians from the end of the Pharaohs in 30 BC until Muhammad Ali in the 19th century (not the boxer). Ali was not actually Egyptian – he was born in Greece and from an ethnic Albanian family; Egyptians are all certainly aware of this but admire Ali as the founder of modern Egypt just the same. Very pro-immigrant of them!)

What we can also say with certainty is that colonialism was never strongly present in Iran, and certainly did not alter the existing class structure. Iran was never India.

"Colonialism" in Iran merely meant "zones of influence" by the Russians and English during the 19th century. Before they could even think of trying to completely subjugate what is now modern Iran, they had to first hack off parts of Persia—which they did. This was all a very short era in Iranian history and certainly, if we are comparatively speaking, in humankind's colonial era. The Anglo-Iranian Oil Company (now BP) lasted less than 50 years; American influence, following their coup d'état against democratically-elected Prime Minister Mohammad Mosaddegh lasted barely 25 years. In contrast, Algeria "was France" for 132 years— under complete subjugation: political, economic, religious, linguistic, cultural, etc. Furthermore, the imperialist exportation of oil is far less societally-damaging than, say, the imperialist exportation of cotton - that requires deep, strangling tentacles into every area of agrarian and commercial society.

Iranian culture escaped this devastating impact, and this has huge ramifications for understanding modern Iran's sense of and habit of independence. Much like the incorrect use of "neoliberal" and "privatization", the use of "colonization" when referring to Iran only distorts the truth and hinders understanding of modern Iran.

This lack of being colonised crucially meant Iran never had many major structural obstacles to economic and political modernity, which so many other countries still suffer from today. The fact that modern Iran's societal structure does not suffer from colonialism's legacy of poison is rarely appreciated, but certainly Iran is thankful for it.

Another unappreciated but key historical fact is: modern Iran's economy has always been state-run and centrally-planned.

Reza Shah (1925-1941) operated the economy via the policies of statist mercantilism, meaning that the Iranian economy was totally protected, as it would be into the 1970s: there was no compact with Western imperialists for major foreign domination of local goods and manufactures— only for oil. The Iranian bourgeoisie was only the Shah's coterie and chosen few, and not independent, self-centered, world-trading/world-conquering merchants like in Western Europe. Subsequently, this small class could not impress upon the national culture with the weight of their Western counterparts, thank God. The lack of a sizable bourgeois class is as important a historical fact, and as unusual, as Iran's lack of colonialism.

The lack of colonization meant that there was also no comprador class waging economic exploitation against their fellow Iranians on behalf of foreigners; the only part of the bourgeoisie dependent on foreign capital were those who existed to extract oil. Imagine your own developing country without (or without still having) a comprador class? This is yet another huge historical advantage explaining Iran's success in achieving political advancement – the number of reactionary forces were extremely small and highly concentrated in Iran.

I hope the reader is appreciating in just how many profoundly different ways the Iranian economy developed, as compared with both Western nations and colonised nations.

2nd half of the 20th century: Iran's economic uniqueness grew & grew

Given that he was in total control of the economy, Reza Shah was forced to redistribute some oil wealth in order to guide the economy in such a populous nation—of course, he did not redistribute much. His successor, Mohammad Reza Shah (1941-1979), continued with state mercantilism—he used drastically increasing oil revenues to enrich his person, of course, but he was also forced to make enough investments to complete Iran's change from an agrarian to semi-industrial nation. In short: he was making so much money from oil that only an idiot wouldn't have made the basic investments he did: he couldn't have spent it ALL on himself and his coterie.

(He certainly did appear to try, as evidenced by his shamefully extravagant, shockingly egotistical and totally reactionary "2,500-Year celebration of the Persian Empire" in1971. The four-day event was called "the Devil's Festival" by Khomeini, and showed the obvious need for immediate revolution. Modern supporters of monarchy (which are almost wholly located in the Arab and West European worlds) need to ask themselves if their own monarchs are really much less extravagant…and then join Iran in modernity.)

This era of limited morality and sensibility is known as the White Revolution (1963-1978), and it was instituted specifically to avoid a (Iranian Islamic) socialist revolution. During this era Iran advanced from the periphery to the semi-periphery of the global economy thanks to proper investments in infrastructure and basic industries, such as steel: in the 1970s Iran went from producing no steel to the level of France and the UK by the 1980s.

However, despite this advancement to semi-industrialism there was STILL no major bourgeois class!

Unexpected, but true: In 1973 just 45 families owned 85% of private industry in Iran. Yes, this is "capitalist" —very —but just as not all "capitalism" is "neoliberal", not all "bourgeois" classes should be considered the same.

As socialist-influenced demands for more land for peasants increased after World War II, what the Shah essentially did was reduce the landholdings of the biggest gentry and provided them compensation by handing the new industries to a few of them - i.e, he bought off the ones he preferred and made them beholden to him, the central planner. The 54-year Pahlavi dynasty created only a teeny-tiny bourgeois class.

Furthermore, the genuine Iranian middle class – with decent-paying but stable jobs – was essentially limited to those who held government jobs: government workers were just 5% of the workforce in 1976.

So in 1979 Iran had a tiny bourgeoisie, a tiny middle class, a tiny industrialist class, an even tinier comprador class: indeed, Iranian society had quite a distinctive structure. However, we can surely imagine that the shahs' insistence on repeatedly increasing the concentration of their power must have made them increasingly unpopular, and thus ripe for toppling. This over-concentration proved fatal to the royal class when the military failed to stand up for them in 1978-9.

And the military truly had no reason to: in yet another deviation from the global norm, pre-1979 the military had no role in the country's economy. The shah always feared a military coup, so he purposely kept them poor and dependent, and he constantly manipulated the top leadership to avoid the rise of any one general. This explains why the armed forces could not —and often would not —aid him in 1979.

This lack of military involvement in the economy was yet another unique economic feature of Iran's. In the US, for example, there is no doubt that their economy is essentially centrally-planned by the Pentagon, which is the world's largest employer.

(In this sense, the "privatisation" of state assets to the (state-linked) Revolutionary Guards (which is not the national army) is a sort of rebalancing more in line with the global norm, and certainly in line with the socialist idea that the state and its organs should hold all the major economic assets. However this concept requires much more explanation in the next chapter, and is also present in the discussion of the Basij.)

Iran's economy was always state-run, but 1979 made it for the People's benefit

I think you'll agree we have a lot of 20th-century economic uniqueness to recap: no constrictive and uber-reactionary colonial structures, total state planning of the economy, protectionist policies to promote Iranian development, a tiny foreign colonialist class and just a handful of compradors working with them in a single sector, a tiny domestic bourgeois class, a shamefully-meagre middle-class, a weak and unstable military ... and let's not forget another hugely important economic aspects which is unknown to Westerners – Islamic financial culture which includes a huge role for charity and which precludes the rapaciousness and insane compound interest of Western financial culture.

Iranian economic development has never been typical, and thus resists the usual clichés. Use such clichés and one reflects their ignorance, and also render your ideas useless to Iranians.

Undoubtedly, there were totally different social forces at play which produced very different groups than have been normally found around the world. Iran was, and still is, often quite unique.

But if we want to give a parallel, we can say that Iran developed more like South Korea. After all, these are the two countries whose UN Human Development Index increased the most from 1990-2014. This is absolutely no small feat for either one, and certainly lessons for other, less successful nations must abound. I have often cited this UN gauge regarding Iran to show what all Iranians know and what likely forms the practical basis of the Revolution's solidity in 2019: since the war with Iraq ended, the government has massively succeeded in transforming Iranian society for the benefit of the masses.

However, their results did not stem from the exact same approaches: in South Korea the Park military dictatorship decided the economic plan and controlled a small bourgeoisie's relationships with foreign capital with the same strictness as the English did for their 18th-century colonial subjects. The huge difference is that in Iran the state was not just the main driver of growth but was also the main recipient, as opposed to private industry.

And that fact largely explains other huge differences: such as why South Korea is filled with US troops, whereas all the US bases dedicated to subjugating Iran are around but not inside Iran. South Korea's commitment to capitalism also explains why US corporations are now all over South Korea, whereas in Iran you buy "Niks" and not "Nikes", and you shop at the bazaar and not Wal-Mart. This also explains why, tragically, it is "South" Korea and no longer just "Korea". One hopes that reunification happens soon....

South Korea is a common comparison for Iran, but incorrect: the best comparison is China. In fact, the two share so many common experiences, beliefs and institutions that it is the basis of Chapter 4, *Structural similarities between Iran's Basij and the Chinese Communist Party*.

So by the end of the 1970s the state WAS the capitalist sector - they owned it all, and much of what they didn't own outright they controlled informally. This also means that Iranians have always seen the state as the natural driver of a centrally-planned economy; or at least they certainly have been prepared for the socialist concept of central planning and central ownership as much as any other country.

The problem under the Shah was: it was not for the People's benefit - not enough economic redistribution of wealth. The 1979 Islamic Revolution obviously changed that, and only a liar, ignoramus, or anti-religion fanatic would deny it.

Given all these facts, the economic heritage of the Islamic Republic of Iran is difficult to define, but we must agree that Iran under the 20th-century shahs was nothing like a "bourgeois capitalist state", "colonialist state", nor a "neoliberal capitalist state". To this Iranians proudly said, "Hooray for us!" But they also said, "But down with the shah!"

This section should make clear that Iran's revolutionaries thus inherited an economy totally ripe for total nationalisation, as well as an economic mindset which had known nothing other than central planning. This was a huge advantage which helped produce the vast redistribution of wealth post 1979 in Iran. Whether this was luck, the good grace of geographic determinism, Iranian ingenuity or some other force is not important - who cares about credit? What's important is to see things clearly in order to understand Iran from now on, because what I have mostly read in the West is a bunch of ill-informed nonsense.

I do not expect that non-Iranian and non-economic (and non-good) journalists will know the basic outline of economic history in Iran, but it is amazing that they do not know that Iran's current economy is not only centrally-planned but almost entirely centrally-owned...because for nearly 100 years of modern history the vast majority of Iran's economy been under national control! This is not a new event! Tap tap tap - hello? Is this thing on?

The oil price boom of the 1970s threw the Shah's 0.01%-centered system into crystal-clear relief, and so it was scrapped in favor of Iranian Islamic Socialism. And that is where things get even more economically different!

Is Iran the most state-run economy in the world today?

You will have to read the next chapter to get the complete answer, but I can only think of one country which has more state control – North Korea.

With the revolution the property of the Shah and his coterie, which controlled 70% of the nation's capital, came entirely under anti-capitalist, revolutionary, national control. This percentage of state control would, amazingly, become significantly higher in the coming years.

1979 certainly wiped out the undemocratic state planner (the shah), the bourgeois class (reading this from Beverly Hills), an army which was not Guard-ing anything remotely Revolutionary, and put Islamic Socialist revolutionaries in charge: they were tasked with creating and implementing a completely new system unseen in history... and that they did.

It had to be a "new system unseen in history" because the Iranian revolution was not just intensely nationalist and Islamic but hugely against capitalism-imperialism: therefore, there was also an uber-intense demand to decouple from the entire international political system. That necessarily implies decoupling from capitalism as much as possible.

Indeed, because there was this popular demand to decouple from capitalism Iran's nationalism could never - and is never and should never - be called "fascism" or "reactionary". Khomeini's "Neither East nor West but the Islamic Republic", is no mere slogan but an ideology of both independence and revolution, and that most certainly included the economy. Contrarily, most Eurozone nationalists don't want socio-economic revolution but merely independence, and this makes many of them neo-fascists.

That anti-capitalist goal was undoubtedly met and preserved: today, Iran is incredibly un-globalized and at the bottom of all such tables ranking international economic connectedness. You can buy a fine pair (for the price) of Niks, however.

All of Iran's economic planning and development remained state-planned and state-owned, but here is the difference: pre-1979, there was no talk of redistribution, of economic justice, of social justice, or of anti-privileges; post-1979, this was explicit philosophy of the state and the promoted discourse. There can be no false claims that Iran's "Islamic economy" isn't a welfare state deeply concerned with social justice; it sits fundamentally opposed to the neoliberal model. To implement this is why Iran's economy remains so controlled by the state, both constitutionally, in practice and informally.

Westerners don't have the facts about Iran's unique (revolutionary) economic structures. I concede that uniqueness does complicate easy understanding, but Western mainstream media would never retell Iran's success in redistributing wealth.

What this final section will show, as well as all of the next chapter, is how Iran took the existing state capitalist model and built upon it something totally new - Iranian Islamic Socialism.

Background for the bonyads, because there is no Western parallel

Forty years is long enough to have realised that Iran's economy is structurally totally different.

There is massive, massive, MASSIVE misunderstanding about Iran's unique (revolutionary) economic structures and ideas, some of which are often inadequately described as the "Third Sector" (the first two sectors being "Public Sector" and "Private Sector"). I am not discussing the "Second Economy / Black Market", which is yet another sector.

If this "Third Sector" phrase is unknown to you, it is likely because this is a sector which does not have a Western parallel. Frankly, a better name is the "1B sector", because it is entirely accurate to say that this is indeed a part of the Public Sector. I will use "1B sector" in this book because it is the most accurate.

Being Public Sector is like being pregnant - you can't be "just a little" of either. Well, actually you can - 20% is considered a controlling stake in a company, and a state can certainly have a smaller stake than 20%. However - and this is detailed in the next part - Iran never goes less than 51% state control in seemingly anything worth having, and certainly not in any industry of even moderate importance. BP tried that with us - Iranians were not converted.

No account of Iran's economy can be complete without these so-called "para-statal" organisations which are somehow called "para-"... despite being under the government's control. I will explain one of them, the *bonyads*.

When the WSWS penned this extremely broad and unexplained generalisation - *"huge sums paid over to the Shia religious establishment"* - I assumed they were talking about the state religious charity cooperatives (*bonyads*), for which it is very difficult for Westerners to even conceive of.

To put it briefly: the *bonyads* became major economic factors when the Islamic Republic of Iran nationalised the assets of the Shah and his 1% and... gave them to charity.

Totally pure capitalism from those hypocritical Iranian Islamic Socialists, right? It's amazing what all the hardcore neoliberal capitalism charities get up to, as we all know, and especially Islamic charities!

But that is how around 10-20% of the Iranian economy came under the control of state religious charity cooperatives. However, the administrative apparatus of the *bonyads* can go back 1,200 years - these are embedded, grassroots organisations.

Let's quickly talk about the role of charity in an Islamic economy - it is much more than just some free soup. Many Iranian politicians even talk of Iran being an "alms-based economy"...which seems like a stretch to me, but I certainly get where they are coming from.

Charity will always have a significant role because of *zakat* - the Islamic obligation (charity being one of the Five Pillars of Islam, which all Muslim groups agree on) of giving (usually) 2.5% of your profits to charity. In Iran, this is a voluntary decision, and the giving is to imam-sponsored instead of state-sponsored collectors (unlike some Muslim countries). $1 billion was given in Iran via *zakat* in 2017, but not all *zakat* is reported, so it is likely much more.

Because Iran is Shia, there are not 5 but 10 pillars, one of which is *khums*: Shia businessmen are expected to give 20% of their profits to their local mosques for charity. Now you understand that Iranian politician I just mentioned! I have no figure on *khums*, but you get a good *khums* and you can build a new mosque or something overnight. This helps lead to false perceptions of "millionaire mullahs", which I will soon address.

This works very similarly for Jews in the West: religious people come knocking on the door of your (Jewish-owned) shop and ask you to give some of your profits to support the community - it's certainly not capitalist. Nor is it what some readers are thinking - "religious extortion": extortion is for personal and criminal gain - not community gains. The underlying thinking here is that one has made their profit off the community, after all, so they must give some of this profit back – unlike in the West, no tax attorney can help you cheat. Of course, I'm sure many Western commentators will find a way to mistakenly label all this charity as "neoliberalism", LOL.

An underlying rationale for both of these economic levers is the idea that religious people can provide welfare as well as the state can - that has certainly been the case in Iranian history. So the *bonyads* were already needed and useful in Iran - the Revolution made them here to stay.

An introduction to Iran's 'para-state' sector: The key word there is 'state'

The only question is how much money they should have under their charge. The 1979 Islamic Revolution decided that too - rather a lot.

They made sure that much of the economy would be run with a religious – and not capitalist - goal. This is a hugely important (and by default a socialist, or at the very least a "Islamic socialist") fact of the Iranian economy. However, it was not just handed over with no strings attached - this is not a Western capitalist bailout of bankers! Nor are the *bonyads* some sort of Iranian mullah-version of the Clinton Foundation - which was often accused of existing to funnel money to the Clintons to fund their lifestyle in return for political access and favourable political decisions.

The *bonyads* now employ millions of people, and the goal is certainly not cruel capitalist efficiency – workers there have far, far more rights and job protections than when they were privately-held. Perhaps because Westerners don't like to see religious people in charge of anything, this is mistakenly labelled "corruption" instead of "avoiding unemployment and poverty". The goals, motivations and practices of the *bonyads*, which are totally removed from Western capitalism, simply cannot be dismissed, not labelled, or mislabeled – you are free to come up with something better than "Iranian Islamic Socialism" if you like, but do NOT call it capitalism.

The *bonyads* are not just in consumer goods but have been awarded parts of more sensitive economic sectors; the same goes for the Basij, another co-operative foundation. However, it's the Revolutionary Guards (also known as *Pasdaran* or *Sepah*) who have been handed partial control of the big portfolios, sectors and projects upon which the country's well-being depends: oil, telecommunications, large-scale development and construction. This was obviously all by plan (and not "market forces", LOL), and all of these groups, their political backers and their employees have collectively discouraged private competition because their ideology is that the state should control it — they prefer the *bonyads* (and Basji and the Revolutionary Guards) to Western capitalism (and thus Western capitalists).

The main complaint about the *bonyads* is that the factories and businesses they were awarded became more economically inefficient, but... *the entire point* of taking the money from the capitalists' hands and giving a large part to charity is inherently to oppose the cruel efficiency of market capitalism.

Capitalists will thus always talk badly about the *bonyads*; their mere existence will cause the West apoplexy, and the idea that they could spread to other Muslim countries causes profit-based terror.

The *bonyads* report directly to the Supreme Leader - not only is he the religious leader of the nation, he is the ideological leader of the modern, social justice-obsessed principles of the Islamic Revolution. People have different opinions on the role of the Supreme Leader, but we should all agree that Khomeini and Khamenei are not hard-core capitalists.

This decision has both pros and cons: they are not concerned about making money, but about providing social services, jobs, wages, etc. Khamenei is not the CEO of the *bonyads*, making decisions for shareholders and not workers, of course. In effect, the *bonyads* give the "soul of the government" - the Supreme Leader - a direct and influential hand in the economy. One may be against this, but one may not call this "capitalist"!

The *bonyads* are not under parliamentary supervision, causing a lack of transparency and accountability.

The *bonyads* pay no taxes. This reduces government revenue, technically, but in reality it is yet another redistribution measure as it is obviously an implicit government subsidy of economic development, employment and charity.

The *bonyads* can also technically make investments and commercial plans apart from the government's five-year economic plans, which does create redundancies, competition and inefficiencies. However, considering that the Supreme Leader, and many other religious leaders are tied to the *bonyads*, and also to the government, and are also heavily-involved in long-term economic planning, it is not as if the *bonyads* operate like economic loose cannons totally divorced from the democratic planning centers. The head of one of the largest bonyads, Ebrahaim Raisi, came second in the 2017 presidential election with 38% of the vote and is one of the leading candidates to follow Khamenei as Leader.

The *bonyads* are, from a practical and legal point of view, under government control... but not much parliamentary or executive control... but they are under total judicial and Supreme Leader-branch control. It's simply a unique (revolutionary) system, but do NOT call the *bonyads* capitalist.

There is widespread agreement in Iran that the *bonyads* absolutely could and should be made more transparent and efficient...but that they absolutely should remain *bonyads.* One may be an ardent atheist, but no socialist would prefer to see a *bonyad* emulate the worker treatment of a company like Amazon, correct?

I'm sorry to bring up these realities, because if there's one thing Westerners don't tolerate about Iran it is trying to understand its nuances.

Do you really think the average CEO is more ethical than the average mullah?

You must have a lot of faith in capitalism... that's a funny kind of faith, to me.

Not only do Westerners accuse the *bonyads* of being capitalist, they say it much more harshly. They accuse: "These must be fronts for 'millionaire mullahs'." Of course Westerners are very cynical when it comes to religion or money, so when the two intersect….

Truly, this is only an issue for Iranians who are obsessed with being anti-government and want to believe the worst about it. Most mullahs in Iran are barely middle class—it's an inherently absurd argument. Do priests in your country really live lavishly?

At the highest levels of the religious establishment is there money? Sure, and with *zakat* and *khums* there always was and always will be, but in many ways mullahs today are poorer than ever: in pre-modern times being a mullah meant you had formal studies, which meant your family had to have some money to send you to school in the first place. Take Rafsanjani, the stereotypical "millionaire mullah" —how many people know that he was already rich before becoming a revolutionary? He comes from pistachio money, which is very big money in Iran.

The idea of "Millionaire Mullahs" came from the uber-capitalist magazine *Forbes* in 2003, and by their longtime Russia editor, no less (Russia in the age of Boris Yeltsin, when *Forbes* reporters were probably feted like kings while the average Russian plunged into unwanted, underserved socio-economic and cultural despair). Why on earth we (especially leftists) would accept *Forbes'* account of the *bonyads* is totally beyond my comprehension! I can assure you that this book has given you more objective information about the *bonyads* than *Forbes* will ever write about Iran in sum and until that sweet day when they go banktrupt/shuttered by the revolution. They hate *bonyads*, and any kind of charity which do not garner rich people a lot of very public credit (and tax credit) for.

Do the *bonyads* have a lot of money? Yes, but there is a difference between being stewards of money and being

CEOs. They are expected - by the people, press & government - to actually do something with the money, factories, subsidies and workforces they are handed. A *bonyad* leader cannot be Gordon Gekko, of Oliver Stone's famed movie about 1980s US capitalism *Wall Street*, and liquidate parts of a *bonyad* for his personal profit, LOL. If a *bonyad* leader dies the *bonyad* is not transferred to his eldest son like in England, LOL. A *bonyad* leader cannot "go public" and sell shares... and sell them to non-Iranians, too, hahahahahah. LOL, I am really having fun thinking of ways the *bonyads* do not conform to capitalist rules!

Regardless of how funny or not funny I am: a mullah driving a Maserati, living in a palace, throwing lavish parties and living like a rap music video - the Iranian press would die from happiness at such a story because it would be so big and sell so many papers! The idea that Iranian *bonyad* leaders are all living massively corrupt, unequal, high-off-the-hog lifestyles is an absurdity and it also ignores Iran's highly-critical press. Other than that... *Forbes* article spelled some difficult names right, at least. However, and this is most damning of this false, hypocritical Western criticism: if a *bonyad* leader did lead such a lifestyle he would merely be like *almost every single Western business leader*!

But *bonyad* leaders are not Western CEOs and it is inaccurate to imagine them as such... not that anyone in the West has enough information about the *bonyads* to imagine them at all. There are major structural and cultural limitations on anyone's possible desire for unrestrained personal enrichment, shareholder enrichment, and profit-at-any-costs; the West has structural components *expressly designed to remove any such limitations*, and which do not exist in Iran, and that is not something which can be glossed over by anyone seeking the truth about modern Iran.

Therefore: there can be no question from leftists that the *bonyads* are indeed superior in every way for society than the continued presence of the previous capitalist class.

Perfect? No. Ways to get them better? Yes. Capitalist? Go away kid, ya bother me.

However, more explanation of the 1B sector is needed. This section on the *bonyads* hopefully primes the pump for readers to realize just how unusual Iran's economy is with these so-called "para-statal" organizations. I hope I have clearly shown that not only are the *bonyads* not capitalist, but they are also not "para-statal" - they are not separate from the branches of Iran's government.

For the past 100 years Iran's economy has been hard to get a handle on, but the last 40 years have truly been unique. Hopefully this chapter sheds some light on things, but much is left obscure, because Iran's economy is truly revolutionary in conception and practice.

That's why clarifying the much-discussed but rarely-implemented "privatisation" is the inspiration for the next chapter.

Chapter 3
What privatisation in Iran? or Definitely not THAT privatisation

*J*ust as everyone falsely assumes that Iran's economic history followed the standard colonial model (it didn't), that their political cleavages are the same as the West's (they aren't), and that Iran trails the West in modern political thought and democratic structure (they don't), it is little wonder that Westerners assume that "privatisation" simply must be the same as in the West. It isn't.

To quickly spoil the ending and prime the pump for accepting the fundamentally unique nature of Iran's economy: the "selling" of state assets to other state-controlled institutions -like the Basij, the Revolutionary Guards and the bonyads (state religious co-operatives) - is not "privatisation". Even if you disagree with that declaration after reading this chapter, you will certainly concede that it is undoubtedly not THAT "privatisation" which Westerners imagine.

"Privatisation", when used in the Iranian context, is a hollow catch phrase; just like when "neoliberal" is absurdly, inaccurately and impossibly applied to Iran.

But why privatisation at all, if Iran is economically (Islamic) socialist?

Well, there are money crunches because of war and sanctions, and Iran still needs to pay wages and pensions and keep the economy functioning, brainiac... but this is not a very complete (or polite) reply.

Trotskyist Socialists like the World Socialist Web Site – who claimed "Islamic socialism is a sham" –often have a real inability to put themselves in Iran's shoes. They insist on forcing their shoes onto our feet due to their overwhelming urge to Monday-morning quarterback (instead of supporting and learning about actually-working socialist ideas).

The WSWS knows a bit about Iran... but often only enough to be dangerous. For example, they write that Iran, "amended Article 44 of the constitution, eliminating the stipulation that core infrastructure remain government-owned."

It's good they know about this obvious, rock-hard socialist foundation of the Constitution of the Islamic Republic of Iran, which mandated the existence of three economic sectors – public, cooperative (what I call the "1B sector") and private, and with private designed to be the smallest.

However, Article 44 was never "amended": in 2004, after much discussion at all levels of government, the Supreme Leader declared – in total accordance with Iranian democracy – a new interpretation of Article 44. The new interpretation is that some industries – but not oil, main banks, key transportation, etc. – could be privatised, but never more than 80% (20% being generally considered a controlling interest in a corporation). This is obviously in direct contradiction with the false but attention-grabbing claim that Article 44 was "eliminating the stipulation that core infrastructure remain government-owned", to say nothing of the possibility of reduced ownership while maintaining retention of government control. "All or nothing" is rarely the case in politics or economics, but it does sell newspaper and force mouse clicks.

But were they privatised, and to that extent? I can give you a resounding and short answer: not in the slightest. The reasons are described in this chapter, but let's first consider why Iran became persuaded to reduce some socialist economic controls – why the new interpretation in the first place?

Let's examine the situation for Iran in 1989: the Iraq war gutted Iranian oil infrastructure just when they needed it the most, oil had dropped to $15 per barrel (adjusted for July 2017 inflation, and which was the lowest price since 1973), the war cost 60-70% of the government's entire annual budget, caused $1 trillion in damages, dislocated a million people, killed 1 million Iranians, created hundreds of thousands of needy veterans, damaged 67 cities and 4,000 villages. In short: the war cost Iran more money than it had earned in oil revenue during the entire 20th century.

That was the situation on the micro-/national level, and yet Iran persisted during the war with implementing socialist-inspired economic plans. Indeed, this is likely why Iran prevailed. That notion was summed up well in 2018 by Ismael Hossein-Zadeh, a professor of economics at Drake University (USA) and a regular contributor to the very prominent leftist website CounterPunch:

"Indeed, the plan of a war economy should not be very difficult for Iran to implement since it has a relatively successful experience of carrying out such a plan: during the 8-year war with Saddam Hussein's Iraq, Iran embarked on an extensive state-guided economic management that effectively provided for both its military and civilian needs. Because of the revolutionary atmosphere of the time, and because of the corresponding spirit of generosity, selflessness, social cohesion, and national unity the country was able to effectively withstand both the military and economic wars launched against its territory and its people."

I can put a more negative spin on it: in 1989 there was nothing to distribute and equality was largely achieved –

nearly everybody was broke and in mourning.

Western leftists are also totally unsympathetic to the historical anomaly Iran found itself on the macro-/international level, which I personally find fascinating and compelling: In 1989 Iran was a nation which was certainly among the most radical and most successful in terms of the application of leftist economics (via the war economy); a nation only recently acclimated acclimatised to leftism - and leftism is always accompanied by many trials and even more errors, as leftism has very little historical experience to draw from – and almost solely during wartime conditions; a nation which just lost its political unifier and charismatic national hero with Khomeini's death in June; a nation which was a war-devastated society, but still bent on implementing the most amount of revolutionary Shi'ism in global history... this nation was then totally abandoned by Western leftists as the Eastern Bloc and USSR collapsed!

Thus, at a time when Iran was trying to patiently explain the importance of ideology over money, "It's the economy, stupid," became the mantra seemingly worldwide until 9/11. At a time when Iran needed a friendly mentor – even a non-Islamic one – a huge part of Socialism collapsed, just as Iran had emerged from foreign aggression and added its flag on the rostrum.

What if Iran had not been faced with this depressingly solo leftist march after 1989? This is a fascinating historical fantasy to contemplate! A combined USSR, Eastern Bloc, China and Iran certainly seems to imply greater success in the neo-imperial Muslim World, at the very least. Iran certainly suffered from bad timing.... Yet despite all the cold and hot war, Iran has not only held on but thrived. In 2019 they stand as the world's last great revolution, and about that there is no doubt. It also undoubtedly true that since 1989 socialism has been at its nadir, but this book contends that if the non-Muslim world had been able to appreciate Iran's leftism, then socialism's recent record would not be so very depressing.

In 1989 there is absolutely no doubt that there were many people in Iran, and at the very highest levels of government, who wanted to maintain the huge amount of state ownership, but who was helping us? Nobody. Our allies, our would-be allies evaporated. Our enemies only switched from hot to cold war, although sanctions are indeed the modern "siege", and thus are not "cold" at all.

I raise these points to give historical context for the so-called "privatisation" that began in Iran: the global crisis of confidence in leftist economies and economics after 1989 surely must have affected leftists inside Iran as well, no matter how resolutely leftist they wanted to be. To use Mao's phrase, "capitalist roaders" were truly going full throttle for the first time since 1917, but everyone outside of Iran was dogmatically insisting that a religious person couldn't also serve as a crossing guard.

Of course, despite all these things working against the Iranian economy and the worsening of sanctions in the coming decades, the economy has never collapsed expressly because Iran was (and remains) so committed to nationalisation, central planning, price controls, subsidising essential goods and services, to fundamentally socialist economic ideas, to Islamic ideas of morality, to post-Liberal Democratic ideas, etc.

But make no mistake: the massive anti-capitalist nationalisations are the essential economic legacy of the 1980s, and they can neither be forgotten nor dismissed because they remain the foundation of the economic thought, experience and practices of the Islamic Republic of Iran today. The WSWS may lament the new interpretation; another view is to point out that the entire West has no similar socialist economic constitutional clause in their own countries Iran to possibly re-interpret.

'Privatisation' in Iran ultimately re-distributed money to the poor, not back to the rich

That seems paradoxical, but only if privatization is viewed through Western (non-revolutionary) definitions.

In short: A broke government cannot afford to pay more salaries and pensions; thus, new structures were created to fuel employment and stimulate production, and to reduce the state bureaucracy and intensely socialist regulations. However, they were not capitalist structures and certainly not globalist or neoliberal capitalist ones. It's even more to Iran's postwar credit when we remember that these were precisely the types of economic structures which were being adopted across the West, in places like the nascent European Union (1993) and Eurozone (1999).

The best parallel for Iran's economic evolution after 1989 is, once again, China. However, China after 1976 and not after their liberation and revolution in 1949.

Following the Chinese Socialist Civil War (my accurate re-naming of their Cultural Revolution (1966-1976)), which saw an intensely democratic refocusing of economic resources away from urban areas and towards the far more populous rural areas, the physical and (especially) human capital of China had become not just far more advanced but far more egalitarian than ever.

(This has been indisputably documented by people like Dongping Han, a rare case of a person who not only was from a Chinese village but who actually investigated the effect of the Cultural Revolution on 82% (in 1976) of China's population – villagers and peasants, eschewing the usual Western focus on minority groups such as urbanites, technocrats, professors, artists, monks and those forced into exile for their adherence on right-wing ideologies. Indeed, for the rural areas the Cultural Revolution was – and this was its stated intention – a true great leap forward in education, industry, socio-cultural progress and democratic empowerment.)

And what phase in China's socialist journey came after this huge progression in the human, cultural and physical capital? The turn towards limited capitalism, shepherded by the Communist Party and now headed by Deng Xiaoping. Post 1989 Iran followed this same trend: after all, the period of 1980-9 also saw a state-sponsored Cultural Revolution and thus great leaps forward in education, socio-cultural progress and democratic empowerment.

The reality is that socialism is one big trial-and-error process – they have not perfectly followed the dogma of Marx or anyone else. Those who actually work in politics – politicians, journalists, grassroots activists – must produce tangible results, unlike the ivory tower theoreticians. And, on a level totally removed from any dogma, things have gone pretty well for China during their various socialist epochs; epochs which are characterized by a very human, very natural, very palpitating waxing and waning, and then more waxing and waning, of socialist fervor. Crucially, while fervor and passion waxes and wanes the bedrock of China's domestic socialist commitment, structure, policies, controls, laws, etc. have not greatly been altered since 1949.

Returning to Iran, revolutionary fervor had been sustained at a wartime pitch for a decade – quite a period of waxing. Whether it was due to a waning of socialist fervor, or the fact that Iran's Cultural Revolution had produced tremendous human capital, or the fact that socialism may indeed need periods of "socialist-style capitalism", or the fact that there was a global crisis of confidence in socialism, by 1989 there was massive support (even among the hard-core left) for new President Hashemi Rafsanjani's plan to privatise the non-strategic sectors in order to promote immediate production; also, foreign borrowing to rebuild also seemed unavoidable, considering the economic devastation. This lack of production and lack of capital was an urgent problem, and few non-Iranians consider this context of deprivation in 1989 - ivory-tower socialists remain untouched by such urgent realities, of course. But where else could the much-needed money come from? Furthermore, opposing this meant opposing both the democratic will and the vanguard party in Iranian Islamic Socialism - the clerics.

But this is where we can stop crying for how rough Iran had it because (and this is what Westerners simply refuse to understand)... just because some in Iran wanted to somewhat-privatise the economy, that does not mean there were not others who still wanted to maintain a huge measure of state control.

I say this over and over about Iran: observers simply do not appreciate that there are multiple groups, ideas, philosophies, political parties, so-called "factions" at play in Iran (although I have never heard of the US Democratic or Republican parties being called "factions"). There is also a modern, structural balance in the 1979-penned constitution; there has been political plurality since the war ended; there is a very vibrant and openly critical press; there is definitely no single ideology other than "guard and progress the country and the revolution". Beyond that – it is a free for all, like any modern society! The idea that Iran is not pulled in many different directions by many ideas – democratically – is totally wrong. Failure to understand is this will only lead to your misunderstanding, because your foundation – that Iran is a totalitarian society – is totally incorrect and without factual basis.

So just because President Rafsanjani said "privatise" – Iran is not a dictatorship...Iran got rid of one in 1979, remember?

Given this reality of pluralism, it should be easy to comprehend why a policy of pure neoliberalism could not possibly succeed in 1989, or in 2019, when so many still advocate for a command economy (war economy) of a socialist-egalitarian nature? Many openly say the only solution to the West's current cold war is to return to the war economy, with coupons, rationing, command economy and mass mobilisation of workers for government projects. This "faction" is rarely reported in the West, but it is significant (and certainly anti-capitalist).

What gets more press, and is a larger "faction", are those who promote a "resistance economy". This stresses import substitution - using domestically-produced substitutes for what you can produce rather than importing foreign goods, for the sake of employment, industrialisation, modernisation and self-sufficiency. This is most ardently promoted by Khamenei and Mahmoud Ahmadinejad, but has been supported on some level by literally everybody and for years because this was also an ideological part of the war economy. The resistance economy is supported at all levels of government in dramatic fashion, just some more dramatically than others – again, there is a pluralist, democratic pulling in multiple directions in Iranian politics.

Again, given this pulling, the idea that a Western-dominated, neoliberal, globalist lobby has ascended to absolute, dictatorial dominance in the Iranian government is patently absurd, defies logic and is inaccurate. It also demonstrates total ignorance of modern Iranian culture and history.

Furthermore, Western capitalist media are eager to exaggerate the tiniest lemonade stand in China into proof that they are "not socialist", so why would they call Iran anything but "capitalist"? They want to fuel ignorance, as that advances their own capitalist ideology.

However, to the WSWS and many other Western leftists, any support of a capitalist lemonade stand apparently makes one "neoliberal" and seeking to humbly "accommodate" the globalist order, when that is not at all the case. Franco-German Rothschilds, America's Waltons and the English monarchy have made zero headway in Iran.

Let's all begin the ending of this idea that Iran has gone from mass revolutionary economic nationalisation to Wall Street-istan. The reality is that such ideas should have ended in 1979.

Rafsanjani era – from 70% to 100% state control over the economy

I hope I have established that the idea that the Western approach to privatization – or even the unique Iranian approach - travels through Iranian society totally untouched by opposition from powerful state actors, groups, and lobbies is totally inaccurate; it only makes sense if one has no knowledge of Iran's laws, structures, history and current culture.

Yes, after the war the government allowed more entrepreneurship and created some free trade zones in southern Iran... but they also created price-controlled cooperatives to get poor people basic goods. Again – push and pull, two revolutionary steps forward then only one step back, cycles of revolutionary vigor waxing and waning and then waxing again.

Of course, only out-of-touch leftists would condemn all free trade zones out-of-hand, as they fail to acknowledge that free trade zones allow a country to learn quite necessary new industrial and practical skills from foreign nations, which can then be used for national development. The idea that the free trade zones in the modern I.R.I. are creating a new comprador class like in 17th century Latin America is simply absurd.

Did this create a new bourgeois class? No, it was groups like the state charities (bonyads) who were incorporated into these free trade zones, which are state-controlled organizations under control of the "Supreme Leader branch". The Iranian Revolutionary Guard, which oversees the mass-membership Basij and its co-operative foundation, both also participated in privatisation – these are two more state groups which, like the bonyads, actually own factories, businesses and banks, etc. There is no Western parallel for these 1B structures.

Were companies privatised during the Rafsanjani era (1989-1997)? No – because they almost always handed to state-controlled organisations. Furthermore, this so-called "privatization" was only partial - rarely more than one-third of a company. Eighty percent was legally allowed, but that occurred extremely rarely, due to the pluralistic, democratic view and practice of "privatization" in Iran. The government retained absolute majority control over and over and over and over.

These facts are not at all mere nuances, and certainly contradict claims that Iran "went capitalist". Indeed, I rather get apoplectic when Westerners talk so sweepingly about Iranian "privatization", because it is clear they have only glanced at such headlines and then made sweeping generalizations which are entirely self-referential.

Because people will not believe me, I quote from Anoushiravan Ehteshami's Iran: Stuck in Transition. The negative title indicates why it is available in English in the West, LOL. I quote him to show what every Iranian knows: privatisation is not, was not, was never intended, and could never be "privatisation" like Westerners conceive of it.

"So, by the end of his (Rafsanjani's) presidency, 86 per cent of the country's GDP still came from the state-controlled sector and the remaining 14% also included the share of the powerful foundations which worked closely with the state."

So the allegedly-rabid capitalist Rafsanjani (which is inaccurate, because he was also an Iranian revolutionary and thus against unfettered capitalism), who is the godfather of the neoliberal Reformist Party (also inaccurate – he had many ties with Principlists), successfully privatised much of the gains of the Revolution (another inaccuracy, he actually increased it), and thus privatisation has destroyed Iran, made a joke of their Revolution, and shows why "Iranian Islamic Socialism is a sham" (to quote the WSWS).

Uh… if you say so. Just don't say this in Iran and expect to be perceived as credible.

And yet this is all accepted as the truth among Western leftists despite the fact that by 1997 you had 100% of the major and legal components of Iran's macro-economy controlled by the state! This is greater than Cuba today, where the state-run economy is only 70-80% of total GDP – I am not calling Cubans "socialists in name only", but calling Iran "non-socialists" is obviously absurd.

These are the types of absurdities one must endure from Western leftists as an Iranian leftist…. Perhaps I am the fool for trying to explain, but I assume that some are listening and can also admit that they were wrong, mainly because they lacked the key facts. I do not blame Westerners for being misguided: as I wrote, a ban regarding good news on Iran and a ban regarding good news on socialism equals total ignorance about modern Iran in the West.

But the irony here is that Westerners, left and right, keep saying that "Iran has privatised" and Iranians have been saying for decades, "What privatisation are you talking about, LOL?"

Those who are reading this book perhaps now agree that they need to totally return to zero - the way to do this is to realize that: this was never privatisation to begin with. In reality, the government gave shares to these 1B sector foundations/cooperatives mainly because a war-ravaged state simply could not pay the money they owed (mostly for pensions). In the most accurate sense, these shares were never intended to be "sold" but were mainly debt settlements. Again, this is not some minor nuance!

I contend that the West only calls this "privatisation"

because they know that the phrase "de-nationalisation" has negative connotations – indeed, you simply never read that phrase in Western journalism. I think the average, patriotic person would raise an eyebrow at ever such mention.

But as regards Iran, the bonyads, cooperatives and Revolutionary Guards – those who got governmental approval to buy these very minority portions of state industries – were all actors who are all under state control…many can fairly insist that "de-nationalisation" is not the right word to describe the economic practice which took place in Iran, either. But that is Iran –revolutionary.

I think I have demonstrated that when it comes to "privatization in Iran" the misunderstanding is TOTAL, and caused by both slavish dogma to ivory-tower socialism and a high tolerance for misinformation and inaccuracy on the part of the Western left.

Indeed, Iranian-style privatization should have been followed in the West after 1989! Imagine if the Eastern Bloc and Russia had abandoned socialism, and yet also made constitutional commitments to 1B sector institutions, instead of embracing wholesale (and true) privatization? Surely the catastrophic drop in living conditions in these areas would have been largely averted; surely their societies and workers would benefit from greater stability and cohesion. What is the reason nobody paid attention to Iranian-style post-1989 "privatization" – Islamophobia and anti-religious bigotry, of course. And, of course, constitutional commitments to the1B sector is not some sort of the "Third Way" – it is socialism, and the 1% of the USSR and the Eastern Bloc betrayed the socialist desires of their 99%, sadly.

Anti-socialist dogma and pro-capitalist revisionism on the part of Western rightists is expected – they will do whatever they can to obscure, slander and misreport on Iran's unique economy because they want everyone to follow the Western capitalist model. But even though the Western left would rather die than admit it: they should have been trumpeting and implementing Iran's economically socialist policies – would have saved them a lot of grief.

Iran did not drastically change after Rafsanjani, either. From 1997-2005, the Khatami era, these competing forces, ideas, philosophies, parties and "factions" did not just evaporate.

Khatami, despite being an allegedly privatisation-loving "Reformist" like Rouhani, did not seriously try to turn the economy to the right. He mainly focused on cultural and domestic political ideas, while his economic policy remained totally in line with the dominant themes of Iranian Islamic Socialism (Iran operates on 5-year central plans): promoting social justice at home, decreasing oil dependence, increasing foreign trade contacts but with huge amounts of oversight and no laughable "neoliberal" total deregulation, increasing entrepreneurship and competition with the state but only with huge regulations and extremely slowly, increasing domestically-produced exports to earn money in a typically mercantilist and state protectionist fashion, and bolstering the importance of the 1B sector.

In 2004 the constitutional control of "mother industries" got its new interpretation. People who know probably nothing of all I have written up until now likely said back then, "Oh, they're going to privatise the entire percentage of the economy the state controls." Oh, all 100% of it, eh? That's because you think that all those anti-capitalist forces which fought, won and installed an anti-capitalist revolution just disappeared, hmmm?

Not so…. Parliament (the non-Liberal Democratic embodiment of these forces), backed by the Council of Guardians (democratic embodiment of Iran's vanguard party – the clergy) in 2004 immediately shot down all actual efforts at foreign investment through privatisation: two Turkish companies were not allowed to buy into two "privatised" industries. The meaning was clear: privatisation could not be "neoliberal" nor "globalist", because it refused to allow domination of the national economy by foreign capital. I think readers can see how extremely significant that decision was, and how it certainly was a unique, contrarian decision in the post 1989-world.

The constitutional re-interpretation was initially pushed by the Rafsanjani-headed Expediency Council, which acts as a smoothing liaison between Parliament and the Guardian Council. I would say Iranian history is clear: there is more chance of this interpretation being changed than of Iran embarking on a massive Western-style privatisation plan for which there is no historical or cultural precedent, in either modern or even monarchical Iran.

The primary force in Iran in 1979 and 2019 is patriotism, which is why I call it "Iranian Islamic Socialism".

However, we need to realize that the socialist economic influence in Iran goes further than patriotism, because the opposition to "Western-style privatisation" extends to domestic capitalists. Iranians clearly do not approve of reducing state control of the economy – full stop.

Ahmadinejad era – more 'privatisation'…from the state sector to the state sector

The Ahmadinejad era (2005-2013) is also misunderstood. Ahmadinejad, a former Basij member and an ideological ally of "Mr. Resistance Economy" Khamenei, was against privatisation in general and also foreign investment.

And yet there was also far, far more "privatisation" than ever: by the end of 2010 – the "Golden Year" of privatisation – 275 state companies had been "privatised" worth $630 billion. Indeed, Iranian contradictions abound!

But only to the uninitiated: just 1/3rd went to the private

sector. Again, the huge bulk of it went to the Basij, the bonyads, the Revolutionary Guards – all state entities. This wave of "privatisation" actually expanded the government's payrolls and bureaucracy – it didn't shrink them!

Clearly this is yet another dagger in the idea that Iran "privatisation" is akin to the Western form. What kind of a privatization makes the economy more publicly-owned? A totally misnamed privatization, that's what. Yet the most uninformed commentators not only called this "privatisation" but "neoliberalism"! Catch-phrases may suit the West, but they do not apply to Iran because Iran has a different culture and different governmental model.

Chinese commentators should know better – they get the same Western "fake news" treatment. And do Chinese Communist Party-controlled companies not qualify as "state-owned enterprises"? Of course they do, and they must – they are dependent on/controlled by the government and thus contradict the definition of capitalism. China defies capitalist clichés because they, too, have a different culture and different governmental model from the West... yet they are absurdly called "neoliberal" as well, mainly because such claims allow Westerners to flatter themselves and to reject the idea that socialism can not just exist but thrive.

Returning to Ahmadinejad's first term (2005-9), the amount of state-owned enterprises allowed to be purchased by the private sector instead of the 1B sector was even lower – just 19% .

It should be clear what occurred and why: the Iranian state, under massive foreign economic attack, needed a way to raise funds from within the country, as they distrusted foreign investment. They did not want to create a seemingly-totalitarian society where every citizen officially works for the government (as is the case with other Persian Gulf nations, such as Saudi Arabia or especially Qatar), as this rather defies the heterogenous nature and inclinations of the average Iranian (in my opinion). The government would likely have been overthrown by the People if they went full-bore Western capitalist (not that the government ever wanted to grant local capitalists such latitude). The government would likely have been overthrown if they sold the country's assets off to foreigners (not that the government ever wanted to). And so they expanded the 1B sector to take some financial pressure off in order to keep maintaining revolutionary ideals.

The 1B sector also has the incredibly important advantages of being inherently pro-revolution, pro-constitution and pro-government – their existence, continued success and advantages are due to the revolutionary government, after all. Thus the success and expansion of the 1B sector – in stark contrast to Western-style privatization – thus increases the stability of a constantly-under-attack government.

The 1B sector rewards those members of the citizenry who are the most supportive of the revolutionary government, and simultaneously makes them even more reliant on the government. That is a complex sentence, but vital; that is also essentially a one-sentence description of the Basij, to which I devote the next four chapters of this book.

And it sure beats the hell out of selling off your country to foreigners who care nothing about you and your neighborhood. It also beats neo-colonialism.

Iranian-style privatization took debt off the government books, improving the domestic financial situation, and also raised much-needed funds (funds they could not get anywhere else) by permitting the de-nationalisation of a small percentage to the private sector while still retaining massive majority state control.

Workers in France would currently kill for the level of nationalisation and the level of "de-nationalization" Iran has. I don't know when they will get it: In 2018 President Emmanuel Macron announced a plan to privatise 15 billion euros worth of state assets – that represented 15% of all French state assets. Please see things clearly: the French "mixed socialist" model is in its death throes during the Age of Austerity, but the 5th Republic was never anywhere as socialist as the Islamic Republic of Iran. Not even close. It's quite sad that France will soon have even less state control over the economy to influence jobs, prices, pensions, etc. Now THAT is neoliberal capitalism, and it can't be found in Iran.

Please don't compare Emmanuel Macron with any Iranian leader

What we can say with total clarity about Iranian privatisation is that it was not "privatisation" as the West conceives; it was very limited "privatisation", and not done in a way which ended the People's controlling share of the economy. Iranian privatization was resorted to in order to raise government revenue amid global sanctions, and it might even be increasingly looked upon as a logical but always-cautious step in the evolution of successful socialism (thanks to China's success).

I return to Ehteshami's discussion of Ahmadinejad's privatisations, because my analytical summary is likely to be considered biased, despite its clarity and foundation in facts known by the average Iranian:

"This did not amount to the transfer and control of assets previously owned or controlled by the state to the private sector. Indeed, even where the private sector was a beneficiary, it still needed state support (in terms of using ministerial contacts for securing assets being offered to the public, finance for its acquisitions, access to soft loans, elite-linked partners to shield from future state interventions, minimizing tax commitments) to ensure control of the enterprises being offered."

This is reminiscent of how the Shah tapped his preferred coterie to benefit from his semi-industrialisation drive, as I described in the previous chapter. This is also reminiscent of China, where their 1% is entirely beholden to the government for their riches and can be stopped immediately if they become corrupt or defy Communist central planning. Just as in China, if the bonyads, Basij or Revolutionary Guards deviate from central planning, are too inefficient, or are too corrupt, then the Iranian government has enough measures and control to yank them back into line. Capitalism, and especially neoliberal capitalism, has few to none of such measures.

But Ehteshami is making my same point: what privatisation in Iran?... even when it is the greatest level of privatisation!

So, no, the government did not sell to the highest bidder, as is the case with Western privatisations.

Furthermore, the minority-stake privatisations to the private sectors absolutely had to deal with a ton of ministers, government shepherds and government regulations. Is it supposed to be easy? It is supposed to be easy... in Western privatisation, but not in the Iranian style.

I hope leftists are realising just how misled they have been. But wait – you are even further away from the truth. We must always recall that these state-affiliated 1B sector companies pursue decidedly non-capitalist policies in a societal doubling down of the amount of socialist-inspired everyday policies in Iran!

In short: the goal of the 1B sector is never capitalist efficiency – they are not trying to squeeze out every bit of profit possible – the goal is to provide jobs, goods and wages which can be introduced to the national economy. We should be able to see why Western capitalists and the Western media look at Iran's 1B sector with both rapacious greed and total contempt for its idealistic objectives. The idea that Iran's 1B sector is somehow more "corrupt" than Western corporations and businesses – where unbridled greed, inequality and disregard for worker protections are admired, promoted and legally protected – is completely laughable. But just as Iranians have a different idea of what "corruption" is, Westerners have a different idea of what "privatization" is….

The non-capitalist goals of the 1B sector require more examination and explanation than I have offered here, but it is detailed in the forthcoming analysis and description the Basij, whose economics are governed by the Basij Cooperative Foundation.

Privatisation: Largely forced by the West – wanted and yet unwanted

Never raised in the West is this inconvenient reality: that the West's support of Iraq's war, the West's endless economic and military pressures, and the US, EU and UN sanctions, forced the privatisations. The WSWS and other Western leftist critics act as if Iran both started and allegedly ended a massive revolution simply on whims of fleeting passion. From the WSWS pamphlet:

"The Islamic regime made certain social concessions to Iran's workers and rural toilers in the first flush of the revolution. But these have been systematically rolled back, and at an accelerating pace…."

I think I have proven how this is hyperbole from the WSWS, and that it hides only a grain of truth, and a tiny grain even as grains go. That "pace" is basically that of a snail: those initial concessions certainly went farther and deeper than anything west of Russia ever, excepting Cuba;

any dashes towards privatization necessarily start from 90 meters back in a 100-meter race in Iran, and the pro-privatisation runners soon find they are must run while being pelted with rotten vegetables.

I hope this chapter has demonstrated just how little "privatisation" has gone on, and also how the democratic political forces at play in Iran seem to certainly prevent a wholesale shift to a Western mindset.

This is the key summary to understanding the longevity of the socialist-inspired components of Iran's economy:

"Privatisation" is completely the wrong word because it has only strengthened the government's hold on the economy, and its success in maintaining socialist-style redistribution policies... and the economy cannot shift to the right because no political group in Iran's pluralist system has the political weight to reverse it without massively ending their own popularity.

Such a movement is political suicide; modern Iranian history has shown it essentially gets scuttled by its many opponents before it can even get it started; if such a movement to the economic right was actually implemented *en masse*, we would be foolish not to expect rather serious resistance from the Iranian workers and citizens who would both suffer and feel betrayed.

Western-style privatisation simply cannot be tolerated in Iran – no political group could pay that price and survive. This is obviously because of the decades of modern political anti-capitalist discourse both before and after 1979 which is ingrained in Iran's unique and revolutionary culture and among the populace. Iranian culture is definitely unique in this sense.

For example, France's Macron absolutely can pay that price. And he is: his popularity plummeted because he sped through "reform" after "deform" to treacherously and unpatriotically place France on the neoliberal, Anglo-Saxon track. If he and his totally inexperienced party (full of "civil society" businessmen - not politicians, and certainly not true grassroots activists) don't win a single vote in 2022 they will not care one bit – they will return to civil society and be feted by the Western capitalist community despite the damage they inflicted on French society. But just as Iran has structures, ideas and possibilities which have no parallel in the West, the West also has many structures, ideas and possibilities which have no parallel in Iran… thankfully.

Michel Temer in Brazil is another person who absolutely could pay that price. He had an astoundingly low 4% approval rating in 2018, but the accurately-titled "parliamentary coup" and shamelessly capitalist-fascist rollback in Brazil could not be stopped – culminating in the election of neo-fascist Jair Bolsonaro in 2018 - because their government structure is bourgeois (West European) and because Brazilian culture has not been changed by several decades of decidedly revolutionary thought.

The groups in Iran associated with this "privatisation" – and I do not mean shareholders, but the millions of workers in 1B sectors, their family members, those who oppose neoliberal capitalism, who support the ideals of Revolutionary Shi'ism, etc. - are succeeding and will not give it up their success willingly; their political, intellectual and cultural backers are not about to give it up, either; many mullahs are not about to quit the clergy and use their government contacts to thrive in the private sector (unlike Western politicians).

Ultimately, for Iran to completely privatise (and I am speaking here of privatisation to only national bourgeois, not foreign bourgeois), you would have to demolish not just the structure of the government, but the very psyche of an Iran which is decidedly revolutionary on the global spectrum. I cannot imagine that anyone would fail to agree with that if they were to look at modern Iran objectively?

Even if Western leftists cannot accept Iran as revolutionary and (Islamic) socialist, the capitalist-imperialist leaders of the West correctly see Iran as a threat to right-wing ideas. That is why in February 2019, as I make the final proofread of this book (please excuse the errors I surely overlooked), 60 Western nations and their allies are meeting in Warsaw with a single objective: how to contain Iranian progress, how to destabilize Iran, how to end Iran's modern revolution. They are not meeting to congratulate Iran on their alliance with reactionary forces….

Given all the leftist economics, of course the West must destroy Iran's economy in 2019

Invasions of Afghanistan and Iraq did not lead to main imperialist goal - the hoped-for invasion of Iran, and that is why beginning in 2010 anti-Iran sanctions began to really hurt. The West simply could not allow Iran's economy to thrive and continue to set such a bad (yet ignored) example.

The sanctions can stop anytime – all Iran has to do is play ball, i.e. let the West buy in, and thus wield influence in Iranian politics. However, this important part of the narrative is never remotely intimated: sanctions were stepped up because the West realized that they *would never be allowed* to buy into Iran's economy in the massive, dominating way they are used to.

Even if Western leftists often don't understand economics, Western rightists do: they read about the 2010 "Golden Year of Iranian privatisation" in *The Financial Times* and *The Economist*, made a few calls, realised they couldn't buy a slice of Iran, and got mad. Sanctions are their way of getting even.

Such a fundamentally capitalist analysis goes a long way in explaining why in 2012 the sanctions truly hit a global record in terms of harshness, injustice and lack of humanity. Only Cuba and North Korea can sympathise.

That year the US sanctioned Iran's central bank, the main route for settling its export profits, and banned any other national bank from buying Iranian oil, while the EU installed an embargo on Iranian oil, banned all trade with the EU, froze (stole) all Iranian central bank assets, barred all trade insurance, and barred all banking. Oil exports dropped by two-thirds. By October the *rial* was down 80% from the past year; the 2013 economy would be a shocking 25% smaller than its growth trajectory previously indicated – it was brutal siege warfare.

The sanctions hurt everybody because that's what they were designed to do –paralyse the Iranian economy, cause pain to everybody, death to many, and foment civil war over to the horrible situation.

Given the fact that this is all obvious fact and not opinion, it is amazing what a one-sided story is presented by leftists such as the WSWS: that cuts to social programs were

"neoliberal austerity", instead of being forced by sanctions. It was as if Iran were cutting programs for the same reason Francois Hollande and Emmanuel Macron cut social services in France?

The appalling ivory-tower stance of the WSWS in 2018 boiled down to this: howling condemnation for trying to work with the capitalists (only half of them, Europe, as there is no rapprochement with the US) in order to end these horrific sanctions, and combined with muted condemnation of the capitalists' sanctions on Iran.

The economic warfare is specifically targeted to subvert Iran's socialist economic policy, as socialism requires patience, long-term approaches and solidarity over immediate, individual need. Given the increase in 2012 of the sanctions on the Iranian state, in the 2013 Iranian presidential election every single candidate's economic plan – from left to right – was based on more privatisation: the only question was "how much" and "to whom".

The only true capitalism in Iran – the Black Economy

It's not as if the US hadn't been limiting Iranian access to banks prior to 2012, but it really became all-out war then . The sanctions forced Iran into being a heavily-cash economy – no bank would give us a line of credit, after all: with Iranians it's "payment up front", and that's only when they condescend to do business with us.

All this cash obviously increases the chances for corruption. Liquidity in Iran is thus excessive – it is not tied up in investments, and only the rich have liquidity, of course. They speculate on real estate and goods and don't invest properly because it's not secure. Iran also attracts highly-capitalistic people, because there is higher reward to compensate for the higher risk for doing business with Iran. This worsens the economic situation –it is not the government's fault, but the fault of Western governments.

Neither can the government be faulted for the existence of the Black Market – this market is citizen corruption by those who for their own selfish gain won't follow the People's laws, as well as corruption by innocent people who are forced into moral compromise due to terrible situations caused by mainly non-Iranian factors.

I promised a complete answer to this question in the previous chapter: "Is Iran the most state-run economy in the world today?"

I can't fully answer that question - because of the Black Market. But, as I wrote in the previous chapter, take out the Black Market, the average shopkeeper and the carpet industry (which is a cottage industry, full of domestic part-time workers) and I would say – and there is no clear data I can point to, nobody has such information – that even after the "de-nationalisations" Iran is still very similar to 1997, when the state controlled 86% of the economy and informally controlled the other 14%, although the part which is informally-controlled (1B sectors) has increased. Certainly, people smarter than me have affirmed that 100% of the economy is controlled (not owned) by the State; ask any Iranian (and I have asked many), and they will likely agree with this assessment, even being as drastic as it is.

These are the types of information which are never revealed but which are common knowledge to Iranians. These are the types of information about which few Westerners are exposed to by their Mainstream Media. Nor should this high level of state control be surprising - Iran has been close to that level for about 100 years.

This means that likely only North Korea has a higher percentage of state control, as they do not explicitly recognise private economic activity. And is North Korea "not socialist" economically?

But back to the Black Market. If you're looking for unfettered capitalism in Iran you are only talking about the Black Market – it's perhaps 15% of the entire economy, but that could be an exaggeration. It is obviously just as big a threat – culturally, economically, morally, politically – to the Iranian system as it was in the USSR, where decades of tolerance for the Black Market was obviously one of the prime reasons the USSR fell. China, seeing this, runs perpetual anti-corruption campaigns; indeed, the Cultural Revolution was a literal parade of corrupted factory bosses, farm team leaders, Party cadres, teachers, etc.

In October 2018, with the JCPOA half-dead, Iran waged an unprecedented war on currency traders, completed development of a national cryptocurrency ahead of almost every other nation (and for obvious reasons – cryptocurrency is a Godsend to Iran, as well as to the entire world), and cracked down on other Black Market financial instruments to regain control of the Black Market.

Controlling the Black Market would increase tax revenue, obviously, but what people likely don't know is that Iran has very few taxes by modern standards, and certainly not in almost any country of comparable size or development. Farmers pay zero tax, and one-third of 22 million guild workers pay no tax either. Nearly half the economy is tax-exempt, and tax revenues compose just 7% of government revenue. This rate is over 20% for most Western countries and 16% for OECD members, because they capitalistically tax labor and not production, unlike (Islamic socialist) Iran.

The only significantly Iranian industry in which the government is not involved is the hand-made carpet weaver industry – that is totally privatised, as it is a cottage industry which long predates the Islamic Republic. Carpets comprise around 1% of GNP, 2 million full- and (mostly) part-time jobs, and sometimes 20% of our annual non-oil exports. However, it may simply be impossible for the state to control non-machine-made carpet production. However, they do need to ensure that workers' rights and safety are properly regulated, which is no easy feat when so many carpets are made in private homes.

(Iranian carpets are so good it's amazing that the entire world doesn't buy them: if I am honest, I think you are all true savages for walking around on bare floors in your cold residences, and I can't possibly imagine how you live that way! A room without a carpet is a room without a soul. How can one prefer the monotone ("chic") Western carpets instead of the Iranian explosions of color, geometry and order? Floors are universal – like the mousetrap, there is only one possible solution: nice carpets, right? Of course. So let's focus on ending the sanctions so your nation can massively import some nice carpets in order to pull your lives together and stop living like savages. Even Iranian nomads have carpets, and they have no floors!)

Do Western leftists want Iran to remain under sanctions forever?

We can really say that since 2013 Iran has seen a situation of nearly unparalleled cold war, considering how much more valuable Iran is to the world economy than Cuba or North Korea, and Iran's much larger overall economy (top 25 globally).

The desire of the Rouhani government to create "mutually beneficial" (the government's constant mantra) capitalist deals– in order to call off the European side of the West's war on Iran, to raise money, and to increase the quality of Iranian industry – must be seen in this honest, balanced context.

Just as I have proven that "privatisation" is a word which is only used because Iran's revolutionary structure has rendered the English economic language inadequate, "neoliberal" is a terrible, terrible term to call the deals by the Rouhani government. I covered those deals for PressTV in France (which have not been implemented, sadly – Europe has not kept its word and honored the JCPOA) and they were indeed joint ventures, technology transfers and 50-50 deals. As I said repeatedly then and say so now, this defies the definition of neoliberalism, where the bigger corporation wins; all capitalism is not "neoliberal" – how can one be a journalist (or an active leftist) and not realize this?

In 2018, despite the increasing signs that Europe was not going to honor their treaty, Iran still refused to obsequiously play by the rules of capitalist diplomacy: As France's Total Oil dawdled on the bellwether project between Iran and Europe, the $5 billion South Pars gas field project, Iran's ideology (along with their pride) insisted on doing something considered extremely rude in Iran – handing them an ultimatum: Total had 60 days to negotiate the exemptions from the US which Total said they needed... or China takes over. In November 2018 Iran announced that China had taken over Total's role, but there is some indecision at the time of publication of this book, as the US has reportedly put pressure on China to drop the deal.

"But wait," you say, "If China takes over they'll have 80% of the project – doesn't that contradict the government's claim of 'mutually beneficial deals' and maintaining the People's control over resources and industry?"

A reasonable objection.... Perhaps the most important detail is to remember that the Total deal was for just one "phase"- a phase is generally planned to have a daily production of 1 billion cubic feet (28 million cubic metres) of natural gas – out of around 30 total phases. Iranian companies run nearly all the other 29 phases completely. They do have joint ventures on one (sometimes two) phases with Russia, Brazil, South Korea, Italy, Venezuela, Angola and Norway, but Iranian know-how and Iranian profits are the big winners here, even if 1 out of 30 phases is not majority Iranian-owned.

Really, really big winners.... The South Pars natural gas field, along with Qatar's neighboring half, called North Dome (which is the reason why Iran and Qatar will always have good relations) has nearly as many recoverable reserves as all the world's other natural gas fields combined!

I have crunched some numbers and determined its total value: roughly, a bazillion kajillion dollars (rounded upwards).

So, keeping this in mind, and the fact that we are talking about just one phase, $5 billion is rather a small portion of that astronomical sum. If Iran gives $4 billion to China to learn the latest extraction technologies and train the Iranian workforce, thus permitting Iran to extract the remaining bazillion kajillion dollars worth of gas (less $5 billion)... then this is clearly not a "neoliberal capitalist" deal, but a balanced, fair, intelligent investment. If Iran wanted to give $4 billion to France, and if this could encourage France was able to twist away from decades of US-led Cold War on Iran... that is clearly not a betrayal of any Iranian Revolution's values but a price which should be gladly paid to protect the nation.

It's not great that Iran becomes so beholden to one source – China – but the West are a bunch of liars and deal-breakers: what can Iran do about that? What they have never been willing to do is give up their ideals and the Iranian people to create a shah-like 1% which seeks "accommodation" with global capitalism. Such an accusation is preposterous....

Conclusion: Iran's economy is under unjust attacks in reality and in leftist intellectual circles

The WSWS wrote - absurdly, inaccurately and in a sensationalistic fashion - that Iran has "*pursued neoliberal policies*".

Iran has not, and cannot, go whole hog over to neoliberalism, and this chapter illustrates why. It's "fake news", in the post-Trump parlance of the US. Selling a very small portion of Iran's oil industry to neo-imperialist France cannot possibly make Iran a "neoliberal" in any honest sense of the term. Nor does the effort make Iran a rabid capitalist: embracing some capitalism does not deny Iran's socialism, nor North Korea's, nor Cuba's, nor China's, etc. Not only do they not understand Iran's economy, nor Iran's oil industry, but I don't think places like the WSWS read the fine print, as

I do, on such deals.

Furthermore, cuts to social services in Iran cannot be rendered comparable to cuts to social services in Western nations – the motives are totally different. Such false equivalencies are based on the total unwillingness to comprehend the economic context of economic shortages created by foreign sanctions on Iran.

If I am being precise, it is impossible for Iran to pursue neoliberal policies, which are based on reduced government spending, private over public ownership, pre-socialism ideas of deregulation, a free market domestically and free trade abroad regardless of ideology (even Zionism). This chapter has shown just how repugnant all of these ideas are, in a democratic way, *to a huge mass of Iranians*. "Neoliberal", after all, is the extreme-right form of capitalism, and I would imagine the number of adherents in Iran to this form – which clearly violates multiple key tenets of Islam – to be a tiny minority.

The WSWS wrote: *"Declared Khomeini, 'As long as there is Islam there will be free enterprise.'"*

This is obviously only a problem for the most radically anti-capitalist (which few are), but I want to clarify the situation: yes – the Koran explicitly sanctions trade. So, I see the total abolition of capitalism as un-Islamic, and many Muslims do as well.

What the Koran also does – radically then as well as now (as the Revolution of Islam was an immediate political, social and economic revolution, unlike Christianity) – is to repeatedly forbid cheating in business practices, usury (compound debt and loans at exorbitant interest rates) and, by logical extension, the tactics of modern Western finance and neoliberal capitalism. This should be considered significant, and a significant advance, and a significant victory of Islamic Socialist ideology over Western capitalist ideology.

But it is all rather a moot point: Trotskyists cannot even

present Iran (nor China, Cuba, Vietnam, North Korea, etc.) with a working system where some free enterprise isn't necessary to a nation's very survival (perhaps even without the enormous external aggression). Nor can Trotskyists point to any existing system of theirs which works better than Iranian Islamic Socialism. And, certainly, I think very few people among working socialist countries – not parlor socialists – want to abolish all capitalism in a democratic majority. Certainly not in China, Cuba, North Korea, Vietnam, Eritrea, etc.... you know ALL the socialist countries.

Finally, I don't know why the WSWS is so very desperate to portray Iran as having accepted modern neoliberal capitalism? Don't they like little victories? There are many shades on the capitalist spectrum, and every shade away from the neoliberal variant on the far right should indeed be trumpeted as a victory in 2019 because that is *how very bad the situation is for the Western Left*.

The WSWS's failure to properly trumpet Iran's economic rejection of neoliberalism implies that there can be no gradual victories, nor inspirations for other nations, no innovative ideas: all there can be instead is total, complete, already-decided Trotskyism, which will be born fully-formed. My main problem with this refusal to see in shades of victory is not that it is "we want all or nothing" – that is revolutionary idealism – but that it is not desired democratically anywhere, and that it is not actually advancing socialism. But we are repeating the old Stalinism vs. Trotskyism debates on this subject....

Regardless, what these two chapters on Iran's economy have shown – and which the upcoming parts on the Basij will reinforce is: economic liberalisation has a grassroots political price which no group in Iran can afford to pay if it wants to remain a part of Iran's democratic political process.

This is because economic questions are at the heart of Iranian morality and have been for decades; no group has a free hand, nor will.

Iran's economic choices in 2019, and beyond, will have to be compromise between competing groups – some economically (Islamic) liberal, some economically (Islamic) socialist. The only common denominator is: upholding the ideals of the 1979 Iranian Islamic Revolution, which are explicitly anti-capitalist to a large degree, and also to a degree which is almost unparalleled currently in the modern world.

Clearly, since 1979 Iran's economy has undergone drastic changes, seen major economic redistribution to the poor, resisted Western economic attacks, rejected globalisation and coalesced into something which is accurately called "Iranian Islamic Socialism". But what needs to be grasped is just how deep-rooted these revolutionary economic changes have dug into grassroots Iranian society and culture. The next four parts will discuss exactly that, by objectively analyzing something the West has long tried to ignore – the Basij.

I think readers will find this unique institution rather fascinating. They certainly are controversial even in Iran, perhaps because it is such a unique concept. The WSWS did not see fit to even mention the Basij, but I contend that it is impossible to understand 21st century Iran without knowing what they truly are - I think every Iranian would agree this is not an overestimation of the Basij's relevance.

Chapter 4
Parallels between Iran's Basij and the Chinese Communist Party

As every journalist and critic knows, the laziest (and fastest) way to describe something is to present it in terms of something else. This is "the new that", or this is "that combined with this". However, Iranian Islamic Socialism is pretty unique and not very derivative, I think we can agree. I thought about making this chapter the last in this four-part sub-series on the Basij, but I think some frame of reference is needed for Western readers.

What I am certain of is that these four chapters contain the very first objective analysis and the very first leftist analysis of the Basij in Western history. Considering we are talking about 10-25 million Basiji, that is unfortunate – they have been written out of modern history and modern understanding.

The Basij is not communist, of course, but I think you'll find the Chinese Communist Party provides a very apt comparison in terms of structure, goal and societal application. That would be surprising only to those who don't know Iran very well, because since 1979 Iran has followed

China in so many ways, big and small. Few of them are known or appreciated in the West.

For example, Iran is the only other nation which has also had an officially-titled, government-sponsored "Cultural Revolution" (1980-83). It was obviously modelled on the Chinese experience: purging Western and un-Islamic thought was the stated goal (and thus also imperialism and un-Islamic capitalism), whereas in China it was purging corruption (unchecked capitalism and anti-socialist thought) and Confucianism/polytheism/folk culture. This was the time when bus drivers became bosses – something which is lamented by Iranian technocrats in exile – because the bus drivers had a more moral and more modern political ideology. Both were, of course, supremely leftist events on the global political spectrum in the second half of the 20th century. This leftism is why the Chinese progenitor is depicted in the capitalist-imperialist West to be a horror-show of rampaging students; the Iranian brother, just four years younger, is imagined in the West to be a horror-show of rampaging seminary students.

I addressed China's Cultural Revolution in my book I'll Ruin Everything You Are: Ending Western Propaganda on Red China, which is also available for purchase thanks to Badak Merah publishing. In 2019 I also penned an 8-part series dedicated solely to China's Cultural Revolution, by examining Dongping Han's The Unknown Cultural Revolution: Life and Change in a Chinese Village (Han was kind enough to write the forward to my book on Chinese Socialism. That series can be found for free online. The first part was titled: A much-needed revolution in discussing China's Cultural Revolution - 1/8).

In short, China's Cultural Revolution bravely and democratically addressed the age-old problem of the urban-rural divide. Iran, whose revolution occurred 30 years later in the 20th century (and thus after the decades of almost universal country-to-city migrations following World War II), did not have this cultural divide to the extent of the Chinese. Iran's rural population was 50% of the country in 1980, and is down to about 27% today; China's rural population composed 80% as late as 1980, and is down to about 45% today. Clearly, the demographics on this point are quite different. Rather than a Cultural Revolution for the Iranian countryside, during this era it was truly the Great Leap Forward: despite the ongoing war they got things they had never imagined possible under the shahs, such as electricity, indoor plumbing, schooling, health care, literacy, land and infrastructure, etc. Beyond material things, they got enormous democratic and cultural empowerments: The dress of the average lower class woman – the chador and roosari– went from a sign of poverty to a sign of prestige, to give but one example of the elevation of democratic-majority values.

The main points of both Cultural Revolutions were, obviously, "cultural" - to forbid the promotion of Western capitalist-imperialist thought, to combat corruption in every sense with revolutionary vigor (like it or not), to devolve power away from autocratic and Liberal Democratic structures and towards Socialist Democratic structures, and to promote a revivifying of modern political (and in Iran's case also modern Islamic) values. (Certainly, for committed communists Communism is undoubtedly a faith-based & messianic religion. They don't call it "divinely-inspired" but they sure act like it.)

China's Cultural Revolution was more insular and less-Western focused than Iran's. It came 15 years after they had kicked out the Western imperialists, but China's huge size, population, history and geographic situation has always made it more able to totally ignore Western trends in order to follow authentically-Chinese ideas with confidence. However, with Vietnam raging and the US helping to create a communist genocide in Indonesia in 1966, we would be wrong to assume that they did not have the same justified fear of invasion and counter-revolution as Iran did.

Both Cultural Revolutions undoubtedly succeeded. In Iran this was when the ideological battle between global Socialism and a finally-liberated political Islam fought it out publicly, politically and physically to wind up creating "Iranian Islamic Socialism". In China, this was when Maoist-era economic equality was preserved from corruption by empowering and educating the rural areas to a never-before seen degree, thus laying the human and physical capital for the post-1980s boom; when a new generation of youth was given the power to reject the Western siren song in order to truly live the ideals of leftist revolution; and when Western-Russian socialism was definitively changed into "Socialism with Chinese characteristics" by devolving daily control down to the average peasant.

Why four chapters on the Basij?

Because almost nothing is known about Iran's biggest and most important organisation, just as almost nothing is known about the Iranian Cultural Revolution.

The most basic fact of the Basij is: the Basij is an institution which is dedicated to supporting the revolution, the constitution and the government and not any one political party.

The Basij students, technically the largest group, were heavily involved in the first Cultural Revolution, and their spectacular growth led to calls for a Second Cultural Revolution in 2005. This is when Ahmadinejad, the first Basiji president, was elected. A Second Cultural Revolution did not materialise, but there definitely was renewed revolutionary activity in Iranian universities.

Why do I bring up the Basij and the Cultural Revolution?

Because, in my objective view, the Basij are something of a "permanent cultural revolution", or a group seemingly designed for that. This will be made clear in the ensuing parts, but let's return to the Chinese frame of reference to dispel the dominant, narrow, fear-based, Western idea of the Basij – that it is a "militia" or "paramilitary" organisation.

The Basij and the CCP: Want to join the government? Then you likely should join

What kind of a militia has enrolled perhaps 1/4th of the country?

"Militia" is obviously a false term of propaganda because militias and paramilitary groups are usually not under state control and often even opposed to the state. The Basij, however, totally supports the state – that is its raison d'être. The Basij is also totally controlled by the state, subject to its laws, and can in no way supersede the police in fighting crime.

However, not only is the Basij controlled by the state, but the Basij IS the state - or it's getting there quickly… and certainly not in the way many realize.

In China, Communist Party members comprise an estimated 75-80% of government workers – from the village level to the very top, and including their state-owned enterprises. (That figure on China, and many others in this chapter, are according to Jeff J. Brown, author of the irreplaceable China is Communist, Dammit!: Dawn of the Red Dynasty, also available by Badak Merah.) In 2003 the number of Basij members among government workers was 65%; the Public Servants' Basij is the biggest Basij of them all.

The Chinese Communist Party's economic clout is well-known, although the control is technically the state's. (The Iranian government undoubtedly has a greater percentage of control over the economy than the Chinese government – this is not as well-known, but hopefully I have explained that.) The Basij Cooperative Foundation is a huge entity which oversees all Basij operations, veterans included, including over 1,400 companies and firms as of 2007. Subsequent years of so-called "privatisation", especially during the "Golden Year" in 2010, saw the Basij gain even more economic clout. The Basij is overseen by the Revolutionary Guards (often referred to as Sepah or Pasdaran) which has even more economic clout than the Basij.

All of China's state-owned and private companies must have a Communist Party committee. Iranian law says any company with more than 30 employees must have a Basij.

The People's Liberation Army is 100% communist, as are China's police forces. In Iran the Revolutionary Guards and the Basij combine to fill the function of the PLA, but there is also a national army. Eighty percent of new police in 2008 were drawn from the Basij.

Huge numbers of Chinese public educators are communists; in Iran the University Professors' Basij is probably the most influential Basij in shaping public policy.

Being in the Chinese Communist Party is undoubtedly helpful in getting accepted into a Chinese university. In Iran, 40% of undergraduate and 20% of post-graduate university admissions are legally reserved for "active-level" Basij members.

The CCP obviously benefits from massive public funding. In multiple 5-year plans all firms, factories and public companies have been ordered to allocate 1-2% of their profits to development of the Basij.

I hope I have gotten your attention! Still think the Basij is just a "paramilitary"?

The Basij, contrary to popular belief, is not a bunch of armed thugs: it is obviously however a huge part of the government, and thus a huge part of society.

Clearly, the Chinese Communist Party and the Basij have so many things in common that if there is something fundamentally wrong about the CCP, then Iran's Basij likely must share many of the same flaws; the same logically goes for the fundamental positives the two obviously share. Of course, only Chinese and Iranian opinions matter in terms of final democratic judgment.

There is no shortage of similarities which prove rather objectively: these are two institutions which have a great deal in common; that these are two institutions which also have no Western parallel; and that it's obviously better to be a member if you want to rise in these respective governments. All of this necessarily has tremendous implications on how these two countries are run, and what their guiding ideologies are.

What is the Basij, exactly? It's an "apolitical Islamic socialist union NGO", in my view... but proving that requires the next three chapters. Certainly, it is yet another truly revolutionary creation.

However, I think it is best to confine this chapter to the many, often unexplored, political and cultural similarities between Iran and China.

'Neither East nor West'... but giving a cold shoulder to the West implies facing East

It's almost as if Iran knew they had to eventually turn East, but wanted to create and preserve a new sovereignty first.

The attraction is natural, and here is a brief list of their key similarities:

They world's only two Cultural Revolutions; anti-imperialist support (Vietnam and Korea – Palestine and Syria); long-range central planning (both operate under 5-year plans); a vanguard party (Communists – Shia Islam mullahs); a government with open concerns for social morality (as opposed to the "anything goes" West); economic redistribution (as opposed to neoliberal capitalism); tremendous success in socio-economic redistribution (China #2 in increasing UN Human Development Index from 1970-2010, Iran #2 from 1990-2014) and much, much more.

The primary demand of the 1979 revolution was to immediately de-couple Iran from the West completely, but there can be no doubt that the East was never viewed so extremely negatively: no matter how atheistic China was and how shirk (idolatry and polytheism) India was, they were not imperialists. Economically, Iran's democratic primary demand also meant de-coupling from the global capitalist system at any price; Iran did exactly that, and have paid quite a price ever since. Unfortunately for the West, this price has never been enough to seriously consider counter-revolution.

From 1979 on Iran's trade immediately turned towards the global south and east as Iran abandoned Western ties. The view from Iran was likely: "Certainly more trustworthy than the West, and China has no oil - let's do some big business." I imagine the Chinese view of Iran since 1979 has developed along these lines:

"Well, they have some good ideas, but they are really religious and Communism is not a religion, don't exaggerate." And then 10 years goes by. "Well, they beat off Western-backed Iraq – Iran isn't a heavyweight, but they sure punched above their weight there. If they get their oil system back up and running, take their calls." And then more time goes by: "These guys still aren't folding. And you say they had a Cultural Revolution, too? Really? Hmmmmmm. Our economy is really booming, the West is still trying to take us down, and we need to start thinking bigger. Get Tehran on the phone."

And call Iran they did: the result is that Iran is a main hub (and the primary energy hub) of their $4-$8 trillion New Silk Road, or One Belt-One Road project, which sets the stage for many trillions in Eurasian trade for many decades.

Iran and China have obviously come to an arrangement: China accepts that Iran is Islamic, yet are also rock-solid modern revolutionaries they can rely on, and who are actually capable of long-term planning (as opposed to the annual-budgeting West and their quarterly-obsessed corporations); Iran looks the other way on the drinking, gambling and pork-eating. Iran and China have not only a 10-year plan worth $600 billion, they have a 25-year strategic plan. Conversely, Iran and the EU had just $20 billion in trade in 2017 and just $200 million with the US. Iran does not need Western technology when they get the same level from China, and China will always need oil.

Part of the arrangement is also: when it comes to national defense, Iran is on its own. However, if the new Silk Road gets up and running China can't allow the disruption of perhaps the plan's most indispensable nation (Russia could make this claim, but only if they replace any sense of rivalry with one of cooperation) via attack or invasion: a formal mutual defense treaty seems very possible, even if far off. Boy oh boy, imagine that day for Iran? Gonna be a mighty big exhale....

Iran has always been the crossroads of caravans, but China has obviously tapped Iran for such importance because there is such a very large sense of trust. And they should trust Iran: due to Iran's anti-Western, anti-imperialist, anti-capitalist stances, they are undoubtedly the most similar nation to China ideologically and culturally among non-Yellow people. (In fact, Iran is nearly as Yellow as it is Arab, ethnically, and that is no joke – the Turkmen ethnicity are 20% Mongol, genetically, and there are 2 million Turkmen in Iran. But just visit Iran and you'll see countless Iranian faces whose ancestors were clearly from parts north and east of Afghanistan.)

You probably think Iran is pretty pleased about all this is – you don't know independent Iranians!

Many in Iran are so devoted to "Neither East nor West but the Islamic Republic of Iran" that they don't accept these (mostly) mutually-beneficial and certainly not "neoliberal" terms of partnership – they want fewer Chinese goods and more Iranian-produced ones. Iran may not have the population capabilities to be a genuine superpower like China, the US, the EU or Russia – but we're big enough to stand alone, they insist! This strain of defiant patriotism is considered totally absurd in the West – they cannot believe that Iran will not run into China's arms like a scared child if only China would shelter them... just as they couldn't believe that Iran ran out of the West's arms 40 years ago.

China is not viewed as an all-knowing guru and often with some suspicion in Iran – modern Iran has had only bad experiences with superpowers – but they can certainly be a partner and a friend. The West is only just starting to whisper about being (grudging) partners – it seems unlikely that Europe will truly hold up their end of the JCPOA. Friendship with Europe is out of the question due to their Islamophobia and their many wars in Muslim countries –who needs such persons as friends? Iran and the West may not be partners in my lifetime, but they are already firm partners with China. Hopefully Iran and China will soon be friends - and the kind of friends who watch out for each other.

Socially, Iranians don't need friends because they have such vibrant and extended family lives, LOL. But everyone needs friends – what are we, self-centred and selfish capitalists like Emmanuel Macron? In 2018 The New York Times wrote, "'I don't have friends,' Mr. Macron said coldly." I'm not surprised, Manu....

Iran & China – Asian similarity at home and in public

The social similarities between the two precede the creation of socialism: Iran and China are familistic (and patriarchal) states, and this binds them as much as their shared economic and anti-imperialist outlooks.

Compared to Westerners the role of individualism is "suppressed", yet one is also "freed" because your place in the family hierarchy assures you of a stable role and a stable social life. You will not die alone, nor live that way either.

There are just so many Western cultural practices which appear completely bewildering to family- and unity-oriented Iranians. Anglophones do not even, for example, have defined names for many of their extended family members – it often seems they don't even want them over even for Christmas, much less have them over on a regular basis. In Asia there is no dominant history of absolute primogeniture, as in England, Scandinavia, the Netherlands and Belgium even today, where being 2nd born long meant men needed to look elsewhere (or perhaps invade elsewhere) for wealth and status. This idea reminds me of essentially killing – and certainly in a psychosocial manner – your 2nd born son, just as all societies used to often kill newborn daughters because they were too much of an economic burden. You cannot will your entire estate to one person under Islamic law – ending such unfair, divisive practices are among the major social advancements of Islam, which also greatly strengthened the inheritance rights of women; similarly, one could not will all their farmland to just one member of your family in China.

Both Confucian China, Communist China and Iran agree that it takes more than just force to govern – China has the "Heavenly Mandate", where legitimacy is not based on noble lineage but on justness and ability, while Iran has religious authority going back to pre-Islamic Zoroastrianism. It also takes more than just "rule of law" (Which "law" anyway? The law of aristocratic capitalist lawyers, as in the bourgeois (West European) model? LOL, no thank you.) This is the root of the Western emphasis on "order" instead of "justice", whereas in both Chinese and Shia renderings it is perfectly acceptable to overthrow an unjust ruler (this idea was certainly used by Liberal Democrats in the 18t centuries, but was almost totally suppressed once those same Liberal Democrats were the ones in power). It also takes much more than Hillary Clinton's famous "village" – it takes a central authority and planner.

In another important cultural similarity Islam, Confucianism and socialism all view man as perfectible. In Christianity, this is not the case – Roman Catholics emphasize that humans are born into a state of original sin. The Calvinistic idea of predestination is seemingly just as negative regarding humans' ability to improve themselves, as one is simply born into the "elect" (as well as into the "damned"), and thus by nature are supposed to be in charge. Being born into the "elect" does not explicitly enforce any moral requirements or laws on those who are elected – they simply have been born with a God-given moral prestige to lead (residing in their DNA, or their advanced consciousness, or more-moral souls, or wherever) and the rest must follow. Baptists and other Protestant sects also adhere, in varying degrees, to predestination, but not the Eastern Orthodox churches. Indeed, few Protestants are aware of just how much their religion dovetails with their dominant neoliberal political thought….

For Iran and China, the government also has an obligation to morally educate. In the West, this is something which a father and mother seemingly have no right to do past the age of 18 years old– all is an adult's individual choice, especially in Protestant societies. Many Westerners have come to hold that moral choices are now all "relative" and valid (supposedly). Indeed, the phrase "moral prestige" is never heard in the West anymore, and there I think it is presumed to no longer be possible? No senior citizen could invoke that phrase with any Western teenager without being laughed out of the room, and often with hearty seconding by those in middle-age. The West, of course, honors youth and not age, unlike Iran and China.

But moral education is embodied by the Quranic commandment of "forbidding the wrong and promoting the good". These are two ubiquitous phrases in Islam, are two of the 10 pillars of Shia Islam (but not the 5 Pillars observed by Sunnis), and both are explicitly listed in Article 8 of the Iranian Constitution, which calls on people to apply it in their everyday life. Few realize that to read Confucius' indispensable commentaries on the I Ching is to read literally the same thing. If we read Gua 14, in his commentary on the symbol for the concept of "Great Harvest" Confucius wrote: "The superior person represses evil and promotes good, Carrying out the glorious virtue of Heaven." Everybody knows China's farmers have been the most effective and most efficient (and also the most co-operative) for millennia – how did they get there? Well… it sure didn't hurt to promote good and forbid evil for great harvest after great harvest (1,000+ famines – all prior to 1961, of course - aside). I'm sure if I dig deep there is a Western cultural parallel to "forbidding the wrong and promoting the good", but there is certainly nothing explicitly like this in modern Western government structure.

Such moralizing from Western governments is totally absent and often violently resented in the post-1960s West. But while the idea that the government exists to improve societal morality does not exist in these neoliberal capitalist societies, it has obviously not been abandoned in Iran and China.

One should read the penultimate chapter in Brown's China is Communist, Dammit!: He includes, describes and interprets 60+ photos of a local government "propaganda" campaign which is 80% moralising and 20% socialism/patriotism. At first it seems like the book's most boring chapter, but then it becomes the one you can return to and enjoy repeatedly. In Western societies such moral-advertising campaigns would certainly immediately discredit the government which put them up. Signs are only for advertising consumerism, after all. In Cuba, there is no advertising and the only signs are the very occasional "Local Farmers Committee #___ Will Defend the Revolution".

The point of this section is: it should be little wonder that both Chinese and Iranian societies are governed by a vanguard political party which is prone to public moralising and which have insisted (and proven) that "modernisation" is not synonymous with "Westernisation", and that "modern morality" is certainly not synonymous with "Westernisation", either.

But the West ain't all promoting evil and forbidding good….

The similarities between the Chinese and Iranian views of intellectuals

A problem for Western leftists, in my eyes, is that they have been unable to conceive of a domestic moral role for their government.

Quite hypocritically, Western leftists view their governments as capable of enforcing morality abroad (via rightly-despised and tragically-failed "humanitarian interventions", as in Yugoslavia, Afghanistan, Libya and elsewhere), but they feel they should not be seen or heard at home! Please start choosing something else to export to the developing world….

The moral role of governance in the West appears to be: they are supposed to clear a space where all types of morality can coexist. The problem with this is: all governments take actions, and all actions have moral consequences and motivations – such "moral objectivity" is simply false.

Philosophically, Western leftists have been deceived by this concept of "moral relativity" which, while being a quite important lens to view an issue through, does not mean that discussions of the issue should not take place and that a final judgment cannot or should not be levied.

When it comes to domestic morality, Western leftists are ultimately supportive of the neoliberal view of it – i.e., no government regulation. They absolutely fail to make this connection between their economics and their morality. I assume it is because the worth and necessity of secularism and laïcité is an article of faith – it is not based on scientific, universally-verifiable proof – and most people don't like have their articles of faith insulted or questioned.

This is also an example of why fake-leftism thrives in the West, and not true leftism – they assume they are "left" without questioning what modern leftism is or if it has changed. Faith in "moral objectivity" as the most "leftist" approach is simply taken as another article of faith, and taken despite the fact that moral objectivity and capitalist-imperialism have ascended hand-in-hand. Regardless of my assessments here, "no government regulation" in the realm of morality is simply not the view in Iran or China.

What the adherents of the CCP and the Basij believe – and also many Chinese and Iranians who are not in these organizations – is that the government should have a huge, huge, HUGE societal role: a role in promoting religion/ideology, a role in the economy, a role in overseeing the press, a role in stopping offensive displays of immorality, a role in stopping financial immorality, a role in truly everything important, a role even in – to varying degrees – the personal lives of citizens.

Calling for this moral involvement by the government is usually labeled "conservatism' in the West... and yet both China and Iran are both undoubtedly leftist revolutionaries? The failure is clear: on the part of the West, because they are so very, very counter-revolutionary in the 20th and 21st centuries. Their definition of both "conservatism" and "left revolutionary" is obviously schizophrenic and riddled with holes.

This is obviously a mass cultural failure in the West, but it is an especial letdown on the part of their intellectuals.

This letdown may have occurred because there is barely any role for the government in Western intellectualism, as well as barely any role for intellectuals in the government. Occasionally you'll have a Vaclav Havel, but such types are the exception which proves the rule. The two are not supposed to meet (just as religion and government are not supposed to meet) – in the Western view, true intellectuals are supposed to be elite, artistic, rare, apart.

Perhaps most crucially of all, in my view, is that Western intellectuals are never openly considered to be in public service – that would be apologism, sycophancy, jingoism and even corrupt opportunism. Of course, because I work for PressTV, the English-language television news service of the Iranian government, and because I defend the aspects of Iran I think are worthy defending, the WSWS accused me being an "apologist" in the headline of their first article which mentioned me: The working class unrest in Iran: The WSWS replies to an apologist of the Iranian regime. LOL, their epithet is not unexpected nor is it surprising, and for the intellectual reasons I have just listed.

And thus, Western intellectuals are content to be merely public critics... and thus are detested and unwelcome - like all who only criticize - and are never seen by the masses as being part of the solution (rightly or wrongly). Western intellectuals, the Western People understand, are only in it for themselves.

For an intellectual to be openly in public service would mean they are creating propaganda. And yet, stunningly, there is NO propaganda in the West. "Government propaganda" in the West is like a hammock in the North Pole – it simply does not exist.

I repeat: Western governments do NOT do propaganda... unlike all non-Western-friendly governments. This is an appallingly naive yet universal opinion among Westerners! The ramifications are quite enormous; so enormous they cannot even publicly broach the question of, "Is our own Western government feeding us ideological propaganda with this line?"

Ultimately, Westerners view themselves – and their Western democratic systems – as "too smart" for propaganda, and thus their government could never even try it, much less get away with it. Westerners simply "know" when non-Western governments are trying to "pass off propaganda", but such a thing would never be even attempted by their own governments and especially never from their preferred camp of their own government (LOL). All I can say is: appallingly naive, politically unaware and culturally destructive.

Intellectualism and the arts are fine and necessary things, but when nihilism & individualism or capitalism & imperialism are seen as the goals (as they undoubtedly are by many in the West), then promoting persons with proper ideology certainly becomes more important than independence; and more important than class as well, because it is absurd to think that all poor people are leftists and that all rich people are right-wing. Look at American rappers and Lenin for examples of these class-defying examples; class prejudice is as much of a wrong as racial prejudice – intelligent people don't assume.

I think the average (revolutionary) Iranian implicitly supports Mao's view here, which is taken from John King Fairbank's, the "West's doyen on China," (mainly because he was a right-wing imperialist and anti-socialist) China: A New History, which is the top Chinese history book in English-language universities:

"Once the intellectuals had been shown by the Hundred Flowers fiasco (1957 – when Red China tried 'glasnost' and immediately stopped before it went too far, unlike the USSR) to be of dubious loyalty, Mao moved to the idea that a new generation of intellectuals should be trained up verily committed to the party because they were of good proletarian-class background. In the contradiction between merit and class status, he saw it necessary to emphasize the latter. He warned the intellectuals that they were simply teachers employed by the proletariat and laboring people to teach their children...."

China's Cultural Revolution is so important because it initiated the process of pulling teachers and intellectuals down from their lofty Brahmin status they had enjoyed for millennia; while a PhD is still feted like a city-state monarch in modern Germany, thinkers in China now had to prove their social utility by doing more than just saying, "I studied something for a long time, therefore I am above being questioned by you." As China progressed in this modern reassessment, Deng Xiaoping correctly noted that intellectuals are part of the working class – and they certainly should stay there, lest they become servants of power and not the People.

Intellectuals should not be a separate elite, but that's what they are in the West – the negative consequences are obvious to absolutely everyone in the West, regardless of formal education.

It is partially because Iranian and Chinese intellectuals take an open part in supporting and working with their governments that the intelligence of government policy is so superior than the West's: this is proven by their twin silver medals in the UN HDI since 1970 – what else can you call such massive success but the result of intelligent government policy? It is not pure luck, and nor is it the result of riches which were stolen imperialistically.

We should see quite clearly: intellectualism (and what could be considered both "immoral" and "positively intellectual") in China & Iran often aim to serve their Socialist Democracy-inspired governments and their People, whereas in the West intellectuals should only follow their own lights, ambitions, desires and whims… and somehow this will magically prove to be a benefit to all; of course, it mostly only benefits the intellectuals themselves, and their elite class.

In the end, I feel pity for Western intellectuals but especially the leftist ones: they have no government which they feel they can morally support, nor one which supports them. They are all alone in the world, LOL! No wonder they are so disagreeable… it's like they never heard a revolutionary could be happy?! (Of course, how many Western intellectuals know Camilo Cienfuegos, the ever-smiling Cuban revolutionary?) It's also no wonder they often wind up renouncing their leftist ideals – it's hard to feel one must do everything alone.

As China's and Iran's governments continue to support affirmative action policies for the intellectually-politically-morally inclined members of the CCP & Basij, their societies will only get better and better governance… at least theoretically. Certainly, this tactic has worked for them for decades. What appears indisputable is: they will get more revolutionary government. "More revolution" – or at least "more of this unique system" – is what the CCP and Basij appear to have as their guiding lights, and that accounts for their many, many affinities.

You can join, but you aren't going to rise in the Basij or the CCP without being revolutionary

After 30 years of long marches to win over the Chinese People, the Chinese democratically demanded that the Chinese Communist Party govern. The Basij have now had 30 years since their inception, and 10-25 million Iranians are willingly choosing to volunteer and play a par...but they are not being demanded to govern as a vanguard party.

However, they appear to be on their way to majority-control of the government, despite not being a formal political party: the Basij may reach a democratic critical mass where their members are elected into so many positions of power that they effectively dominate Iran's pluralist government just as the CCP dominates China's pluralist government (30% of seats in China's largest national legislative body – the National People's Congress – are held by non-Communist parties), with non-Basiji parties there mainly to keep the government honest. It is certainly trending in that direction. As an Iranian civil servant who is trying to present the first objective view of the Basij in the West ever: I pass no judgment – I only note the trends, and remind that trends change.

I think it's quite worthwhile to note the striking structural similarities between the Chinese Communist Party and the Basij.

Firstly, the Chinese Communist Party – despite being a "vanguard party" and having just 90 million members in a nation of 1.4 billion people – is indeed a mass organisation. Just as the Basij is one-third students, the Communist Youth League – separate from the Party but obviously affiliated – has another 90 million members. Additionally, all public school students are enrolled in the CYL's junior corps, the

Young Pioneers, with around 175 million members. That means 25% of China is involved with the Communist Party, which is very close to the 20% of Iran involved with the Basij (if we take their midpoint membership number – 17 million).

Clearly, both the Basij and the Chinese Communist Party are firstly ways to get youth involved in politics and to provoke the shaping of their political ideology. However, kids in such groups are mainly going on field trips, playing sports, only barely tolerating serious school-like discussions, possibly marching around with toy guns or something like that – compared to serious politics this is mainly day care, but with revolutionary cartoons instead of Disney.

Serious politics is serious business, and these two serious groups take being a truly serious member quite... seriously. When we compare the selection processes for prospective members, we find that they are nearly identical.

From Brown's book on China, talking about how to join the Communist Party:

"You will be assigned a mentor.... You have to fill out an application and write an essay on why you want to become a member of the Party. Your first essay could easily be rejected.... Obviously, reading and learning the Chinese constitution, Party documents, Marx, Lenin and Mao are essential...you take an exam on communism and the CPC....

...you will get a thorough background check. Through local Communist committees, your family, friends, neighbors and colleagues will be contacted. There is not much notion of 'Western' privacy in Chinese society in general, and in the CPC specifically.

One of the final steps is a meeting with you, your mentor and people who know you. It could be colleagues, family or friends. You are not told in advance who will be there. Your dossier is fully discussed in your presence. The good, the bad and the ugly are all laid out on the table for you and everyone to see. You will be told your strong points. You will be criticised for all areas where your peers think you should improve. It is all a very slow, arduous and humbling experience, and you are not even a member yet.

If one does finally convince the work/school/local Party Committee that you have the right stuff, you are accepted on a one-year probationary period…. At this point, a lifelong journey and commitment has begun for the new member. Your surrounding fellow members are educating and observing you the whole time. Are you sincere or just out for yourself? Are you patriotic, hard-working and selfless, or merely selfish and venal?"

And now the application procedure into the Basij, taken from Saeid Golkar's rather obviously disapproving book (and the only Western one available on the Basij) *Captive Society: The Basij Militia and Social Control in Iran*. (I should note that many of the previous statistics on the Basij I listed came from his book, which I review in detail in the next part of this series.)

"… its members are classified into five groups: potential, regular, active, cadre, and special. (Before 2010, the Basij membership consisted of three groups: regular, active and special.) These categories are based on the training that members undergo, the extent of their cooperation with the Basij, and their level of ideological commitment to the IRI (Islamic Republic of Iran).

The regular Basij… has little connection to Basij bases; members only undergo basic training. Legally, a regular Basij member must be at least eleven years old. Beyond the age limit, there is no other limitation for a person to join as a regular member.

…

Members who are at least fifteen years of age, have been a regular Basij for at least six consecutive months and have participated in ideological sessions can apply for 'active membership' status."

…

After initial approval by their base commanders, two separate bureaus in the Basij regions review their requests. The Deputy of Confirmation of Ideological Qualification, a branch of the Representative of the Supreme Leader, reviews their ideological-political qualifications. Their applications are also reviewed by the Counterintelligence bureau to check their security backgrounds. According to a Basij member, these committees 'are investigations on everything. It starts with your school, where you went, the kinds of things you did, how you dressed, what your personal opinions and views are, whether you go to the mosque or not, your reputation around your neighborhood, and so on. They investigate all these things.'

...

According to the new Basij regulations, active members should spend at least six hours per week in their bases and three hours per week in special ideological and political training courses. (I detail this intellectual training in Chapter 6. Spoiler: it is learning the ideas of` Iranian revolutionaries, just as the CCP expects their members to know Chinese revolutionaries.)

...

A small group of active Basij can be promoted to the fourth-ranked called the cadre Basij.... After passing these (ideological-political courses), cadre Basij, who are employed by the Basij organization, become the main part of the Basij base organizations and can occupy sensitive positions. The cadre members are full-time Basij members under short-term contracts (usually three to five years), meaning that they are on the Basij payroll.

...

Special Basij are members who possess military skills and ideological qualities similar to those of IRGC (Revolutionary Guard) members. They become part of the organisation after passing special military and ideological courses, and are committed to serving in the IRGC full time.... All the special Basij members also need to take part in 'consistency or refreshing trainings' offered every year, usually lasting for 5 to 15 days."

The similarities in selection and advancement between the Chinese Communist Party and the Basij should be totally obvious, and they couldn't be much more alike. Their trajectory is also the same: they start off as youth programs, and then the serious youth can make these community-oriented organisations a part-time hobby, and then those really committed to their society and government can join the government bureaucracy full-time, and then those who are really committed to the revolution can join the revolutionary wing of the government (CCP, Revolutionary Guards) and have tremendous political and economic influence.

For the West, and for Golkar, the selection procedures for the Basij (and likely the CCP) are terrifying – it's "an invasion of privacy", it's "indoctrination", it's "only for the special forces of the military".

But for Iran and China politics is serious, and probably because they have to be; if Iran and China had spent centuries meddling in European affairs, I don't doubt for a second that Westerners would be taking the exact same precautions. Furthermore, membership in both of these groups have both responsibilities and privileges, and you don't hand such things to the unworthy, unverified and unmonitored. If these groups are allowed to exist, democratically, then they also require standards to ensure proper public service.

Governments sponsor pro-government organisations… that's what they all do

You have to be pretty native not to realize that all governments exist firstly to protect their own power, eh? Such an assessment doesn't make one an anarchist, either. However, some governments focus their power on raising up the People, whereas some use their power to raise up only the 1%.

So what we have here are essentially two mass organisations, which via internal selection winnow themselves into a "vanguard party" at the higher echelons. For China, the Communist Party will be seen as a natural continuation of their millennia-old civil service examinations. Are all CCP members 100% devoted communists? No, but you can bet at the top they are, a few very-slippery exceptions aside, perhaps; it's obviously designed to be the same with the Basij.

The Russian Communist Party became something of a hybrid: Khrushchev, seeking to overwhelm the Stalinist party/faction, opened the membership floodgates to change it from a vanguard party into a mass party, and this was likely a major reason for the Party's subsequent corruption – ideologically unsound people joined and created niches where corruption flourished, expanded and then break Soviet society apart. Along with the Black Market itself, glasnost, and Gorbachev's catastrophic decision to abruptly end central planning of the economy, the expansion of the Communist Party is seen by many as a primary – if slow-acting – cause of the USSR's implosion.

Both the CCP and the Basij obviously need to have strict human resources tests for their members, and it sure seems that they do. Quite intelligently, China's President & General Secretary Xi has moved to make CCP membership more selective, and it is now harder to get into the CCP than the US Ivy League university group.

It is my objective analysis that the Basij – not having had any Long Marches like the CCP had during which they won their People over – has been made a mass membership organization in order to gradually win over the entirety of the Iranian People to the Revolution.

The Iranian Islamic Revolution is also clearly even more revolutionary (unique) than the Chinese Communist

Revolution, after all – beyond the usual counter-revolutionaries, skepticism of such a bold enterprise would naturally be higher in Iran than in China, which was initially following in the USSR's footsteps. Indeed, the idea that a thing such as "Islamic Socialism" can possibly exist is still controversial among non-Muslims (of course, this is despite the existence of the Socialist People's Libyan Arab Jamahiriya (1977-2011)).

If Iran ever gains the international stability and respect which China has won, I would imagine that the Basij would – like the CCP – start drastically scaling back its membership. I can also imagine that some people would not join the Basij for socio-economic benefits – as some now undoubtedly do – if said stability and respect finally allowed Iran to fully harvest and share its wealth and resources with all citizens.

The Basij appears to have one advantage: if the Chinese do not believe the Party is always watching, Basiji certainly believe that God always is (at least at the top levels, one would assume). I certainly think it is fair to assume a higher degree of ideological rigour on the part of the Basiji versus the Russian Communist Party members post-Khrushchev, at least.

The security roles of the Basij, the Revolutionary Guards & the Chinese Communist Party

The Basij is more than a mere "militia", but they do have a security component just like the CCP.

Iran and China are two countries which insist on rigid political control of their armed forces (but not their regular army). Both are also totally against the professionalisation of the army, but the post-WWII West seems to think that mercenaries and democratic accountability/norms can somehow magically co-exist. Iran and China also tolerate nothing like the essentially extra-legal yet highly-political CIA, FBI or KGB.

Unlike the USSR, the Chinese Communist Party has total control of the military. I return to Brown:

"Chinese leaders have been careful to keep control of the commanding heights of politics through the party's grip on the 'three Ps': personnel, propaganda, and the People's Liberation Army. The PLA is the party's military, not the country's. Unlike in the West, where controversies often arise about the potential politicization of the military, in China the party is on constant guard for the opposite phenomenon, the depoliticization of the military. Their fear is straightforward: the loss of party control over the generals and their troops."

After all, the Chinese Revolution put the Communist Party in charge – NOT the military. That would have made it a commonplace "coup", and not a "revolution".

The same "the revolution did not put the military in charge" goes for Iran, where the Army is a separate but equal organisation with the Revolutionary Guards Corps (IRGC). The Basij is placed in the oversight of the IRGC. The Basij and the Revolutionary Guards are essentially the same thing as the PLA: apart from the army, highly politicized, there to preserve the revolution and the constitution, and thus the important role of the vanguard party (Shia clerics).

In my estimation, the primary motivating ideology of Western armies is patriotism; because this is rarely combined with 20th-century, Socialist Democratic ideas, it can easily devolve into jingoism. That is why these armies so easily engage in neo-imperial invasions, but their increased use of mercenaries also explains this continued policy of reactionary aggression.

Both the PLA and the Revolutionary Guards are about 0.2% of the entire population. They are highly-political and elite posts, whereas the Basij is a mass membership organization. The IRGC and Basij are under the overall Armed Forces General Command, who report to the President and Supreme Leader: What this also means is that they were not allowed to become separate and independent from the government (and thus beyond the reach of democracy), like the CIA or KGB; in these latter situations these "ministries" become rivals to the party and/or the government.

Essentially, the Basij and the IRGC serve a very similar function to the Chinese Communist Party and the PLA – they are a "new branch" which goes beyond the usual Liberal Democratic executive, legislative, judicial and military; they are the "revolutionary branch" in that they are unique among the average political system in the world today, and also because each one of them is dedicated to preserving their modern, popular, 20th-century revolutions. Iran's "Supreme Leader branch" should be viewed as similarly revolutionary, and its creation is what makes Iran "Islamic Socialist" and not "Socialist".

I have not and will not talk much about the IRGC – I thought this book was long enough already - but I can sum them up quickly here:

As, you have read – the IRGC are ranked above the Basij in the government hierarchy, and the most-committed Basij members achieve status in the IRGC. The IRGC is an organisation which, while being part of the Armed Forces, is not at all the same as the regular army. The IRGC, like the Basij and the charity cooperatives (bonyads), and unlike the army, have been given significant control over economic resources in so-called "privatisation" efforts, and more than any other group. The IRGC have been given key stakes in the most important and most sensitive sectors (but not oil) – they are Guard(ing) the Revolution, after all. They have increasingly become politically involved, with many former members in Parliament. Their main political affiliation – as I will emphatically demonstrate with the mass-member Basij – is to the Revolution and not the Principlist or Reformist camps. The IRGC are undoubtedly powerful, due to their increased economic influence, and that makes them very akin to the elite of the CCP, but it is the Basij that most affects the everyday life and culture – I think the two should be looked at as a joint unit.

It would be easy to attribute the many cultural similarities between China and Iran to proximity, their centuries of interaction and trade, the invasion and occupation of Persia by the Mongols, and the rarely-discussed importation of Muslims to serve as the administrative elite during the Mongol Yuan and subsequent Ming dynasty. However, all of that could have easily been moot today – it takes unbiased research on the modern, largely-unknown systems of these two modern countries to explain the plethora of 21st century similarities. These similarities, as well as their alliance and intertwined futures, are hopefully much clearer after having read this chapter.

Conclusion – Expect an increase in similarities between Iran and China

For the Chinese Communist Party the process went: fighting, victory, consolidation, purging corruption, rebalancing ideologically, success, and now more corruption purges and hopefully greater success.

For the Basij fighting began in 1980, victory was achieved in 1988, consolidation occurred over the next two decades as Iran successfully rebuilt and redistributed money and power to the lower classes, and then the Basij's rather indisputable triumph occurred when many of them emphatically backed Ahmadinejad during the 2009 protests following his re-election.

However, this chapter has not really explained what the Basij truly is – it has only given context and a standard of comparison.

Nor has the reader been given enough information to decide many things: should the Basij be supported in a democratic majority inside Iran? Are they worthy of foreign support and emulation? Are they worthy of Chinese Communist Party-like prominence in Iran's government? Do they need a corruption-remedying cultural revolution because they have lost the ideals of the Iranian Islamic revolution, or are they living up to those ideals?

This is the first truly objective English-language examination of the Basij ever: therefore, I do not want to answer any of those questions. The goal here is to lay a solid and informative groundwork on the Basij, which is totally absent in the West. The upcoming three chapters are to inform, and not to sway or render judgment.

One cannot understand Iran in 2019 without understanding the Basij – I think all Iranians will agree that this is a fair guiding principle of this 4-chapter sub-series. I hope readers will now agree that the Basij has many similarities with the Chinese Communist Party.

Chapter 5
Iran's Basij: The reason why land or civil war inside Iran is impossible

Allow me to give a summary of my conversations with well-meaning Westerners since at least 9/11.

Everyone: "Ramin, I'm so worried about Iran! I expect US troops to land in Tehran every time I turn on the news!"

Me: "The Basij."

Everyone: "Ramin, the US invaded Afghanistan and Iraq – Iran is obviously next!" Me: "Yawn...the Basij."

Everyone: "Dubya Bush... no, wait – Barry Obama... no, wait – Trump... they are sure to invade and destroy Iran!"

Me: "So bored... I'd make a pun, but nothing in English rhymes with 'Basij'!"

Everyone: "Ramin, why am I more worried about Iran than you?! You aren't taking this seriously!" Me: "May I please tell you about a group called the Basij?"

And then I allay everyone's very kind fears for Iran, just like I'm going to do for you....

I'm sure that the few Western capitalist-imperialist analysts who have actually examined the Basij simply shudder when they find out what the Basij's full name translates to: "Organisation for the Mobilisation of the Oppressed".

"What the heck…? And there are 10-25 million people in this group?!"

"Oppressed" has obvious leftist connotations, and I'm sure Western readers will confirm that there is absolutely no organisation with such a title and directive in their countries.

Nor one so very popular – the goal has always been to enroll half the country (men and women) in the Basij, in what is reminiscent of the American Revolutionary War ideal of citizen/soldier. Iran has 80 million people so they have far to go, but I can report that their recruitment efforts are not flagging.

The Basij is a controversial group even inside Iran – there is a sort of love-hate relationship. However, as in all such relationships, the key word there is "love": if you have that, you have basically already been won over save for a few disputes. Hate-hate relationships – Iran with Zionism, for example – have no chance at reconciliation or compromise.

What's certain is that during the Iran-Iraq War the Basij were universally loved for their defense of the country and their sacrifices, and they would be universally loved again if Iran were invaded tomorrow. Iran won't be invaded though, because the invading country would lose terribly and overwhelmingly, and this 3-part sub-series on the structure, motivations and tangible realities of the Basij aims to prove exactly why.

I think finally explaining the Basij is important at this time: there is a lot of ignorance about Iran, and many people are playing with fire. When US President Donald Trump has been persuaded to pull out of the JCPOA; when Israel is forced to ramp up their perpetual fear-mongering about Iran to cover up the regular deaths of Palestinians and their inhuman Apartheid; when Iran is making equal-partner business overtures to Europe to end their 40 years of cold war and murderous sanctions on Iran… an enormous, mass membership organisation like the Basij simply must play a part in everyone's equations regarding Iran.

The Basij is a major force in Iran, but they are no mere "militia": their military power is dwarfed by their cultural, political and even their economic significance. This group has no parallel in Western society – the previous chapter compared it with the Chinese Communist Party, another deeply misunderstood and mischaracterized institution in another country also slandered by ignorant Western propaganda efforts.

Bottom line: If I can help end this misunderstanding, people will perhaps realize the difficulties any warring tribe would encounter upon invading Iran.

As far as I am concerned: beauty of the Basij is in the eye of the beholder.

So what is the Basij, really?

At the most fundamental level, the Basij is a mass organization which is dedicated to preserving the principles of the 1979 Islamic Revolution, to defend the Iranian People and to work for the success of Iran.

To say that they are "pro-government" is truly redundant or nonsensical: there is no modern country which has a group dedicated to destroying the government which enrolls 12-30% of the nation thanks to government support... and is still a nation. The only political certainly with the Basij is that they are "pro-Iranian political structure" because, crucially, their voting record is mixed.

Two million Basij fought in the Iran-Iraq War, but they are not a military organisation – this explains why when the war ended they were not disbanded, but expanded. They exist to guard the Revolution, serve the State, and serve the People, so they did not run out of work to do just because there was no more war. We now see that the Basij exists primarily as a domestic socio-cultural institution, not a military one.

This fact means that the most important propaganda to wipe away is that the Basij is a "militia" or "paramilitary". Only a very small percentage of the Basij are armed and involved in military/security operations, and by that I mean – they literally only serve at guard posts at public buildings or as bodyguards at major public events.

Furthermore, "militia" and "paramilitary" are propaganda terms because the Basij is a pro-state organisation – militias and paramilitary groups are often not under state control, and often opposed to the state. Thus the Basij should be considered like the National Guard in the US or any other reserve force – totally under control of a democratic government. The Basij can be mobilised quickly in times of war, but in peacetime the Basij reverts to an active cultural and domestic role, unlike the National Guard.

The Basij are also not comparable to Nazi Brownshirts or Italian Blackshirts. The reason this insult is incorrect could not be more simple: Iran has a modern, democratic, anti-racist, anti-imperialist and anti-capitalist ideology which is fundamentally different from the fascist, imperialist, war-mongering, racist, faux-socialist ideology of those two European groups. No such comparison is legitimate in the slightest, and it is fear-mongering anti-Iranian propaganda not based on facts.

Anyway, the Nazi Brownshirts were disbanded long before WWII, and the Italian Blackshirts melted upon invasion and only proved good for imperialist wars in Africa. Because all three of these groups are mass organisations there are some similarities... but this is like saying that "the Conservative Timbuktu Party and the Antarctic Anarchist Party are the same" because they are both political parties. As I showed in the previous chapter, the Chinese Communist Party is the best comparison: both nations have had modern revolutions which deposed their undemocratic fascists, after all!

Again, the Basij cannot be compared to the xenophobic groups of Europe: Europe has a many centuries- old problem with racism, the Holocaust being merely the latest manifestation. Indeed, modern European Islamophobia – the idea that Islamic culture is inherently inferior, negative, violent, sexist and undemocratic – is just the latest domestically-acceptable manifestation of this historical trend and reality. Iran, however, is the opposite of this because their 1979 revolution was openly anti-racist and anti-sectarian. Combined with the fact that Iran has not invaded a country in 300 years, I simply will not countenance the idea that the ideology in which the Basij are inculcated (described in the next part of this series) is similar to the xenophobic, imperialist ideology of the 20th century European fascists. Case closed.

When we stand up to this fear-mongering, it paves the way for realising that the Basij is something totally new, which is why I term it an "apolitical Islamic socialist union NGO".

An 'apolitical Islamic socialist union NGO' seems like a terrible definition

Well, the Basij is a unique (revolutionary) entity – you come up with something that rolls off the tongue!

If the Basij succeeds and its model is copied – like in, say, Venezuela – they will say, "It's a Venezuelan Basij", and not, "It's an apolitical religious socialist union NGO" – I certainly agree there.

This is a novel definition, and while it's certainly not very catchy it does have the virtue of being accurate:

It is "apolitical" for the simple fact that Basij members have mostly voted for the mainstream Principlist (conservative) Party... and then mostly supported the mainstream Reformist Party... and then mostly supported Principlists again, and back and forth, etc. This is both for president and parliament. Therefore, Basij members do not support just one political party in Iran. One might assume Basiji are all conservative supporters, but their voting record clearly and crucially disproves that assumption. And we should not be surprised at that: because this is a mass organization whose only criteria is to support the principles and structures created by 1979, members are obviously drawn from all parts of society and thus all parts of the political spectrum. Above all, and very often openly and loudly, the Basij are devoted to the post of the Supreme Leader and say they follow his orders; this post was created to embody the moral, religious and political ideals of Iran and the 1979 Revolution. The Supreme Leader is not a mere, transitory "president", and a good description of his primary political role is that of unifier of the different political camps – he also clearly unifies the Basiji, whatever their everyday political ideas, as well. Because the Basij support, at both the ballot box and in everyday life, the entire political spectrum in Iran, it is fair to call the Basij "apolitical".

I think the word "Islamic" could easily be removed from this definition – there are Christians, Zoroastrians and others in the Basij, and not only Muslims. So if one means "Islamic" in the sense that one has to be Muslim to be in the Basij – this word is false. However, if one means "Islamic" in the sense that the principles of Islam guide the Basij, then this word is correct. Much like the "Iranian Islamic Socialism" which guides the country, the Basij is expressly "Iranian" first and "Islamic" second.

It is "socialist" due to its obvious goal of politically empowering the "oppressed" class, for the redistributive and decidedly anti-capitalist policies of the many Basij economic ventures, and for its clear role in uplifting the lower classes via direct social aid. I will explain this in detail throughout this sub-series.

They are a "union" because they are mass organisation drawn from every class and sector of society, and one which is undeniably working towards political, economic and social ends in concert with each other. Some call them a "party", but they do not function like one in the modern sense: most Western political party members are indoctrinated and will vote in almost perfectly predictable ways – as a "political machine" the Basij repeatedly does not vote as stereotypes predict. Tell the Basij to "get out and vote", and the record shows that one cannot predict what will happen. A "union", however comprises voters of often very different political persuasions but who are united by a common job, interest, experience and/or needs, with economics playing a key motivation. So "union" is far more accurate than "party".

They are an "NGO" (non-governmental organization), which is the official government designation and a popular one as well, because they are overwhelmingly unpaid civilian volunteers. This is a crucial distinction, and why "NGO" cannot be left out – these people are giving their time and energy in large part because they love what they do, like any unpaid supporter of any NGO. The Basij do not spend their time marching in military formations but doing things like earthquake relief, planting trees, policing the internet, and all that civil service stuff that activists typically do – that's truly the main role of the Basij.

So it's not pretty, but "apolitical Islamic socialist union NGO" is accurate; it's a big definition, but the Basij has evolved into a very big phenomenon.

The Basij: Too big (and too revolutionary) to grasp, and way too big to attack

Why has nobody studied the Basij when it is such a huge peacetime organization of such voting, political, economic and cultural importance? My answer is this: it is too intimidating and revolutionary to be grasped, for non-Iranians:

- a 17-million person organization, and growing
- mostly joined by the lower classes
- a 40-year old organisation, meaning it is durable, tested and rooted
- embedded in the civil service, political and law enforcement classes
- structurally supported by government laws to create economic and social advantages for members
- economically supported by so-called "privatisation" and central planning, which have created massive economic networks and jobs for Basiji
- only criteria is to be 100% pro-Iranian Islamic Revolution
- is primarily a grassroots cultural group drawn from all levels of society
- is a group which is half youth and 1/3rd female
- all receive basic military training
- physically present in every neighbourhood via Basij "resistance bases", which are often deeply involved in community life
- 60,000-80,000 resistance bases nationwide with 10 to 100+ members in each base
- 3-4 million "active" members who spend at least 6 hours per week at their base
- members join willingly, indicating enormous appeal

This is obviously a huge, huge, HUGE grassroots phenomenon in Iran, no?

Those figures I have given are the midpoint between governmental and private estimates. It certainly appears to contradict the idea that the support for the 1979 Revolution is flagging. Why are all these people volunteering for it, then? They do get benefits, and I will relate those later, but some 17 million people didn't join for solely opportunistic reasons.

Beyond the members, how many people are not in the Basij but still supporters of it? I am referring to the spouses, family members and friends of Basij – they are not Basiji officially, but it's reasonable to assume a feeling ranging from tolerance to outright encouragement in a significant percentage of cases. 25 million Basiji supporters would thus appear to be a low estimate.

This is the key point of this chapter: any force which seeks to drastically disrupt Iran will have to contend with the organized, trained, patriotic Basij… and because I know this, and because the most nefarious plotters in the Pentagon, Paris, London & Tel Aviv surely know this… I am totally unconcerned about foreign invasion. Another foreign invasion of Iran is not the risk of a quagmire - it is an idea which is dead on arrival.

Those plotters already took their best shot at foreign invasion – it was in 1980. Western-backed Iraq lost in the War of Sacred Defense (as the war is called in Iran). It can't happen again – Iran has prepared for that, and their plan is called "the Basij". That is my honest assessment.

Bombs alone simply don't work – ground forces must always hold key areas, after all. The US bombed and chemically-weaponed North Korea and Vietnam to the Stone Age, but it was no matter in the end because they couldn't hold the land. War has not changed this fundamental reality and never will, no matter how loudly jingoistic Americans boast at their local bar. What good is nuking a foreign country when you can't occupy the land and reap its fruits – a war machine makes comparatively little profit that way, and that's why the US has been occupying Iraq and Afghanistan for nearly two decades. In Iran all the West can now do is commit massacres – like in North Vietnam and North Korea – but they cannot invade and hold, and in large part because of the Basij.

In a completely objective view: any invading force which gets through the Iranian army and the Revolutionary Guards then has to go through the Basij. Street to street, house to house, cave to cave, cactus to cactus – a Basiji will be there, just like the Vietcong. They'll call him "Ali in the black pajamas" – and will eventually result in your funeral. This is not to vaunt Iran as special in the slightest - China, Vietnam, Korea and other durably-rooted socialist-inspired nations have also repelled invaders hell-bent on overthrowing their democratic, popular, modern systems.

Therefore: of course the Western media doesn't want to talk about the Basij – it makes "War on Iran" a suicide mission which nobody would support despite massive Western jingoism.

That is the overview of the Basij and how they affect non-Iranians. Digging deeper provides fascinating insights. However, not too many people have done this – objectively – outside of Iran.

Replacing 'zero scholarship' on Iran's Basij with 'bad scholarship'

Given the near-total lack of information, I want to remain objective about the Basij so that readers can decide for themselves. I don't want to give my personal thoughts and experiences. I'd like to state that I am not in the Basij (though there is a Basij Journalists Guild).

That is why I am glad there is at least one (but only one) book on the Basij available in the West. This sub-series will analyse this book's analysis, and it frees me from having to present the Basij all on my own and be subject to accusations of bias.

The book is *Captive Society: The Basij Miltia and Social Control in Iran*, by Saeid Golkar. Golkar has been raised, educated and even taught in Iran. The book is his PhD thesis for New York City's Columbia University.

This is what Golkar's book is very good for: he has provided the West and Anglophone world with the first-ever massive data dump on the Basij. The next two chapters will rely heavily on his research into the Basij, conversations with Basij members and reading of all types of literature – domestic and foreign - on the Basij.

However, his analysis of said data… Well, of course it is coloured by his political views, as social data always must be. This is not mathematical or astronomical data – "political science" is not a "science" in the slightest, whatever the pretensions of its professors.

I think the title already makes it abundantly clear: this is the first book about the Basij in the West, and it is also the first book against the Basij.

Just as my recent book on China (*I'll Ruin Everything You Are: Ending Western Propaganda On Red China*, Badak Merah Press), exposed the reactionary, anti-socialist views of John King Fairbank, Harvard's first-ever China scholar – Golkar's main virtue is in providing data, but not in the ability to provide a balanced, progressive analysis. Their research – but not their ideological conclusions – can be used to provide more accurate answers about China and Iran, respectively… but only when more modern and democratic political ideas are applied. They are both very much like medieval astronomers who carefully watched the stars and logged their data, but insisted on retrofitting their answers to the preconceived notion that the sun moves around the earth, or that the planets must travel in perfect circles instead of oblong ellipses.

I don't want to condemn Golkar as totally unrepresentative: there are people in Iran who do not support the Basij... but few Iranians I know view the Basij in such an unfairly one-sided manner. His reviews in Iran, however, have not been as lenient – Basiji websites call the book "insulting to Basiji" and "Iranophobic". Considering that they already know much of the data he has provided, and that he amazingly refused to include even a single positive trait or anecdote of the Basij, I can certainly understand why they don't view the book as useful or honest.

I'm trying to remain objective: his book provides data, and that is necessary for the West. All I can do is examine the data from my own perspective, and then try to remove that bias as much as possible; but Golkar did not do this, I believe. He routinely omitted any positive views, opinions, analyses and facts regarding the Basij, and that is bad scholarship.

Naturally, I tried to find out a bit more about Golkar to discover his political-ideological tendencies. Golkar's favorite person to retweet on Twitter appears to be Francis Fukuyama, who famously declared the "End of History" upon the fall of the USSR, with the capitalist-liberal West European model to reign supreme forever, to the great consternation of leftists and the great delight of right-wingers. Golkar is mostly interviewed in the West by Gareth Smyth, a journalist mostly affiliated with *The Financial Times* and *The Guardian* (the only Western review of the book is by Smyth in *The Guardian*, the UK's "fake-leftist" newspaper nonpareil). These media are neoliberal capitalist and 100% anti-socialist, so Golkar likely has an affinity with these views; or perhaps Golkar is just happy to be interviewed by anybody on his favorite subject (and as a journalist I partly understand that). However, as a journalist, I know that I will be called to Judgment Day before I get a call from either of those two media, because I am neither capitalist nor imperialist. Golkar appears to be trying to make a name for himself with that part of the Iranian diaspora which left Iran following the Green Movement of 2009 – he is definitely not trying to get invited to speak at Basiji events! Considering how big the Basij is in Iran, Golkar is not trying to get invited to many places in Iran, period, it seems….

I'm going to start at the end, with the very final paragraph of the book's conclusion: the final paragraph should sum up and reveal what Golkar's true feelings for the Basij are, what his motivation for writing the book was, and what are his personal ideological and political aims.

"With the expansion of the Basij's involvement in Iran's social, political, and economic life, the opportunity for the country's peaceful transition to democracy will decrease dramatically. Because many Basij commanders and members have been co-opted by the IRI, it is not implausible to think that they will resist any serious attempts at government reform that would jeopardize their positions."

Undoubtedly, this states that Iran is not a democracy, as Golkar says they need to "transition" to it. I find that to be inaccurate and rather indicative of a negative view of the Iranian political structure - Iran is not Liberal Democratic, but that is not the only type of democracy, and every political scientist is likely aware of that. His very final sentence implies that Basij members and commanders are opportunists or dupes, which is also rather negative.

I will be accused of reading too much into it, but there appears to be a complete sentence which has been hidden:

*"**With the expansion of the Basij**'s involvement in Iran's social, political, and economic life, **the opportunity for** the country's peaceful **transition** to democracy **will decrease dramatically**. **Because many Basij commanders and members** have been co-opted by the IRI, it is not implausible*

125

*to think that they **will resist any serious attempts** at government reform that would jeopardize their positions."*

In condensed form: **"With the expansion of the Basij the opportunity for transition will decrease dramatically, because many Basij commanders and members will resist any serious attempts."**

This talk of a "peaceful transition to democracy" is very reminiscent of the coded language used for an armed attack, as it was for the Western "humanitarian interventions" in Yugoslavia or Libya and elsewhere. The goals there were always to bring "democracy". Certainly, Golkar seems to begrudge the Basij their ability to "resist" changes of his political preference.

Golkar also indicates what I have already stated: the Basij is now a permanent, embedded feature of Iranian society which will certainly "resist" a great many things.

Is my "hidden sentence" paranoia?

Well, his final chapter is titled, "Basij Members – Islamic Warriors or Religious Thugs?" Such comparisons would be expected in an American imperialist's or Zionist's view of the Basij, as both are stupid stereotypes and not scholarship. They are also both apolitical descriptions - they view the Basij via a purely religious lens, which is quite in keeping with the usual tactic to discredit Iran and to circumvent substantiative discussion.

Only slightly less mildly, but still negatively, half of all chapter and part titles contain the words "control", "repression" or "suppression" – these are all quite loaded terms which academic scholarship is supposed to eschew, I think we'll all agree.

After reading the book with an open mind, it is my opinion that such clear bias is why this book is "about" the Basij, but also "against" the Basij... and that is bad scholarship. The Basij have their detractors in Iran, but from start to finish

Ramin Mazaheri

Golkar's book evinces an undisguised and unadulterated antipathy for them.

Very surprisingly, he certainly refuses to admit the possibility of even a drop of possible ideological sincerity on the part of members, which is certainly extreme. It is as if the Iranian Golkar doesn't know any devoted Basiji, or that he has never seen a Basiji be helpful? In his insistence to present all Basiji as mere opportunists, he is certainly giving Western readers the false idea that this group will entirely melt away when confronted with domestic or foreign violence. Some will, inevitably, but some definitely will not because they do have ideological sincerity.

Tellingly, regarding Golkar's personal political beliefs, the book is devoid of even a single reference to the class struggle, Marxist economics and the equality-centered ideals of socialist democracy. Iranian Revolutionary Shi'ism, truly the ideology of the revolution, contained ideas, principles, structures and slogans from all these sources. Golkar could have written just one time: "The Basij fails in all of these socialist-inspired areas," but he does not even broach these concepts as being important alternative lenses through which to view the Basij (indeed, he may not possess such intellectual lenses). This makes me think that not only does Golkar not like the Basij, but he does not want to promote the ideals of 1979 in any way, nor does he want to promote socialist ideals either.

Golkar has done plenty of research – in Iran, talking to Basij members, reading Basij literature, finding obscure Western journal articles on the Basij – and his extensive bibliography is a testament to that. It is the vast bibliography of a top university-level work, which it is.

But an extensive bibliography should never be enough to satisfy, because a big bibliography cannot make – to give an example – an inherently reactionary and capitalist view not reactionary or anti-democratic. Technocratism can never be allowed to govern, only to advise with data – everyone living in the post-Great Recession Eurozone should be well aware of the social chaos that results from putting people into power on the basis of their "technical qualifications" instead of their ideological-philosophical-ethical-economic views. Of course, such a view is common in socialist democracy, but anathema in liberal democracy.

It seems to me that in recent years there is a trend in academia to make the bibliography and footnotes just as long as the actual work itself – padding out the size of the book with footnotes mainly of interest to academics and journalists, at the expense of examining a phenomenon with a diverse range of ideological lenses, and also at the expense of presenting actual new ideas. Golkar, as a political science scholar, is supposed to be conversant in a divergent range of ideologies and he is supposed to relay these ideas to us non-academics – hopefully presenting new ideas thanks to his intellectual cross-pollination. By failing to at least discuss socialism he has not provided that necessary range whatsoever, and this marks his book as a clearly right-wing one. Indeed, his book is a well-researched right-wing tract, and I wonder if those at his PhD thesis reading in New York City even cared that his work was essentially an anti-Basij public relations exercise and not true scholarship.

And so I will not be browbeaten into accepting Gokar's "authority" just because he has provided the trail of his ideological investigation into the Basij. Ideology counts. Fairness counts, too, and this book is so devoid of the Basij's positives one is left wondering if 10-25 million Iranians are capable of knowing right from wrong, which is an absurdity.

But the book should be read because… well, it's the only game in town. There is NO other book in English or Spanish. There is a single book in French, but an extremely narrowly-focused one: *The Advent of the Young Basiji of the Islamic Republic of Iran: A Psychosociological Study* (L'avènement des jeunes bassidji de la République islamique d'Iran: Une étude psychosociologique), by Alain Chaoulli (2013).

I now return to Golkar's very first paragraph, in his preface. This paragraph is when the author primes the pump for what the reader is about to receive, setting the tone for the entire book.

> *"Although the organization has millions of members (known as Basiji) and pervades all aspects of Iranian society, there are only a few scholarly works on the subject and even fewer available in English. With the expansion of the Basij across society and its increasing power inside of the Islamic Republic of Iran (IRI), it has become essential to study the Basij and **its role in controlling Iranian society, which have led to the persistence of the IRI in post-revolutionary Iran**."* (emphasis added)

I have made the same point and have the same goal: understanding 2019 Iran is impossible without awareness of the Basij. But Golkar shows the inherent bias of his thesis when he says we should study the Basij to see *"its role in controlling Iranian society"* – that is a fundamentally unsympathetic, negative view, and we must realize that this antipathy towards the Basij is the ideological principle he will use to guide his readers. My goal is simply to unveil the Basij for Western readers – you can say if the Basij is beautiful or ugly; this should have been Golkar's goal, and the goal of Columbia University, which supported this work.

I, too, have pointed and will point to the Basij as a force which has *"led to the persistence of the IRI in post-revolutionary Iran"*… but I think Golkar's implication is clear – he is not pleased that the Basij has helped in the IRI's *"persistence"*. This is his right as a person, but as a scholar… well, I guess it's also his right to be completely biased – no law against it, after all.

As this chapter is essentially a book review, I include this judgment about it: this is a book about Iran, but it is not very sympathetic to a huge number of Iranians. I fundamentally dislike books like that – how can my own humanity be increased with such a view? Golkar may not like the Basij, but he should have at least given their point of view and explained why so many sincerely support it – it is not as if we are talking about a handful of radical outsiders, after all. This was the bare minimum of fairness – it was discarded. That is my impression, and that was his mistaken choice.

But Golkar does not own data, and not even the data he has unearthed. Therefore, in between his conclusion and his preface Golkar and I certainly battled it out in the fight for accuracy, which has always been my primary journalistic watchword (over the more typical "objectivity").

I'd like to finish by returning to the headline of this part – the reason why the Basij makes foreign invasion and also "civil war" impossible. There are two simple, overwhelming reasons why the Basij will prevent a large-scale civil war: Firstly, a fight between the pro- and anti-Basij would truly be a bloodbath even greater than the US Civil War, for the fact that the US back then was truly two different countries. There would be no "Reconstruction" possible in Iran because pro- and anti-Basij are in every village, town and city, and even in every family. Pro- and anti-Basij are totally intermeshed and inseparable. Perhaps if the Basij was a small group such a fight could be possible, but the government has been able to recruit so many Basiji that civil war against the Basij is impossible. The Basij are not going to wage civil war against the non-Basij because it is obviously un-Islamic; because they are patriots; and, if one prefers practical reasons, because there is no reason for them to do so, as they are already aided by and heavily involved with the government.

This lack of clear divisions and the obvious omnipresence of the Basij means the division is not physical, but ideological: the Basij are an idea which is impossible to eradicate, after 40 years. Thus the question will always be one of democratic balance, compromise and negotiation – an unblissful but peaceful coexistence, perhaps.

The next two chapters will describe the unique structure of the Basij, its legal and cultural roles, its unique goals, and its exceptional influence on Iranian society.

Armed with all the facts, readers can then judge for themselves the merits, or not, of the Basij.

Chapter 6
A leftist analysys of Iran's Basij... likely the first in the West

*P*erhaps the biggest surprise of the World Socialist Web Site's proposal was that it lacked even one mention of the Basij. After all, it is a 10-25 million-person organisation mainly drawn from the working class – surely the WSWS would at least mention it?

I think I can explain the oversight: the WSWS and the Western left stopped paying attention to Iran shortly after 1979, after they defied Western assumptions, classifications, ands expectations - they fell back on their fervent belief that religion is eternally in conflict with leftism. Such ignorance helps explain why 21st century leftism is perhaps strongest, apart from China, in a non-Western region – heavily Christian yet often-leftist Latin America.

But the omission forcefully reminded me: The West knows *absolutely nothing* about the Basij.

Perhaps older readers think of them as being cannon-fodder and mine-clearers from the Iran-Iraq war; younger readers may solely associate them with the political street battles during the historic 2009 unrest following the re-election of Ahmadinejad. Both of these views stem mainly from Western propaganda and essentially tell us nothing about what the Basij really is or does. From A to Z, or perhaps B to Z, the West knows almost nothing about this all-important group in Iran: about its start, motivations, support, successes, problems, structure, etc.

I would imagine that Chavista Venezuelan readers, for example, will be very interested to learn about the structure of the pro-government and government-sponsored Basij – it is obviously similar to what Chavistas aspire to, given how they engaged in political street battles in 2017 to defend the progressive aspects of their government. Those battles were three times as deadly and far bloodier than Iran's in 2009. Chavistas supporting Venezuela's Bolivarian Revolution certainly would like the kind of governmental, legal and economic support the Basij receive for supporting the Iranian Islamic Revolution. But the two countries are fundamentally different in that Iran has had a sweeping revolution, while Venezuela keeps playing by the rules of West European (bourgeois) politics; the former was a hard and emphatic revolution, the latter is a soft, unfinished and quite precarious one. Venezuela has held - by my count - 20 national elections since 1999, likely the most in the world during that span, but in February 2019 Juan Guaido has been recognised as Venezuela's interim president across the West, despite never having received a presidential vote. No nation would think of appointing an interim Supreme Leader for Iran…and this is just one of the many advantages of having had an emphatic revolution instead of one national election per year (which have not garnered Venezuela the democratic respect of the imperialist West, which is unsurprising).

Cuba has something very similar to the Basij – their Committees for the Defense of the Revolution (*Comités de Defensa de la Revolución*) , but they do not have the economic clout and economic involvement of the Basij. This is why the 4th chapter made an in-depth comparison with the Chinese Communist Party, as it is the best comparison I can think of.

I got a visit from the CDR one time while working as a reporter for PressTV in Havana:

They visited the private residence where I had rented a room– somehow they had heard that a journalist was there. Perhaps they heard it from local CDR members, or perhaps just from the government itself, as I follow all the rules when working in Cuba, unlike many other foreign journalists (who are then confined to the shadows and thus cannot show the positives of the country or its people).

It was one older military man, and two neighbourhood members of the CDR. They took notes, asked political questions and were polite, open and serious. I quoted Fidel, they quoted deeper Fidel, and after 45 minutes they left more confirmed in an analysis they held upon first meeting me: Iran is Cuba's *hermano*!

And when they left I thought: "Hmmm, so that's the Cuban Basij? Nice guys…."

Of course, we are on the same political page: I was not there to undermine Cuba with my journalism, but just the opposite. But knowing that *el barrio tiene ojos* (the neighbourhood has eyes), and that this neighbourhood was located in a country under constant Western cold war, was not a foreign concept to me and thus no problem at all.

However, many are not comfortable with this idea within Iran and elsewhere, and it's an idea which is often associated with the Basij. However, the Basij is so big that it really is associated with anything and everything in Iran….

What exactly are we dealing with when we talk about the Basij? Let's dig deeper

Many, but not all, of the following statistics on the Basij comes from the book *Captive Society: The Basij Militia and Social Control in Iran*, by Saeid Golkar.

The fundamental unit of the Basij is a "resistance base", and these appear in every social area: mosques, neighbourhoods, factories, offices, schools – anywhere people gather. Undoubtedly, this is the most important level of the Basij because this is where people interact; this is the root of society. There are probably 60,000 – 80,000 such bases in the country (keeping in mind that there are 72,000 mosques), and about 75% of them are in urban areas because Iran is an 75% urban country. The Basij does not create any urban-rural divide; rural Basij are said to be more ideologically committed to Basij ideals, and there is probably a grain of truth in this stereotype.

Each of these groups has two resistance teams of at least 4-5 people apiece (therefore, "resistance teams" are technically the smallest subset of the Basij). Each Basij base has roughly dozens to over 100 members, all cooperating ideologically. There is essentially only one requirement to join the Basij: one must support the 1979 Islamic Revolution, the Iranian Constitution and the unique political system of Iran.

What are these bases concerned with?

All aspects of society. They must have at least seven specialised groups to form a base: security/defense, rescue and relief, culture and propaganda, social services, construction, educational groups and morality police. And then they can expand as they are able to in fields their members are interested in, such as: telecommunications, ideological/political groups, physical education, art, intelligence and counterintelligence, etc.

Where are these bases found?

In more than 20 branches in every sector of society. There is the Workers' Basij, the Employees' Basij and the Guilds' Basij, with career specific branches for doctors, lawyers, artists, clerics and journalists, etc. There is the Women's Society Basij (the main one for women), the Students' Basij, the University Students' Basij, the Teachers'

Basij, the University Professors' Basij, the Urban and Rural Basij, the Tribal Basij, and the Mosques and Neighbourhoods' Basij. Of course the biggest, like the largest union in seemingly every country, is the Pubic Servants' Basij. But the bases are generally found according to residence – the Basij is primarily a neighbourhood institution, after all.

The Workers' Basij has 1 million members. Each workplace with more than 30 workers has been required by law since 2011 to have a Basij base – this obviously can provide the workers with the benefits of increased solidarity, communication and chances for workplace and socio-political involvement. Thus, the Basij appears to be a rather clear indication of increased political empowerment of the working class.

Western leftists often object that all worker organisations must be totally independent of the government and, in consequence, such groups thus have a generally adversarial or collaborationist relationship with the government: this is not the opinion in working socialist countries like China, Cuba, Iran, etc.

I note that Western unions usually appear to be allied more with their elite political class than with their working class members (and certainly not allied with society as a whole) despite their greater perceived independence. In France, for example, unions have signed off on every major austerity measure since 2010. They have crippled every social movement during the Age of Austerity because they are so easily bought off with targeted concessions (divide and conquer by the government). France's nascent "Yellow Vest" movement rejected any union involvement (at least during the initial 2.5 months) for exactly this complicity.

Contrarily, it certainly appears logical in socialist-inspired nations workers and government are and should be closely intertwined. If Iran had independent trade unions the oil workers would have an undemocratically disproportionate influence, full stop. However, it's just a fundamentally different system: (Western, bourgeois) Liberal Democratic, with the focus on individual rights and free choice, versus Socialist Democratic, with the focus on equality, unity and the collective.

Independent and individual unions, as France proves, are rather fundamentally anti-nation; this is why Iran doesn't allow them. Nor Cuba. But the labor model of both Iran and Cuba are unfairly slandered and libelled for not conforming to Liberal Democratic standards... which they explicitly refuse to do all over their societies!

Both models have pros and cons, sure, but recent data shows that Socialist Democracy is undoubtedly more successful: in the past 40 years unions have totally failed the average Western worker, giving back gain after hard-fought gain. Conversely, the Iranian middle class has gone from 5% in the late 1970s to over 30% today - that one big union is doing something right to lift so many workers out of poverty over the exact same time period and amid Western hot and cold war. Given these two drastically different records of success, I can't imagine why anyone would say the Western model is the one to emulate today – they clearly need major restructurings, at the very least.

The Construction Workers' Basij often gives its projects to the Engineers' Basij, in a carbon copy of two related unions working together in the West.

The Artists' Basij, like any socialist counterpart, is supposed to make art which promotes revolutionary ideals and the government, and which confronts Western propaganda.

The Journalists' Basij was one of the last ones created, probably because we journalists are notoriously unwilling to join anything. I am not a member.

The Religious Minorities' Basij is for Jews, Christians, Zoroastrians and others.

The list goes on and on.

But for those like Golkar, *"...the Basij has successfully destroyed independent civil society in Iran."* That's an exceptionally strong condemnation, but is it accurate? Is it necessarily a bad thing?

The ultimate backer of "civil society" in 2019 is France: Emmanuel Macron became president, and the two mainstream parties were shunted aside, partially due to his call that "civil society" should govern instead of the entrenched and deeply scandal-ridden politicians. A French people, who – per global polls – could not be more alienated or cynical about their domestic politics, clearly saw Macron as a better option than careerist, Liberal Democratic politicians - this is an idea which has gained currency across the West ever since bourgeois-led voter disenfranchisement efforts began to be gradually reversed after World War I.

West European (bourgeois) government – and especially in its modern, pro-globalist form – is, according to many, essentially a way for the richest parts of civil society to independently dominate the government: their lobbies, their lawyers, their contacts with political leaders, their campaign financing, the better trajectories of their privileged children... all serve to make civil society not truly "independent" at all, but tools of the 1% who are thus legally enabled to impose their will on society and the nation. Given that "liberal strongmen" like Macron are governing via executive order, or that the democratic votes of nation-members in the European Union are routinely ignored by Brussels, it is clear that the individual citizen is losing a significant amount of power and quality of life in this system despite all the talk of "independence", "freedom", "rights" and "choice".

Socialist democracy has a clearly different ideal: government under strict control of the not-1% and the not-bourgeois classes; group independence and personal freedoms take a backseat to this effort. There are, however, leftist ideas which demand total independence from the state

– these are "anarchist", and have yet to be implemented in any nation.

Having read his book, I contend that for Golkar the Basij have *"successfully destroyed independent civil society"* simply because they reflect it in such an obviously full manner. The Basij are clearly a method of state-sponsored grassroots social organisation in Iran, and because the system's only unifying political goal is to protect and promote the 1979 popular revolution, the rather obviously anti-government Golkar simply cannot support their flourishing.

However, we can all see that the Basij are clearly divided into numerous interests, and by doing so there is bound to eventually be not just cooperation but also competition between these interests – that is called "politics". This also explains why the Basij do not comprise a unified voting bloc: by being drawn from all levels of society it is impossible to prevent the appearance of many competing ideologies and ideas about how to protect and advance modern Iran.

Furthermore, Golkar repeatedly indicates that because all these groups and unions are protected and promoted by the government, they are somehow not independent but under total government control: "Basij as a form of social control" is essentially a paraphrase to the corollary of his title *Captive Society: The Basij Militia and Social Control in Iran.* Certainly, not everyone in Iran views it in the same manner as Golkar, because they keep joining them and keep them running (for free).

Golkar's view is less interesting and far more extremist than the point I am trying to make: clearly, the Basij is far, far more than just a "militia", as is commonly reported; it is clearly present in seemingly every significant social organization and every neighborhood, and is open to all... save those who want an entirely new political system from the one which was popularly and democratically installed. Thus the Basij should be considered grassroots, democratically representative, and authentic.

What exactly does a Basij member do inside a Basij?

"Ok, so we're all organised – now... what the heck are we"?

So this is what the Basij essentially is: a bunch of relatively like-minded people getting together, debating, and then performing social actions together which they deem it positive for the community. I would say the Basij is mainly a "hobby of social service" which takes up a few hours each week from active members. Certainly, this is not a "militia" who spend their time bayonet-stabbing dummies with Benyamin Netanyahu's picture and whipping themselves bloody in the name of God.

First, what must be answered is the question: "What are we?" And that requires training, study and discussion – this is like any serious organisation: the Basij must have an organised mentality.

So what do they study? If you join the Basij you are obviously interested in and want to talk about politics, religion, ethics, history, society and contemporary global events. Therefore, they are mostly just like you – because why else are you reading this type of a book? Just like a Basiji, you have volunteered for this. (And I thank you and hope you like it!)

Introductory training has courses like "Basij Ethics & Etiquette" and "Quran fluency", but Active-level members (the members who can honestly say they are involved a few hours a week) and Basij team leaders must know contemporary Iranian politics, the history of the Iranian Revolution, the situation in Palestine and of other relevant contemporary socio-political events, matters and affairs. To get a job in the Basij bureaucracy full-time means they must have all the above, and also take courses such as

"Leadership Ethics", "Islamic Ethics, Discipline & Education", "Islamic Commandments", etc. Of course, in an Islamic Republic the Quran and Islamic ideology are going to be prioritised.

I believe that only people who are totally unfamiliar with the Quran or who are rabid secularists view this as an a priori negative influence. Such a view is certainly anti-democratic, and should be considered in 2019 to be uncultured due to its intolerance. Regardless, it is fundamentally invalid to say that religion and politics cannot intersect, or that leftism and religion cannot intersect; certainly, leftists have no problem with saying that rightism and religion intersect! Where the Basij ideological training falls on the global political spectrum is up to the reader; I only say that Iran, being revolutionary, is often rather difficult to pinpoint, and that case-by-case analysis always yields more precise answers than generalisations. Golkar has provided, what I would say, is the first right-wing analysis of the Basij in the West - this is the first leftist analysis, and I encourage readers to honestly consider the Basij's placement on the global political spectrum after finishing this chapter and book.

There are four main ideological training sessions each year which are offered to Active members. Golkar discusses the Basij's "Awareness" session, which was a 3-day, 40-hour program that was taken by 1.4 million members in 2003, and which was conducted like a basic university lecture course.

What's more interesting is their "Righteousness" plan, because it is more similar to the culture of a Basij base, as there is give-and-take discussion:

> *"Students form a training circle of 15 to 20 people, and sessions are participatory and conducted like seminars. A high-ranking Basiji or clergyman is chosen by a Basij commander as the educator and is responsible for encouraging students to participate in discussions and to ask*

any questions they may have about Islam, ideology, or current political issues. The educator, in turn, is expected to provide them with convincing answers.... The seminars themselves are devoted to an analysis of current political and social issues; book-reading sessions focusing on ideological works; courses on Islamic culture with the focus on jihad (The struggle to please God and the effort to follow His path, not waging terrorism, of course. Jihad is one of the 10 pillars or "ancillaries" of Shia Islam.) and holy defense; and Quranic sessions... the most important textbooks in this program... come from the writings of the late IRI theoretician Ayatollah Morteza Motahhari."

Motahhari, along with Ali Shariati (who is the only Iranian Revolution-era name Western leftists may drop but whom they rarely actually read), were perhaps the two main thinkers of the Iranian Revolution, with Motahhari focusing more on ethics and also Islamic democracy (how silly of Motahhari to focus on something which many Westerners are convinced cannot even exist, LOL!).

Because of Motahhari and Shariati, they also study something else which will sound revolutionary to many – Occidentology, or the study of the West. I bet the reader of this book has heard of "Orientalism" and also, thanks to the indispensable Edward Said, why Orientalism is now synonymous with ethnocentrism, Islamophobia and racism.

Fortunately, modern Iran is not guided by the outdated 19th-century racist "ideals" of Orientalists. What is certain is that Iranian Occidentology is far more politically advanced and sympathetic than Orientialism, which Western Europe began with the Napoleonic invasion of Egypt and which colours – in a reactionary, racist and Islamophobic (though I would say "Islam-ignorant") fashion – their thoughts on the Muslim world today.

"Thus, Occidentology for university students and professors in the Insight plan is about 'the critique of modernity; crises of

modernity (ethical, identity, environmental, economic, and philosophical); the principles of the modern West (humanism, technology, nationalism and capitalism, tolerance and democracy); the Islamic revolution and the West (conflict or compromise); and secular science and religious science."

I'm sure it covers Marxism and socialism as well, but these are two terms and philosophical lenses which are totally absent from Golkar's book. It is also unclear if Golkar believes that "modernity" is something which was limited only to the West, even though things like the industrial revolution, the rise of the nation state, public education, etc. were global phenomena.

The only thing from that passage which should alarm or shock Westerners is that Westerners certainly have no similar modern-based study of Iran or of the vast Muslim world. Occidentology is a way for Iran to learn about and even from the West – not to swallow it fully, and not to be content with lazy Western stereotyping. If this is what the Basij are studying – the West should and could only reap what it has sown, no?

To be in the Basij as a full-time worker – to work in the Basij's bureaucracy – is to commit to a serious measure of lifelong political learning, discussion, commitment and involvement as yearly seminars are required. In this sense it is no different from any political party anywhere. However, it is not a party and more similar to a typical worker's union because, again, there are different political views among Basiji which they subjugate to the idea of a greater common good.

The office of the Supreme Leader is charged with developing the ideological-political training of the Basij, writing the textbooks and pamphlets, preparing the course syllabi, training the instructors, etc. To Golkar, such control is evidence that mass brainwashing for the conservative so-called "hard-liners" is taking place, which is why now is a good time to discuss how Basij voting patterns defy categorisation despite Golkar's overarching thesis that the Basiji are socially-controlled.

The Basij are clearly political – so what are their politics?

Khamenei has paternalistically fostered the Basij's growth and stability – nobody champions them more. Golkar and Basij detractors say this is for Khamenei's selfish reasons of political manipulation; Khamenei says it is because they are (in his words) the ideological guarantee of the success, moral worth and essence of the Iranian Revolution.

The irony – or perhaps the beauty – of the Basij is this: even though the Supreme Leader "controls" the Basij by picking its leader and authorising its ideological directions, Basiji are not being controlled politically.

In 1996 the Basiji helped the conservatives remain the largest party in Parliament, with then-president Rafsanjani's new Executives of Construction of Iran Party running second. This was the first time the Basij became openly involved in politics. The Revolutionary Guards, who sit atop the Basij in the Iranian government's hierarchy, and the Supreme Leader were likely content.

But just one year later, in 1997, 73% of Basiji members voted for the Reformist Khatami for president. The Basij then "reverted to form" to help the Principlist (conservative) Ahmadinejad win two terms.

But then they obviously aided Rouhani, a Reformist, to win an outright first round victory in both 2013 and 2017.

The two camps have often swung back and forth in controlling Parliament and the largest city councils during the last three decades.

If the Basij are all political humanoids, Khamenei's robot-designing skills leave much to be desired!

This shows the truth: the Basiji are not guaranteed right-wingers – they are regular citizens who can swing either direction like so many modern voters across the world. A Frenchman who would have never even uttered a word of support in public for the National Front in 2007 may have voted for Socialist Francois Hollande in 2012, but then for the National Front's Marine Le Pen in 2017, and then might conceivably vote "far" leftist in 2022!

Above all, because the 10- to 25-million member Basij are so clearly drawn from all members of society, the pluralistic political structure of modern Iran seems to ensure that a group as massive as the Basij can never all vote in one way. Therefore, the idea that the Basij are used as "an arm of conservative politics" – something which is constantly repeated in the West – appears to be rather directly contradicted by their voting records. The Basij – and this is my personal experience, as well – are obviously not conservative, nor reformist, necessarily. Categorisation politically would be, in fact, wrong... except if we classify them as both patriotic (pro-Iran) and pro-Islamic; however, being pro- or anti-patriotic is rather easy to understand, but being "pro-Islamic" is certainly much harder to define in Iran as it is all a question of degrees. Therefore, the only political classification I would make, if pressed, is "patriotic".

Economically, Basiji seem to strongly lean towards socialist principles – being mostly drawn from the lower classes, as everyone in Iran already knows and which I will emphatically prove in the next chapter, *Iran's Basij: Restructuring society and/or class warfare*.

While some are staunch backers of Ahmadinejad, it is no exaggeration to say that the vast majority refuse to follow anyone but the Supreme Leader, whether Khomeini, Khamenei or (we assume) his successor. (Indeed, I would say that the most important question in Iran is if the Basiji will remain so intensely loyal to the next Supreme Leader – if he is not sufficiently popular... that arguably spells major problems for the stability of the Iranian system.)

Certainly, this debate was quite public and quite emphatically decided in favor of the post of the Leader when Ahmadinejad floated the idea of running for president in 2016, which contradicted the legal two-term limit. Almost universally, Basiji openly proclaimed that their political loyalty is with the Supreme Leader. Their argument boiled down to: presidents come and go, but the Supreme Leader is permanent; there is no doubt about what he stands for, and no doubt that he works with either Party controlling the Parliament or the presidency. Whether Khomeini, Khamenei or the next one, I think they will back the post – indeed, the post of the Supreme Leader is one of the most innovative political concepts of the Iranian Islamic Revolution, serving as the glue that holds the different governmental branches and political parties together. Khomeini's genius was his charismatic ability to be that glue. I would add that the Supreme Leader represents the "soul" in the structure of the government of the Iranian Islamic Republic.

In the West, identity politics prevails and people often vote for "personalities" and not party, and this has culminated (or perhaps not even yet) with the elections of Donald Trump and Emmanuel Macron. Certainly in the West, "respect for the office" has clearly dropped dramatically, and with fair reason – does anyone imagine Trump or Macron to be very "soulful" people? This allegiance to a post which incarnates a mix of modern revolution, religious morals and patriotism may be viewed as an anachronism, as bizarre, or with envy – that is your call.

But the inability to see Iran as a modern electorate with a modern pluralistic democracy is why the West cannot understand the Basij: they incorrectly see Khamenei as a "faction"... as if he is trying to create obstacles for the

Reformists when he is mainly trying to mediate with the limited amount of power he has been constitutionally given. Again, that's what Khomeini did so well – his political genius was not intellectual, but social: he was so effective in charismatically bringing different groups together by making it crystal-clear where he stood, by relating it in a manner which anyone could understand, and by clearly living his principles.

The West does not realise that, just like their nations, the two mainstream Iranian political parties have some, but not total, support among the people; they have some, but not total, access to state resources; they have some, but not all, political levers to get their way politically. I reiterate this reality repeatedly, but we should not expect Western mainstream media to begin reporting on Iran in the balanced manner informed reporting requires. Calling the Basij or Khamenei or the Reformists a "faction" is like calling the American Democratic Party or France's *Les Républicains* a "faction" – you could, but you'd be accused of trying to mislead people. No such sensible restraint exists for Iran; no blow is too below the belt; all political parties are trying to selfishly "consolidate power"; the Basij is just a "militia". Sure – great reporting, pal....

Lastly – and for good reason lastly – the military role of the Basij

Anyone who has read this far realises that the idea that Basij is a "militia" or "paramilitary" or "armed thugs" is totally, totally inadequate and wrong. The vast majority of Basiji are not involved in security operations; when they are involved, all they do is mostly guard buildings and act as security details at events.

The wartime sacrifices are what make the Basij so often venerated in Iran, like any veteran in any country. It is very easy for Westerners to ignore this: in America wars are only held on other people's property and thus are viewed from a distance (although they are no longer permitted to actually view them in American journalism); in Europe, wars and holocausts are only things which happen on European soil – those they committed elsewhere are less important.

Prior to 2009, the main connotations Westerners had with the Basij were the stories of teenage soldiers being used to clear mines. It is either forgotten or never-understood that Iran was in no way militarily capable of fighting the far superior Iraqi army. The Shah, in probably his most fatal of blunders, kept the army totally divided and weak so that they could not threaten his absolute economic and sociopolitical control. So not only were they incapable of suppressing the People's revolution despite the installation of martial law, but the national forces – which also saw a post-1979 Revolutionary purge – were not at all capable of resisting the Iraqi invasion. This is why child soldiers were used – they simply had to be.

The wartime stories of Iraqi soldiers were, horribly, the same as Americans in Korea: a barefoot farmer or teenager attacking you with a garden rake still requires the use of a bullet, and eventually you run out of bullets, or you are so totally disgusted by the piled-up bodies that life and military victory no longer hold any meaning. That, tragically, is the only defense of a poor nation, which Iran certainly was in 1980. This is the Basij's birth pains, and the legacy they would certainly draw upon in case of another invasion. It is admirable history of self-sacrifice, to put it mildly.

The history of the Islamic Republic of Iran shows that in times of threat the Basij's role becomes militarised, but in times of peace, the Basij return to a cultural role of societal and political involvement. The fact that the Basij did not end its duties after 1988 shows that it is primarily a domestic and cultural institution, and not a security one. The US invasions of Iraq and Afghanistan caused an increase in state and domestic support for Basij. For all the post-2009 denigration of the Basij, in case of an invasion any objective analysis would have millions - but not all – of Basiji preparing to defend even those who domestically opposed them in peacetime.

Those relatively few Basiji who are armed are a key part in Iran's decentralized battle plan in case of foreign invasion, which is evidenced by its name: the "Mosaic Doctrine". Such decentralisation means the presence of armed forces and command centers nationwide. This is only acceptable in a country which embraces their military and its doctrines. It is certainly the opposite of a capitalist-imperialist force: a garrison or fort separated from the People, and despised. Golkar quotes a top Iranian military member to describe the Basij's security role in case of invasion:

> *"'Basij paramilitary volunteer troops are playing a decisive role in the country's asymmetric warfare strategies…. What makes up for asymmetries in wars against countries which enjoy technological superiority and hi-tech military tools and equipment, are faithful and highly motivated troops…. …(The Basij are) a faithful and motivating force playing a decisive, fundamental and pivotal role in asymmetric battles.'"*

What this means practically is: Basiji in speedboats in the thin areas of the Persian Gulf swarming big US navy boats, and it certainly will work… though it does rely on *"faithful and highly motivated troops"* who will likely have high casualty rates.

But I would be quite pleased to see the faces of invading troops the moment they see how forbidding the mountains are in Iran. Iran is even more mountainous than Afghanistan: the Hindu Kush is steeper, but the Zagros Mountains alone are twice as long, and slightly steeper than the Rocky

Mountains. The Alborz Mountains are steeper still. So the Basij are blessed with terrain from which to fight down from – invaders will have to come up the hill. Just as Rome only prospered because it had the Alps to its back and the sea to its front, Persia/Iran has only prospered because the Iranian Plateau is similarly protected - by mountains, seas and desert in every direction. I clearly ascribe more to the concept of geographic determinism than the idea of Roman or Persian cultural superiority....

The Basij are not a professional military, but they have some training... and a lot of ideological training, which is far, far, far harder to inculcate than military training. They will also have tremendous local support. All of this means the Basij will not make it easy, to put it mildly. They certainly seem set up to be a Vietcong of the 21st century, as Iran would likely also fight for 30 years to preserve their sovereignty. I think it's not wrong to say that many Basiji, who are dedicated to preserving the modern and popular 1979 revolution and the government and the nation, will be fighting for decades from ideology alone. And then we must also realise that like all invaded nations - they have nowhere else to go. Not all 10-25 million Basiji will be effective "terrorists", as they are sure to be described in Western media, but a few million will be rather a lot to deal with, right, military analysts?

So I hope Washington and Tel Aviv are reading – if a few thousand armed ISIL members can't be taken care of easily, how can millions of ideologically-politically-militarily-trained citizens be easily defeated?

They can't. It's not the army, nor their superior weapons – victory in war depends on the People. Since 1980 the Iranian People have been more than adequately organised to be prepared in case of attack.

Were Paris to be attacked, however, I'm sure it would be total chaos – you'd have the police, and that's it. Were Havana to be attacked, there'd at least be those three dudes from the CDR who came to my apartment to question me… at least three dudes in every neighbourhood and village, that is. Were America to be attacked there would be no domestic organisation for their resistance other than, "How many guns do you have?" (which is indeed a lot of resistance), and the local police (which is indeed a lot of police).

This is why an "invasion of Iran" is so absurd to me. Lots of bombs, ok, but what do the aggressors do when the bombs stop? No country has yet been bombed into complete annihilation if a large percentage of the People resist instead of secede, and the Basij resistance bases are set up exactly for that. When the boots go toe to toe, the Basij is a tremendously solid third line to protect the goal, no?

This chapter has discussed the structure, the ideology-politics, and the security aspects of the Basij – all things of interest to non-Iranians. However, the next chapter is the more crucial one for those who really want to understand Iran, as it discusses how the Basij is drastically reordering the class structures of the nation.

In essence, it answers the questions: beyond ideology, why do people join the Basij? Why do women support the Basij more than men? What is the Basij doing with the money, factories and jobs which have been transferred ("privatised") to them? Why is there strong internal opposition to the Basij? What are the economic and social benefits people get from being a Basiji?

The answer to these questions are all essentially "class"… and while I remain objective in the next part as well, I must concede that I am predisposed to answering most social questions with the answer of "class". Maybe I overemphasise its importance, but I don't think so. While many leftists refuse to discuss religion, we all agree that the class lens is perhaps the paramount way to examine a society.

When I examine the Basij what I see is expressed in the title of the next chapter - *Iran's Basij: Restructuring society via class warfare*.

Chapter 7
Iran's Basij:
Reconstructing society
via class warfare

*T*o summarize: In any objective analysis, there is no doubt that the Basij is rebalancing the social and economic power in Iran in favour of the lower classes. One's view of this may be "positive" or "negative", either "right" or "left", but it does not change the fact of "rebalancing".

What Golkar himself makes clear, with plenty of statistics and research on the Basij from inside of Iran, is that the Basij mainly come from lower and middle class families. Iranians would have been shocked if he had said otherwise, as this merely verifies the common assumption, which Golkar acknowledges:

> *"As of the social origins of Basij forces, there is a general view that they come from the poorest and most marginalised groups of society". Elsewhere: "In fact, Iran's 'oppressed' appear to be the major source of recruits for the Basij."*

Golkar provides no shortage of statistics which prove: the main source of Basij recruits are people who need government welfare programs which promote socio-economic equality. So it should be unsurprising that the full Farsi title of the Basij uses the term "oppressed", which in

Iran refers to the exploited and underprivileged classes who suffered under the aristocrats and monarchy. To use a common theme of mine in my written journalism, 1979 was a "Trash Revolution", or to use an Iranian term which means essentially the same thing about Iran's revolution: it was a "Revolution of the Barefooted".

There should be no doubt that class prejudice has existed in Iran and still exists in Iran, just as in every country: many Basiji are considered "Iranian Trash", and Trash everywhere is denigrated by their nation's rich, technocrats, their so-called "Talented 10th Percent", and their fake-leftists. However, it is inherently reactionary to judge someone's merit by their completed level of education, their parents or their neighbourhood. This is why much of my journalism is dedicated to insisting on socio-economic and cultural respect for "Trash", whether in Iran, China, France, the US, etc. However, such respect can only arrive via socialist-inspired revolution.

Poor people are the backbone of the Basij and the government supports the Basij, so do the math and we can finally start replacing the usual and inaccurate definition of the Basij – the idea that it is a military-minded militia. Security, defense and force are not the primary concern of the Basij - the Basij is a group which serves as a government-supported welfare and affirmative action program, with the majority of its members hailing from the lower classes, in return for supporting and propagating the ideals of the 1979 Revolution and the Iranian Constitution.

I remind the reader that Iran's middle class was 5% in 1976, but it is now well-over 30%. I have often posited an undeniably positive thesis about the 2009 unrest: 1) it heralded the permanence of this new middle class, and 2) it showed that the lower classes will not tolerate any attempt to dramatically change the political trajectory of Iran until they reach the same level of moderate prosperity as the nouveau middle class. I will explain this analysis in detail later in this chapter, but I bring up the issue now because the Basij clearly has played, is playing and will continue to play a major role in reshaping Iran's class structure.

Obviously, over a timeframe where the Western middle class has been gutted, the Islamic Republic of Iran has undeniably lifted over 20 million people out of the lower class. All will agree that this is the primary goal of socialism – government concern goes towards the poorest members of society first.

However, we should see – from a class analysis – why support for the Basij is less often found in the middle and upper classes: they simply do not "need" what the Basij offers its members. Indeed, from a class analysis the upper and middle class may even feel the Basij threatens their gains, or increasing their gains further. From a class-cultural analysis, it is a regular occurrence in all revolutions that even if mummy and daddy benefitted directly from a revolution, their subsequent generations may not be properly-schooled in this reality and history and thus can easily become rather anti-revolution. They "forget where they came from", to use a common phrase.

In the previous chapter I described the educational and cultural training sessions for Basiji, and also how they are divided into "Resistance Bases" where members can focus on a broad range of activities for social, personal and neighborhood improvement. What I did not mention is how all these activities necessarily require government subsidies for the following: classrooms, educational materials, paying salaries, recreational facilities, camp infrastructure (sports, religious, language, cultural), the chance to visit religious sites (travel expenses, lodging, food), entertainment clubs, and many other besides. These are obviously especially prized by the lower classes who cannot afford them as often as Iran's middle class. Thus, at the lowest grassroots level, the Basij clearly provides something to those without much means. The importance of this cannot be under-estimated, even if middle- and upper-class citizens can take such privileges for granted.

The government also implements a tremendous amount of "affirmative action" programs for the Basij, which I will also explain in this chapter; given that the Basij are mostly from the lower class, this logically has an undeniable impact on the class structure of Iran. It is true that this is not the open class warfare of "declared socialism" because it is granting priorities based on Basij membership and not class, but the effect is very close to being the same and the intent is only marginally different. It is up to the reader as to whether "motivations" or "results" are more important. Iran is not an openly socialist government, but that does not mean there is "no socialism".

For example, according to Iranian law, 40% of undergraduate and 20% of post-graduate university admissions are reserved for Active-level Basij members – this is obviously of huge importance for poor people trying to advance their socio-economic status. Western affirmative action is mainly based on race or ethnicity, and sometimes class as well – regardless, such policies have declined precipitously in the last two decades. For example, in 2003 the US Supreme Court banned racial and gender quotas for university admissions.

No group joins the Basij more than students – children and teenagers (age 11-18) make up 30% of total members. Golkar relates how for poorer students the Basij is clearly a way to advance, succeed and to reshape society: *"Being a Basij gives students special privileges, allowing them to enroll in schools that are often the best public schools available in their city...."* They also get discounts on text books and prep courses.

The Basij is more popular among rural students, as half of rural students are in the Basij. As is common worldwide, rural areas are more likely to be poorer than urban areas.

But it is key to accept that most of these students come from poor backgrounds. In 2003 more than half of Basij summer camp members came from a family with a minimum of six members (including parents, and it's possible that grandparents were not even included in these surveys even though this is a typical occurrence in Iran); 76% of their parents did not graduate from high school; many were recent movers from country to town; these are all likely indicators of a lower economic status.

One-third of university students are Basij, showing that the Basij-prioritisation programs are being applied almost fully. We can objectively see how the Basij are getting "smarter", and this makes their ascent and permanence even more likely in any objective analysis.

Western journalists love to talk about the youthful demographics of Iran's population, and they love to talk to Iranian youth... but almost only from the upper class (and preferably female and attractive). This is primarily because mainstream Western (and thus capitalist) publications are only interested in supporting and emboldening the rich, comprador and bourgeois classes in foreign nations. So Iran is not alone in this one-sided, class-based sexualized coverage – read about any primarily-youthful non-Western nation in a Western media, from Cambodia to Caracas, and you invariably find it is the upper-class who is quoted, with the accompanying photos just as invariably being of pretty young women. Crucially, IRI-supporting Basiji youth are a huge counterweight inside Iran to this oft-quoted upper-class, and play a very important democratic role. Sadly, Western journalists systematically ignore or self-censor Basiji students out of their every one of their stories. By ignoring the Basij non-Iranians thus have received a fundamentally unbalanced picture of Iranian youth, and this reality cannot be stressed enough.

For employment in the public sector Active-level Basij members also get priority, which is – in effect – another affirmative action program. In 2003, 65% of government employees were Basiji.

From an objective view of how revolutionary governments remain stable, this makes sense: the only requirement to join the Basij is to support the 1979 Revolution and thus the government, so it is natural that Iran wants civil servants who are the most committed and supportive. This is also exactly what China does.

I think a major problem with Golkar is that he seems to rather obviously want anti-government (anti-Revolution) citizens to be promoted in government, but... what government hires and then promotes citizens who are open political dissidents? Dissidents are not mere "political opposition", let's not forget. In my effort to provide the first objective analysis of the Basij in the West, I make no judgment here – I just think Golkar is asking for the very unlikely, if not the impossible; on a theoretical level, every government primarily exists to protect themselves... but the good ones include protecting their People as well. The reality is that many governments do not, and this is most glaringly evident in the Eurozone during the Age of Austerity.

Government jobs, in every nation, are far more stable and protected than in private industry, and thus always are highly prized among the middle and especially lower classes. This is a reality which many upper-class people do not grasp; it also explains why they are often in favor of the neoliberal idea of reducing the size of government.

Working-class Basij have very compelling reasons for continuing with the Basij even after procuring a government job: it's a state-protected resource to defend their job and their working conditions in solidarity with their colleagues. This is why there are many Basijs (Or is it "Basijes"? Nobody has cared or dared to write about the Basij in English so that may be the first time Basij has even been pluralised in English journalism, LOL. I'm sure the Associated Press will take note and update their 2019 stylebook accordingly.) in so many workplaces. As previously mentioned, every company over 30 employees must have a Basil, by law.

There are undeniable, direct economic benefits one gets for joining and being active with the Basij, and these will be discussed later: what I have listed are ways in which the poorest levels of society are uplifted if they join the Basij and how they Basij are structurally supported. Structural support also exists on the economic level: In multiple 5-year plans all firms, factories and pubic companies have been ordered to allocate 1-2% of their profit to development of the Basij, and there are also tax breaks for donations to the Basij.

Some things are abundantly clear: the Basiji is primarily staffed and supported by the lower classes, and the government is using the Basij as a way to uplift the socio-economic lives of the Basiji. Political ideology plays a part in this uplifting… and that is opposed by those in Iran who feel that not joining the Basij should not exclude them from the exact same government aid. I imagine many in China feel the same about the Chinese Communist Party. However, I also think that Basiji are undoubtedly giving something back to society in return for their benefits.

Women like and participate in the Basij more than men

Being a mass membership organization, women obviously must have a huge role.

The Basij is – I would say – an essentially feminine organisation: after all, the Basij is primarily a social group, and women are more socially-oriented than men, in general. It is also idealistic, and thus quite romantic. For most it is Islamic faith-based (though open to non-Muslims), and women make up the backbone of every faith. Furthermore, the Basij is akin to the Cuban Committees for the Defense of the Revolution in that it acts as a neighbourhood watch; neighbourhood watches are mostly for gossip and not physical confrontation, and women like to gossip more than men, generally. Furthermore, telling people "not to do this little thing" and to "do that little thing" – in a "mother hen" aspect I describe later – is also more anathema to men, who generally prize personal latitude and freedoms more than women.

Add in the social welfare aspects, and it is little wonder that, "*For example, they* (women) *participate more frequently in Basij maneuvers then do their male counterparts.*"

Polls also show that women have a higher opinion of the Basij and welcome the prospect of membership more than men.

This probably blows Western people's minds: "Women actually *like* the Basij? I thought they were being forced into straightjackets from which they had to somehow cook lavish meals and impeccably clean the house?"

In fact, what seems objectively clear is that joining the Basij is liberating and not restrictive for women: "*Equally important to these social activities, being a Basiji provides women, especially those who come from conservative families, with opportunities for social mobility. In addition to finding a better job and earning a higher salary, these opportunities include the chance to marry well and forge a space in society independent of their families.*"

Golkar repeatedly makes vital declarations and startling conclusions such as these, and yet he never even broaches the idea that the Basij serves as an affirmative-action program which is even remotely positive...?

I think that many need a moment to regroup with some fundamentals: the Iranian Islamic Revolution was a massively-supported revolution, inspired by among the most modern political thoughts of its era and combined with among the most modern views of Islam - we should not be at all surprised that the Iranian Islamic Revolution produced institutions which sought to uplift society's most oppressed minority – women. However, most Westerners cannot imagine that 1979 produced anything but negativity and oppression for females because they have been subject to constant Islamophobic and anti-Iran propaganda.

By law, Basiji women have priority in selection for government or semi-government jobs – again, this is de-facto (or ideological) affirmative action. For example, they get licenses to start nurseries easier, a major source of female employment. They certainly can expand their social network out from the usual (quite extended) social network in Iran – the family.

Non-Iranians have a deranged view of Iran when it comes to women, mainly because they think: Iranian women hate modern Iranian culture, that Iranian culture was made entirely without their input, and that all Iranian women find it repressive. But Iranian men can back me up on this: if repression exists, it is women who are the-equal-if-not-better agents of repression in the home and neighbourhood, LOL! This is almost even acknowledged by Golkar, who I'm sure knows exactly what I mean:

> "Generally, women are seen as agents of social change, but their roles as agents of political order are rarely studied."

Yes... quite. The idea that women are perpetually passive, helpless, always-violated members of society is fundamentally insulting to the power, brains and ability of the female gender. Of course, Western women are paragons of progressive virtue and could never even subconsciously act as agents of a reactionary-imperialist-racist political order. That's why Iran should scrap the Revolution and emulate the West, right? Yes... quite.

So, when there was a recent 1 million-signature campaign to decrease societal discrimination against women, Basiji women – while of course not opposing such a campaign – concurrently initiated a 4.5-million-signature campaign to protect the hijab law and other things we Iranian men get ALL the blame, LOL.

Basiji, especially women, study Iranian revolutionary and philosopher Ayatollah Morteza Motahhari's book *Women's Rights in Islam*, and it is significant that in the long-ago, in bourgeois revolutions of the US and France there were NO women's rights components, whereas in Iran women's rights books are foundational texts.

In Islam, as should be already well-known, men and women are equal but have different rights and duties. It is my humble opinion that Western women perceive "modernity" to mean that they have only "rights" and not "duties"; men, however, still have "duties", mainly because they are falsely assumed to have always had "rights". Such an analysis of Western men is faulty because it is fundamentally based on gender instead of class; it is fake-leftist and based on divisive "identity politics". Men of the lower classes have – just like women – been subject to terrible societal oppression by the rich; indeed, far from dividing us the class analysis unites us all the most.

This idea of men and women being equal but different is perhaps typically Asian, as it is the exact same philosophy behind yin and yang: neither yin nor yang is superior to the other; both have the same attributes and strengths which the other contains, but which are less prominent and concentrated.

Golkar, like many men and women in the West, but unlike in the Muslim world, appears to believe that Islam and feminism are incompatible, and also that only unintelligent and uncourageous women could support modern Iran: *"By increasing the quality of the education, ability, and socio-economic position of the female Basiji, the regime ultimately weakens its foundations, influencing its traditional religious interpretation of the role of women."* Many will view that sentence as nonsense in many ways – Islamic tradition is not the result of women being uneducated – but when it comes to Iran and women no view is too outlandish.

For example, Golkar quotes Golnaz Esfandiari, a longtime journalist with Radio Free Europe and former chief editor of Radio Farda, both of which are a 100% anti-Iranian propaganda tools of the US, just as BBC Persian is from the United Kingdom, regarding the Basij Babies program, which is organized by the Women's Society Basij: *"The 'Basij Babies' program suggests that some in the IRI believe that children should be indoctrinated not only at elementary schools but even before that – as soon as they are born, in order to prevent them from turning into potential critics or independent individuals who want to decide about the way they live and do not base their decisions on the rules set by the Iranian establishment."*

Obviously, it is scientifically impossible to indoctrinate a baby… the idea itself is absurd. A baby has no capacity for political thought, and have been scientifically proven to be stupider than dogs until around two years old. Such wild hyperbole, with logic and common sense totally thrown out of the window, is expected from Radio Free Europe but not from academics. However, Golkar's book proves that he is not an objective academic just as Esfandiari is not an objective journalist – both have an agenda. In their apparent zeal for counter-revolution they fatally assume that all readers are dumb enough to swallow whatever they say, and thus they invent or reprint such nonsense.

The Basij Babies program is, of course, a place for like-minded mothers in the neighbourhood to congregate, and where mothers can find other local like-minded mothers for day care and friendship. Maybe they put "cute" Basij uniforms on their babies, as parents often like to do with children, but it is certain the baby would not perceive themselves as being any ideologically different than if he or she was wearing a potato sack… because babies cannot have ideologies! (Perhaps that is why everyone likes babies?)

Furthermore, all elementary schools worldwide have elements of social and ideological-political indoctrination. Socio-political indoctrination is also impossible to prevent… unless you can get kids to stop asking questions, of course.

Both Golkar and Esfandiari (who also writes for the popular American magazine The Atlantic) illustrate that the only way for an Iranian – or anyone covering Iran – to be successful in the West is to be not merely anti-Iran, but to be willing to either wildly exaggerate or invent the most heinous accusations about Iran they can think of. I include Esfandiari's quote not because we learned anything about the Basij, but because it shows how Golkar is repeatedly willing to offer the unsympathetic view of the Basij without ever even discussing the sympathetic view. That is unbalanced scholarship. I have already noted that neither Marxism nor other typically-leftist ideas are ever broached in this work of political science, which makes it bad, unbalanced scholarship.

I wonder if Esfandiari is politically indoctrinating her babies *"as soon as they are born"*? Me, I would focus first on potty training….

How does the Basij have the economic power to provide welfare programs and jobs?

A fair question to ask is: why are welfare programs only open to the Basij, and not everyone?

We must remember that the Basij began as a fighting force: 2 million Basiji fought in the Iran-Iraq War (75% of Iranian fighters, with 550,000 of them students), and, like the G.I. Bill for the US in World War II, there was a tremendous political and democratic consensus that these veterans deserved priority in the postwar era to reintegrate them into society.

In Chapter 2 I explained the nonsense behind the WSWS's indignant-yet-uninformed statement regarding the recipients of the *"huge sums paid over to the Shia religious establishment"* – the *bonyads*, or state charity cooperatives. Just as Iran took 10-15% of the economy from the capitalists and the monarchy and gave it to charity, they used the same resources to create the Basij Cooperative Foundation (BCF), which is the huge entity which oversees all Basij operations, veterans included. So the BCF began as the governmental arm which aimed to help care for veterans and shepherd their return to civil society.

The BCF has grown to over 1,400 companies and firms as of 2007. During the postwar "de-nationalisation" process many state-owned companies were assigned to them, and they were also given priority in buying stocks of state-owned companies. So, for example, when in 2004 and 2005 some Iranian state companies saw their shares privatised, many of the shares were bought by the Iranian Investment Company, which is owned by the Mehr Finance and Credit Institution, which is merely the new name of the Interest-Free Financial Institution of the Basij... so we should see that privatisation is not at all what you thought previously.

Furthermore, not only are these shares not foreign owned, they are not even privately owned! Mehr Bank is the "biggest private bank" in Iran, according to Golkar... and yet is owned by the Basij Cooperative Foundation, which primarily exists not to make money but to care for Basij members and activities, adding yet another layer of "this is not Western-capitalist privatisation at all".

What is exceptionally unique is how anti-capitalist their directive and practices are in their ventures and stated aims: banking (interest-free and low-fee loans to members), construction *("In fact, the IRI has used the CBO*

(Construction Basij Organisation) as part of its economic populist policies," per Golkar), real estate (where they provide low-cost housing), medical industry *("...the IRI pays 80 percent of (Basij) members' medical and health care expenses"*), retail via the Consumer Goods Provision Institution of the Basij *("With hundreds of stores and hypermarket chains, this institution is primarily responsible for providing cheap goods for Basij members."*), telecommunications (free internet access for members) – the list goes on and on.

"Although the Basij commanders have garnered financial privileges by controlling companies, it seems that the economic activities of the Basij are less profit-centered and more oriented towards populism." Considering just how opposed Golkar is to the Basij, and how silent he is regarding socialist economics, this is clearly a major understatement.

But make no mistake: this is the exact same statement made by any Western capitalism-oriented analyst when it comes to viewing the BCF, the bonyads, the companies of the Revolutionary Guards... or the companies of the Chinese Communist Party, for that matter. None are designed to be efficient, which is something that deranges a Western stockholder, but are cooperatives designed to fuel employment, distribute wages to keep the nation's real economy running smoothly, create cheap goods, and reduce the ability of foreigners to destabilise the domestic economy.

This is probably all quite surprising to Westerners but, as this book (and many other articles of mine have proven): the West simply does not understand that these economic practices of Iran which are obviously socialist in nature. Well, Western right-wingers do, most likely. Perhaps the mind-meld Westerner leftists need in order to understand the Iranian is economy is this: the Iranian economy is state-controlled, therefore it is natural that the Basij run a part of the economy.

"Together, all these institutions, including the BCF and its 1,400 clusters, provide many employment opportunities for the Basij… the Basij enterprises are owned, operated and staffed by Basij members…. In fact, the economic activities of the Basij create jobs for both active members and their dependents."

That is why the BCF is a cooperative, and not capitalist. If cooperatives are not "socialist" enough for Western leftists, I guess I should just give up!

"With all the financial assistance provided by the BCF, it seems strange that more people do not want to join the Basij."

Such a statement – a business entity providing a great deal of "financial assistance" to anyone but stockholders or owners - has never been made about any modern capitalist corporation. But this does return us to the first question I posed in this section: why are the Basiji getting priority over regular citizens? The answers to that, and the justness of those answers, I leave up to the reader, but we can get into a fair and public discussion…

Why do people join the Basij? It's complicated

We have answered the "Who", "How", "When" and "What" regarding the Basij, but "Why" has been left for the end.

"The primary function of the BCF in the Iranian economy is to provide for the welfare of the Basiji in different ways. Because materialistic motivations are the main incentive for joining the Basij, the BCF is responsible for overseeing and meeting the material needs of its membership."

Golkar claims *"materialistic motivations"* are the main incentive, and not just here but throughout his book. Objectively, this is clearly the most cynical analysis possible – taken too far, it gives the impression that the average Basiji has joined for hypocritical and opportunistic reasons.

Objectively, I will add: it is also quite often true, and no Iranian would deny it, nor do many Basiji.

This reality does enrage some Iranians about the hypocrisy of Basiji, especially as Basiji may often claim – on an individual basis – to be morally superior to non-Basiji: they often give the impression of being more revolutionary, more religious, more moral, more societally-involved, less selfish, etc.

However, I am not enraged by this possible abuse.

This does not make me unobjective about the Basij, and I am happy to explain why: it's better than Western neoliberal capitalism, at least!

I'd rather have the BCF in charge of a company than some self-interested CEO, right? Iranians all know that Basiji are those who need government welfare more than others – I say: let them take it, because many of them give something back to society; and some gave all during the war.

And what's wrong with the government "buying off" their citizens? That's essentially what they are supposed to do – return our taxes and our natural resources back to us. In the West the taxes of citizens and the People's resources are directed for the benefit of primarily the 1% and their sycophants.

These things the Basij get – a reduction in military service, discounts for some goods, the chance to visit religious sites, a membership card which they can produce to not get hassled by other Basiji, educational materials, etc. These are often only highly valued by those with little. Maybe some poor Basiji – many of whom are religious – will sell their soul for them... but I doubt it. Many are clearly in a position of social and economic weakness, so I am not about to begrudge them some advantages – this is basic leftism.

Golkar never makes such explanations; never focuses on the class redistribution aspects; never even broaches the idea that many Basiji are sincere – he focuses only on the most cynical rendering possible. He even explicitly divides the Basij into three groups: *"the believers, the opportunists and the thugs"*.

For the sake of argument, let's assume they are evenly divided (which Golkar does not assume): even assuming Golkar's clearly-biased arrangement (two out of three groups are objectively "bad"), 1/3rd of Basiji sincerely joining for ideology still likely makes a minimum of 3-4 million people, and that is a very formidable group to deal with for foreign invasion and for domestic politics. I am not here to defend or condemn the Basij, just to examine them objectively, but the idea that 33% of Basiji – and thus 5% of all Iran, at a minimum – are "thugs" seems like a very unscholarly (and insulting) assumption, to me. I would not call 1 of out every 20 French people I have met here a "thug", and Iranians are – to my perceptions – far more mellow.

> *"It is widely accepted that for many people, the most important motive for joining the Basji during the first decade after the Revolution was their belief in the IRI and its leader, Ayatollah Khomeini."*

Golkar desperately and repeatedly urges readers to believe that after the war dissatisfaction and alienation became so rampant that these motivations disappeared, and disappeared completely. That seems highly unlikely. How many people joined because they were true revolutionaries, i.e. their belief in the IRI? How many people joined the Basij because their father, brother, cousin or friend was killed or hurt, and thus became committed to the permanent defense of Iran? Given Trump's JCPOA pullout as simply the latest in an unbroken policy of aggression, how many join the Basij because they perceive Iran as being under permanent cold war attack? How many people want Islam in Iran's government and see the Basij as a force in that direction?

Golkar cites a study of Basij members which revealed that 66% of their friends joined the Basij for reasons other than ideology, while 97% of Basiji self-reported that ideology was in fact the main reason. I must first LOL, because that is all very Iranian: "Your revolutionary outlook is not as good as mine, your Ramadan month is not as pure as mine, my family suffered more during the war than yours, your family prospered more under the shah," etc. Basiji or not Basiji – Iranians are just as difficult as anyone else! But reality is never black-and-white: for Iranians to say 66% of their fellow Basiji are hypocrites and opportunists is likely a mixture of over-condemnation, arrogance and misunderstanding. I do not doubt that material reasons are a consideratble consideration in joining a group which requires your time and effort – and I do not think that is incorrect or immoral – but I think it's unfair to say that so many Basiji are all selling their soul completely to join and get benefits.

I also think that this number is likely inflated by the fact that the largest group in the Basij are the youth, and that it is simply not "cool" to admit that you love your country, the establishment, your neighborhood, God, etc. What I mean is: I think young Basiji don't talk about these "sensitive" things that much among themselves – they, being young, talk mostly just to show off. This would naturally lead to them saying things like "Oh I just joined for such and such materialistic reason – please don't consider me uncool", and then actually being believed by their peers. Such an explanation is not hard to believe nor master psychology – it sprouts from a sympathetic view of a Basiji's common humanity, which Golkar does not have.

As Golkar asked – why isn't everyone joining?

Golkar may just be an economist-type – the "dismal science", which sees everything in cost-benefit equations - but I remind the reader that joining the Basij means you must have some ideological – and thus moral – motivations and reasons for joining. Indeed, how could one tolerate hanging around fellow Basiji on a regular and weekly basis if there wasn't a kinship? It's like a Republican hanging out at the local Democrat center, or a boss hanging out at the local union hall – that never happens (though both should).

Because Golkar is clearly campaigning against the Basij, he cannot accept the obvious reality that one can be in the Basij and yet also be partially discontent with the government. Do Americans in their army or the Republican Party all adore Donald Trump? Of course not. Are they willing to scrap their entire system and start over – not any I have ever met.

I know people who are Basiji and who have told me that they were in it only for some material benefits… but I have never met any Basiji who wants to smash the Iranian system and replace it with something else. I.e., they all support the government on a fundamental level, no matter how much they may complain about it.

I work for the Iranian government – do I agree with everything they do? Of course not – I'm a human being. (I am not even an "apologist", as the World Socialist Web Site pejoratively accused me of being, because I do not falsely defend policies which I do not agree with; nor is the explanation of policies is not a defense.)

Indeed, a smart journalist once told me: "If you support 50% of your media's editorial policies, consider yourself lucky." Promoting someone else's ideas – that's the gig in paid journalism! That "someone else" runs from the CEO to the citizen on the street, both of whom are equally likely to say something quite smart or quite stupid about politics, economics and culture.

Giving a balanced justification of policies one may or may not agree with is paid journalism, and there is no shame in this socially-useful act; what you are reading now is exactly that, minus the paying part. What Golkar has done is to write unbalanced, biased scholarship to advance his personal ideas, his interests and, clearly, his current social class.

So it is in fact normal for someone to join the Basij, accept the materialistic and social positives, and yet still be unhappy with some parts of the government – what government is perfect? But this does not mean that they want to subvert the Islamic Revolution or that, under threat of invasion, they will not fight to defend their home. This simple, real-life concept essentially undermines Golkar's thesis: that all Basiji are being socially controlled to do things which they do not want to do.

People are not as stupid as Golkar may believe – Basiji are getting something personal and intangible out of what they volunteer to do. Are all Chinese Communist Party members rabid communists? At the lower levels no, but you can bet at the top they are. It's the same with the Basij.

A far more telling poll Golkar relays is one which said that 75% of Basiji stated the opportunity to give public service was a factor influencing their decision to join: now that is in line with the psychological assessments I have made, and which totally contradicts Golkar's idea of opportunistic thugs. But, again, it is not master psychology: it's always this mix of selfishness and selflessness in politics. How many of your local-are politicians are truly selfish, venal and out for their own privileges? Twenty-five percent seems about right, in my experience.

As a journalist I can say with some experience in politics of many types: politics cannot be absolutist or else it ceases to function. Philosophers, professors and tyrants can be absolutist, however. Factions of interest and principle exist not just in political bodies but in individual bodies. It is humanly impossible to always act in perpetual and total alignment with one's stated principles – try as we all might – and thus in all revolutionary societies the issue of "hypocrisy" and "opportunism" comes up often. In yet another never-stated assessment is that issues like "opportunism" are never heard in capitalist societies, because they profess no actual beliefs which are not explicitly cynical – such societies inherently assume that everyone is always only looking out for themselves.

Maybe eternal accusations of "hypocrisy" and "opportunism" is the price of living and participating in a revolutionary society? That question leads us to the next section…

Why is there internal opposition to the Basij?

Because membership in the Basij clearly has a lot of privileges.

Iran's government may run what I call "Iranian Islamic Socialism", but that doesn't mean there aren't Iranians who disagree with that philosophy; who favor a Western model and capitalist virtues for Iran; and who dislike the "inefficiencies" of Basiji businesses which they must tolerate.

Basiji are performing public works they consider to be good, but they are often being compensated. That compensation can be financial, or in affirmative action programs, or also in increased social status and influence.

I think it is mostly the last one – "power", and the domestic policing of the Basij - which rubs many Iranians wrong way.

However, I must stress: the Basij's role and presence has drastically, drastically declined from the 1990s, when they came back from the front and were far more severe in their policing. This is to be expected: returning soldiers are going to be more exacting in demanding that the revolution they sacrificed for be strictly upheld; such people need to time to transition away from a "war front" mentality to a "home front" mentality. But things change, and faster than we often realise. No Iranian would deny that in many parts of cities in 2019 you hardly ever see a Basij – it is mainly in poorer areas to prevent drugs, fighting, ensure security, etc. I wonder if the Basij haven't basically become computer geeks – their main task seems to be policing the internet. Only around religious holidays are you likely to see Basij on the streets.

Keeping in mind the new reality, let's examine the Basij history as a whole - "informers" or "revolutionaries", it really depends on your view.

Somebody who knows of a Pahlavi loyalist or an MKO/MEK member – should they be detained for questioning by the government or roam free? The Basij uncovered the Nojeh Coup Attempt in 1980 by Pahlavi loyalists – imagine if that had succeeded? Certainly, the Revolution decided that the Basij-worldview was essentially democratically acceptable, so "informers" is rather harsh, no? The Basij are not there only to harass and annoy people into following the law – they are also there to challenge counter-revolutionary forces. To counter-revolutionaries, this certainly makes them internal spies.

However, the Revolution and the war was long ago for many (but certainly not to all). The government is quite obviously aware that the People resist giving the Basij the powers they had during wartime, which is why they are now limited to acting as neighbourhood watches in their security role. Therefore, the Basij do not operate above the law. When the police are not present, or to prevent the disappearance of evidence, only in such cases can Basij get involved and then they have to send a report to the judicial authorities.

They have also been specifically denied the powers to meddle in citizens' personal lives. Many Basiji wanted this right – they were democratically, officially and publicly denied it.

However, it doesn't mean that this doesn't happen occasionally – I must be objective here. Certainly, it is naive to believe that some Basiji are not corrupted by power and break the laws they are supposed to be such exemplary followers of. The Basij is a mass-membership organisation and the People are not always consistent. But only someone without much analytical capability would allow anecdotal evidence to entirely sway their thinking on any mass phenomenon.

The Basij also often do not do what they are told to do – the most obvious example of this is their refusal to take down innumerable TV satellite dishes. These are banned by law, but many of the People want them… and "the People" include 10-25 million of Basiji, of course. Some satellites do get destroyed, though– it all depends on a neighbourhood's sentiment.

Let's get real: In all neighbourhood watches there is, shall we say, an "informal democratic consensus" which reigns about what is tolerated and what is not, and this varies from neighborhood to neighborhood and region to region. As I mentioned, the Basij is an essentially feminine organisation in that it fundamentally social, but also in how they all play "mother hen" to everybody in a very typical and annoying Iranian fashion. Scratch your head just once in Iran and a female relative is already out the door to get you the proper shampoo for an itchy scalp! One sneeze means they are begging you not to leave the house for three days! Of course, Basiji can fairly point out to me that the chicks survive mainly because of Mother Hen and Father Rooster….

The Basij public checkpoints are not there to offer you shampoo, but they will cut you down to size if you mess with them, and they might even cut your hair! That is no joke….

"Basij membership also offers a sense of empowerment to marginalised strata within Iran society," as Golkar notes, and this creates cultural conflict.

In a major failure and major proof his biased scholarship, Golkar doesn't give a positive everyday anecdote about the Basij – certainly none about Basiji helping a neighbor or improving the community. Golkar does relate a good anecdote which illustrates the cultural class warfare part of the Basij, which is also undeniable. Golkar relates his following interview with a young male Basiji relating a checkpoint story:

> *"It was just to have fun to tease a rich sousol (effeminate)* (this word also carries the connotation of "Westernized", which Golkar failed to note*) kid of north Tehran. With some of my other Basiji friends, we jumped in a car and drove to Sharake Gharb or Miydan Mohseni, we put a stop checkpoint sign up, and annoyed 'rich kids' in their kharji (foreign) cars, and if one had a beautiful girl in his car, we teased him even more. Sometimes, if we didn't like one, we cut his hair to belittle him before the girl."*

This is obviously unacceptable and juvenile behaviour, and which can lead to permanent resentments or even other anti-social practices. On the other hand, it is also exact;y reminiscent of Cultural Revolution as practiced in China.

The reader can decide for themselves if this is acceptable collateral damage for empowering a marginalised strata of society or not. I am merely objectively presenting both sides and am staying out of it: I am a male working in serious TV journalism and thus cannot have long hair.

For many Iranians the Basij are enforcing the Cultural Revolution... every day. "Revolution every day" – is that what revolution truly is? Is that good? Readers must decide that for themselves.

However – knowing Iran – it's not as if this "mother hen" mentality and neighbourhood self-policing wouldn't exist without the Basij, and didn't exist in spades before the Basij. This is something – that Iranians are moral and annoying, and annoyingly moral – which non-Iranian may have great difficulty fully grasping. Non-Iranians unfairly pin all the blame for "moral and annoying, and annoyingly moral" on the 1979 Islamic Revolution as if it was all something created by Imam Khomeini himself! That is totally absurd.

The Basij, I am saying, have not created something totally foreign to Iran. During Ramadan last year in Paris I saw a young Muslim guy standing next to his hijab-wearing sister (I assumed)... and smoking! In the daytime! Let me tell you, why I almost went up to him, and why I almost said, "Brother I don't think you should be doing"... but I didn't... because I'm not in the Basij!

But the Basij step up their patrols during religious holidays like Ramadan, so when one is already tired and doing the best they can to be a good Muslim, such Basjii interference can be met with a cheery, "Thank you! I wish it was Ramadan year round!" or, "Give me a break and mind your own business!" This judgment must be left up to the reader, yet again.

Golkar points out that more than 80% of new police in 2008 were drawn from the Basij. I am not surprised - in China all police are Communist Party members. Frankly, I think both Basij and CCP membership for cops is far better than in France, where 60% of the police force voted for the far-right's Marine Le Pen in 2017: it was likely not for her nationalist economic stance but because she would certainly have given them even more freedom to bust Muslim and Black heads. Cops are cops around the world, perhaps, but I do not see the French police as struggling to be righteous, pure, religious, revolutionary or caring about the emancipation of anything but their early pensions – at least the Basij and CCP pay lip service to such ideas at the bare minimum. Readers must judge for themselves, however.

The Basij, the Green Movement and the unrest of 2009

The Basij's role in the unrest of 2009 was undeniable, and I'm not really going to get into it other than stating this totally ignored reality, which Golkar relates:

"In fact, the Basij response to the Green Movement is the most illustrative example of the Basij's control over civil riots, which continues to this day. Although the government effectively crushed the Green Movement, it was widely rumored that many Ashura (male) and Al-Zahra (female) battalion members refused to participate in suppressing the dissidents, especially during the first months of the crisis. Likely, many did not participate because they had joined the Basij for materialistic or opportunistic reasons rather than out of ideological devotion."

While his last claim is possible, the Basij voting record indicates that, undoubtedly, not only are many Basiji not about to get violent, but also that many Basiji actually supported the Green Movement! We know that Basij voted for both Reformists and Principlists, and that Basiji are clearly on both sides of the political spectrum. However, the idea that there could be "Green Movement-supporting Basiji" is a possibility which Golkar cannot permit to exist, even though it is part of reality. I know Basiji who supported it!

This is evidence of Golkar's sloppy scholarship – denying realities which do not fit your thesis – and is also a way that Golkar willfully increases misunderstanding about the pluralist nature of Iranian politics.

So, yes, many Basiji did not fight in 2009. The vast majority are not "fighters" or in security whatsoever, after all; the majority are teenagers and women. And many were siding with the protesters; indeed, I'm sure many were protesting!

Because the voting patterns of the Basij are all over Iran's political map, there is absolutely no legitimate reason to believe they ALL supported Ahmadinejad's re-election. This is the type of "nuance" about Iran which is not nuance at all, but which is never reported.

The irony regarding 2009 is that Western leftists may openly admire the Committees to Defend the Revolution (who would certainly get physically rough were Cuba ever to actually have protests (other than the Ladies in White)) or even the Chavista brigades, yet the Basjii who opposed the Green Movement – which most leftists, including the World Socialist Web Site, agree was a mostly upper-middle class phenomenon – receive none of this support but only scorn, fear and condemnation. I realize that people are not made aware of the leftist aspects of Iran, its economy, or the Basij, but I chalk this up to the intense hatred of religion by Western leftists. I also chalk it up to the fact that Western leftists do not see Iran as the obvious leftist success it is, and thus cannot see that many people are willing to fight to preserve it. These are all objective realities, to me.

Thus I am not making a value judgment on the Basij in 2009 nor will I – this sub-series is simply to discuss the Basij as it objectively exists. Want to protest for a long time in Iran? Then you may eventually have to deal with the Basij. Most of them are students and women, but a small portion of them are trained to deal with external threats, and what they perceive to be internal threats. A larger part of them are people who are not inclined to violence, but who will commit violence if they feel they are pushed to a certain point.

Violence is – anyone who has been involved in politics already knows – is often violent. I cannot count the number of times I have been tear-gassed while covering political demonstrations in France. I consider myself lucky: I have not been blinded by rubber ballots and do not inspiringly step in front of water cannons. What is certain that the state will fight to preserve its political trajectory, but only in certain nations will citizens fight alongside them to defend the government, as in Iran, Venezuela and a few other places.

Many have, I believe, a fundamentally biased and incorrect view of the 2009 protests because they take an ideological approach – "for" or "against" the government – instead of the far simpler "class" approach. Of course, Western capitalist media never takes a class approach and, being ordered to completely oppose Iran's 1979 Islamic revolution, they can only present coverage of Iran with the angle of, "How can we report any event in Iran with a view as to how it could possibly lead to the downfall of the Iranian political structure?"

People fundamentally fail to see what 2009 really meant: in my view, the 2009 protests showed emphatically that the middle-class in Iran (which used to be so small) had arrived and would not be pushed around; and it also showed that the larger lower class in Iran would not allow a counter-revolution. To me, these are both positive things, and these problems can been smoothed by greater class awareness, solidarity, selflessness and patience. It is unfortunate that people were killed, to say the least, but Iran is by no means unusual in this, to also say the least.

Golkar writes as if there are 2009-sized protests thrice a month in Iran when there certainly are not. That was an exceptionally tense time, and most certainly the worst time for Iran as a whole since the war. I had a ticket to return to Iran during the protests, but Air France refused to fly into

Tehran – I cannot relate to you the anguish I felt every morning as I started up my computer to find out the latest news; I also cannot imagine how much worse it was for expatriate Iranians in 1980, similarly stuck outside of Iran. I did not join the Green Party protests in Paris, because I was not convinced that vote-rigging had actually occurred and I have still not been presented with adequate evidence despite a great deal of personal research.

Golkar may want there to be 2009-sized protests on a regular basis, but he hasn't gotten them. The winter 2017/18 economic protests were not anywhere as large, nor as culturally-revealing, nor as structurally significant as the 2009 protests – they were primarily the result of foreign economic war designed to punish Iran's revolutionary choice.

Conclusion : Is the goal to change Iran to 'Basijistan'?

"At one pole, a small group of people have positive attitudes toward the IRI, join the Basij, and internalize their Basij mentality. At the other pole, a majority of people share a negative attitude toward the IRI and reject the Basij and its culture."

The only undoubtedly true statement in there is that a majority of people indeed do not join the Basij: however, 13-30% of the entire countryhave (and that includes the population of children, who are not even eligible to join) and that is a huge, huge amount.

I include Golkar's quote to set up the following sentence, which follows the above and which also terminates his preface (and thus primes the reader to swallow Golkar's forthcoming analysis of the Basij along with his data).

> *"The result has been a widening gap between the Basiji and the non-Basiji, which has led to the increasing alienation of Basiji members from society."*

This exemplifies the height of intelligence about the Basij in the West, and it is truly a very low peak they have attained: it is their desire to depict 21st-century Iran as a totally-divided country, on the verge of civil war, to be fought by "Basiji versus non-Basiji".

Black versus white; oppressed Iranian women versus horrible Iranian men; enlightened liberal Greens versus troglodyte Basiji conservatives. It is typical fake-leftist "identity politics", which refuses to discuss the identity of "class" or even "nation".

But the objective reality is: just from the low estimate of their sheer numbers, at 10 million strong – how can the Basij be alienated from society? Can 1 out of 7 citizens in a society be alienated from society? Sure, the Blacks in the US are a similar number and they are alienated and live in a world apart, but there is no modern Jim Crow in Iran for Basiji.

Furthermore, Golkar only looks at 10 million members (high estimate, 25 million) – the Basiji have spouses, and I'm sure they must partially bless their involvement and thus are likely sympathetic. The Basiji have family members – let's conservatively estimate that half their family members are sympathetic. The Basiji have friends – let's conservatively estimate that half their friends are sympathetic. What we now have is a nation of 10 million Basij members.... but also an Iranian nation which contains 50% Basij sympathisers as well, right? Fifty percent could be a low estimate! If the government reaches its goal of half of Iran being formal Basij members... when you add in the Basij sympathisers, or Basij "tolerators", it's impossible for the Basiji to be alienated from society because they are society.

That is a drastic statement, filled with class, cultural, domestic political and geopolitical implications, but that is where I must conclude this sub-series on the Basij.

There are people who will never join and who will never support the Basiji... but it appears likelier that it is they who become alienated from society, and not the other way around. I say this purely based on simple, objective logic, math and common sense. So I think Golkar has it backward: it is the anti-Basij who are more likely to become alienated.

And I think, to show my objectivity, a fair point to make is: if the Basij keeps expanding, is it no longer "Iran" but "Basijistan"?

LOL, that is hyperbole, but the point should be made because it shows how the Basij is no minority "militia" of religious fanatics but a huge cultural phenomenon and a mass-membership organisation drawn from all levels and sectors of society. I do not think that "Basiji" and "patriotic Iranian" are interchangeable, however, and I do not believe it will ever, or should ever, or could ever reach that point.

But I raise the idea of "Basijistan" in order to help illustrate the Basij's massive cultural, political, economic and class effects, and also to show how deeply rooted these have become. Iran has changed a great, great, great deal in 40 years.

I would also, again, look to China in order to predict the Basij's trajectory: once the Chinese Communist Party had proven its worth to domestic society, it began changing from a mass-membership organisation to one that is now harder to get into than the Ivy League in the American university system.

From any objective analysis the Basij exists mainly to preserve the Islamic Republic of Iran... which is a modern, democratic nation whose People support in a massive democratic fashion the system of governance they recently created.

So the question becomes: are the government and society wrong to support an organisation dedicated to supporting the ideals of the Revolution? This is essentially the ongoing question inside Iran about the Basij.

I return to a previous point from Chapter 4: if there is something fundamentally misguided about the Basij, then the Chinese Communist Party must share much of the same traits. Because both groups are so representative of all levels of their respective societies, if there is something wrong with either group then there must be something wrong with the Iranian and Chinese Peoples themselves.

I find that very hard to accept. I may be a leftist, but I am not a mindless populist or class-worshipper: unlike, for example, 1930s Germany, neither Iran nor China tolerates imperialism or racism, much less promotes or allies with it, and I am unfamiliar with any enduring or whole-hearted effort at socioeconomic redistribution led by Western fascists.

But the time for explaining the Basij is done – I hope it was informative.

Even though as an Iranian I am well-qualified to judge the Iranian case, I leave the question of the Basij's democratic and ideological legitimacy up to the reader – I must remain neutral if this to achieve journalistic scholarship, as I have intended.

I will only note that a government earns legitimacy based on the quality of its policies towards its People, and also towards the world at large — at least now some of Iran's policies towards the Basij have been described and can be examined and judged.

My whole point with this sub-series was, simply: The Basij IS.

You deal with it.

Chapter 8
'Cultural' & 'Permanent Revolution' in Iranian Revolutionary Shi'ism

"Trotsky was and, in as much as he lives in his writings, remains the foremost strategist of world socialist revolution. Hence the indissoluble association of his name with the theory and strategy of Permanent Revolution—an association familiar even to those like Mazaheri…."

*E*ven someone like me is familiar with Trotsky, wow!

Well, a supremely important association which is likely not at all familiar to the World Socialist Web Site is that for Shia Imam Ali "remains the foremost strategist of world cultural revolution". Nor are they likely at all familiar that the conscious martyrdom of his son, Imam Hossein (spelled Husayn, Hussein or Hussain in Arabic, and often Hossain in Farsi), makes him "the foremost strategist of world permanent revolution".

This chapter is not to discredit Trotsky, but to show that there is room for all of these heroes in socialism in its fight against social injustice, capitalism and imperialism.

The reason why Imams Ali and Hossein actually outrank Trotsky is because Prophet Mohammad, unlike Jesus son of Mary, led the greatest, most immediate and most sweeping religious-political revolution ever. This fact of humankind's history can certainly continue to be ignored, but it will remain a historical fact. This should be quite relevant to the WSWS in 2019 because the messages of Imam Ali and Imam Hossein have been combined, over many decades, with socialism to arrive at the unique culture which I refer to as "Iranian Islamic Socialism".

All that is on an undeniable socio-political-cultural level. On an intellectual level it is just as crystal-clear: 20th/21st century Iranians re-examined Islam through the intellectual lenses provided by Marxism, Trotskyism, Maoism and other major socialist schools of thought, and this led to the intellectual concept known as Revolutionary Shi'ism. The idea that all of Iran's revolution derived from Prophet Mohammad and Imam Ali - and that it did not also utilise the concepts, vocabulary and goals of socialism - is totally preposterous and false. It socialists who must finally come to terms with Islam, and not the other way around.

All of these facts can certainly continue to not be discussed outside of Iran, but Iran will keep adding layer upon layer of solder upon these two ideas from two different historical eras – the early Islamic era and the modern era of socialism – and certainly all without me clarifying it or commenting upon it.

It is unfortunate – because it shows one's lack of crucial historical knowledge of Asia, Africa, India and elsewhere – that just as Western leftists do not appreciate the political-economic-social revolutionary aspects of Prophet Mohammad, even fewer appreciate the similar qualities of Imam Ali. That will be the basis of this chapter, while Chapter 9 will discuss the related political qualities of Imam Hossein. These are not two figures I have plucked from obscurity – they are the two key leaders of the Shia religion, as well as successful revolutionary political beacons in two different eras separated by 1300+ years.

For the WSWS, Western leftists, and also many Western rightists, religion is not and should not be political. People keep telling this to Iranians as if we have not heard it before... and quite obviously totally ignored them!

> *"It is surprising! For what purpose then, was the Prophet fighting? For what purpose was Imam Ali fighting? Is it not the question of politics? Is it not the fact that criminals are ruling over the people?"*

In these two chapters on Ali and Hossein I will often quote from Revolutionary Shi'ism co-creator Ali Shariati and his *Martyrdom and Martyrdom*, a collection of his lectures on Ali, Hossein and martyrdom.

Westerners may believe that religion and politics must be separated in a government: to use their sacred, beloved and individualistic phrase, they "have that right" in their own countries.

What they cannot believe – unless they willingly wish to remain in confusion and error – is that politics and religion are somehow two fundamentally unrelated socio-intellectual domains: both endeavour to tell us how to live.

It is notable that the Western view also lacks the democratic majority in a global sense – some people find that significant....

What is certain is that if one side does not give up... we will just go around in circles endlessly: Westerners with their dogmatic secularism and rabid *laïcité* (both of which latently support Christianity), and on the other side people like Shariati, myself and billions of others who say: *It is surprising! For what purpose then...*

How imperialism dies: Learning from socialism's mistakes and unlearning capitalist propaganda

The WSWS seems to think that I have invented something new:

"He again insists that socialism in Iran can galvanize the masses only if fused with Shia Islam. This argument is far easier to make if one ignores, as Mazaheri does, any consideration of the pivotal role of the Stalinist Tudeh Party in the development of the Iranian workers' movement."

I am not insisting anything about the galvanising power of Shia Islam in Iran – this is what has already happened. Truly, I am a journalist just reporting the facts. These are facts which are, unfortunately, not reported by many others.

However, this chapter will also provide some new scholarship on Iran: I will show how there is a clear parallel between the aims of Imam Ali and Mao, both of whom attempted Cultural Revolutions after they perceived their initial revolutions to be failing. This is of vital interest, precedent and perspective to all political revolutionaries, and not just Shia and Chinese ones.

But I don't deserve that much credit here because I will use Shariati's own scholarship to show that he essentially proved this historical parallel already... but that he did not know it.

The likely reason is that people like Shariati (died 1977) had not and have not unlearned the anti-socialist propaganda about China's Cultural Revolution, which I have helped debunk in other written works.

Furthermore, Shariati was so powerful because he was incredibly and uniquely adept at employing Marxist perspectives on Islam, but he was also anti-Marxist in the sense that he did not want formal communists to come to power in Iran – he was not inclined to openly laud Chinese communists. Indeed, much of Shariati's writing on communism is negative, and filled with now-outdated ideas that communism is inescapably totalitarian.

While there is much writing on Marxism and socialism on the Farsi-language internet, there is apparently no claim like the one I am making.

Nor is there much on the claims of the next part in this series – the link between Imam Hossein and the need for "Permanent Revolution", but it is at least not the desert of the Imam Ali-Cultural Revolution claim of this chapter.

However, I feel certain these links are easily proven, and that they likely were made by a few dedicated Iranian Maoists during the revolutionary heyday of the 1970s. However, back then Revolutionary Shi'ism was disseminated via cassette tapes of lectures by Shariati and Khomeini and flimsy mimeographs. I'm glad the internet makes the registration of such ideas seemingly permanent. Of course, credit for scholarship is not important to me – I only hope that these ideas are understood and prove useful to sociopolitical advancement.

The continued moral failures of capitalism and imperialism mean that socialism – from an economic and democratic perspective – is the only way forward. Iran, and others, will never give up religion, so that is a non-issue, but understanding historical parallels shows the universality of the human economic-political experience. The ability to appreciate Prophet Mohammad, Ali, Hossein, Jesus, Moses, Mao, Lenin, Trotsky and others as common socio-political liberators draws us all closer together, and closer to the goal of peace and shared prosperity.

This is what makes the above claim by the WSWS rather pernicious, and it marks a turning point in their tract: it's when the WSWS starts to try and appropriate the credit for the 1979 Iranian Revolution away from Revolutionary Shi'ism in order to give it to the Iranian Communist Party. And to give it lock, stock and barrel.

This is why the bulk of their series discusses the history of the Tudeh Party - it is mainly a revisionist work, to its discredit. Both ideologies existed, but one obviously prevailed; both ideologies existed, and to completely ignore one of them is obviously revisionist history and bad scholarship. Their pamphlet thus mainly appears like yet another example of the rather common modern practice of rewriting Iranian history by Westerners, which is misleading, dangerous and self-serving. Of course, Iran is not alone in being victimised like this.

If it was communism which galvanised the masses... it certainly took its time: by the late 1970s communism had already been present in Iran for decades, just as it was in seemingly every other nation in the world. As Iran was never subject to colonial domination, it is a fact that communism had far more cultural latitude and influence than in many colonised nations (of course, the UK, France and the US horrifically repressed any anti-imperialist and socialist notions and groups) - even Shah Mohammad Reza, the final monarch, openly proclaimed himself a socialist. But the truly-atheist Tudeh party members (which were truly few in Iran, where polls show less than 5% are atheists today) faced the same problem the WSWS does today: one may educate the Iranian masses all you want on Trotskyism, but that doesn't mean they will also renounce viewing Imam Ali as a political model the equal of Che, Sankara or the WSWS' blessed Trotsky.

While their series was informative on the topic they preferred – although it was clearly exaggerated to the point of nonsense and revisionism – WSWS readers would have learned much more about Iran if they had instead talked about the enduring political influence of Imam Ali. Indeed, the refusal to even consider the possibility that Ali, Islam or religion can have a positive and enduring political influence is what dooms Western leftism to political marginalisation in

Iran, and elsewhere. It is also creates obvious enmity, discord, sanction & murder.

Imam Ali's failed Cultural Revolution: the ideological schism between Shia and Sunnis

It is truly impossible to understand Iran without at least passing familiarity with Ali and his son Hossein.

In short: Imam Ali, the very first male Muslim, Mohammad's son-in-law, the 4th Caliph to Sunnis and the 1st to Shia – in the historical context of a perceived slackening in Islam's revolutionary, political and moral integrity – cemented the ideological Sunni-Shia schism by trying to implement a Cultural Revolution after the initial political Revolution of Islam.

(The schism was officially created decades before: Mohammad repeatedly and openly declared Ali to be his successor at the event of Ghadir Khumm, but this decision was surprisingly reversed on the very day of the Prophet's death at the Saqifah. This decision installed tribal dominance instead of the will and house of Mohammad, and Ali was not able to resist this decision. Ghadir Khumm is why Shia consider Ali to be the first Caliph, and is truly the root of the schism, but Ali's future actions – described here – would considerably exacerbate it.)

Perhaps all peoples of all times have reinterpreted religion to better understand and to improve the times in which they have lived?

It's certain that many reinterpret religion to make their times more reactionary: drive through the United States and you will hear on radio station after radio station the combination of Christian fundamentalism and anti-government/neoliberal-capitalist ideology. This is no exaggeration – for them the "beast" of the Bible is actually a symbol for the government, and thus makes government inherently evil even beyond totalitarianism. This obviously fits perfectly with the neoliberal view. There is also plenty of airwaves reserved for "prosperity gospel", where faith in God is merely a method to make you rich (and neoliberals are very glad that you really on Him instead of higher taxes on the rich). These are obviously not distortions of a failed or reactionary Christian creed, but of a failed capitalist-imperialist one.

Instead of hysterically reinterpreting Jesus as a way to make money, the application and promotion of leftist perspectives on Ali and Hossein provided more inspiration for the common masses than the Tudeh Party ever did or probably ever could.

Leftists fail to see that Prophet Mohammad was also a political revolutionary

Don't worry: this section will not be long, nor will it involve quoting the Koran. I could do that, but many leftists have closed ears, and the Koran repeatedly: "God confounds whom He will" (couldn't resist that one short quote!).

What this section will recap is the political, humanitarian revolution which Prophet Mohammad created. These basic historical, sociological and political aspects of Islam are facts which cannot be denied, and should be, at the very least, of intellectual interest to politically-minded atheists to reflect on. Similarly, I think it is very difficult to understand any religion without having a political understanding of its social aims, so this section could help some Muslims understand the historical path of Islam more fully.

As I have written often before: Shariati was just one of many, many similar Iranian political thinkers who are intensely Muslim and also politically leftist. His work is marked by superb political insights combined with an intensely urgent and open concern for morality.

For an example of his gifted political insights, Shariati noted that the social origins of Jesus and Mohammad – the two Abrahamic prophets of whom we have definitive historical proof – were not the aristocratic origins of Buddha, Confucius, Lao Tzu, Zoroaster, Aristotle, Plato, etc. Indeed, all the founders of schools of pre-Enlightenment thought in Europe, China, Iran and India fundamentally supported their aristocratic, elitist, hyper-conservative political establishments. Contrarily, the primary Abrahamic messengers (including Moses, who was born to an enslaved people and then orphaned) were drawn from the People and openly opposed the existing power structure.

This vitally important lineage helps explain why the main Abrahamic prophets were explicitly sent to free people not just spiritually and morally but politically as well. Unlike Buddhism, Hinduism, Confucianism or Taoism, "Abrahamism" has always been decidedly political and decidedly against the establishment: Abraham against the ruling polytheists and his father the idol-maker; Moses against Pharaoh; Jesus son of Mary against a slave-owning, imperialist Rome which lacked political or financial compassion; Mohammad against the oppression inherently imposed by polytheism (the humorous and sad delusion that God or gods are actually working against you, instead of loving you), the meagre cynicism of materialism (scientific, not material), aristocratic privileges, social castes and tribal divisions.

Indeed the Western-created "Sunni-Shia divide" could only have been created by non-Muslims because Mohammad ENDED tribalism, sectarianism and nationalism, and every Muslim is aware of this. This is easily proven:

watch any gathering of Muslims and you see people of all hues and ethnicities – it is beautiful, politically, and the direct result of the humanitarian revolution espoused by Islam. This is absent among the insular "chosen" Jews, and far less present among Christians; indeed, the presence of multiple races in Christianity is largely due to their legacy of forced conversion, a practice explicitly barred in the Koran.

All of this helps show why Islam is the undoubted updating of Abrahamic thought. Yet Mohammad had a mission of unification because he repeatedly confirmed the previous Scriptures of Judaism and Christianity (the Torah (Old Testament) and New Testament) in the Koran, and because he also created a unification of time, space and ideology by pointedly declaring Islam to NOT be a "new" religion – it is simply a continuation of the one true religion of monotheism, which was started by Judaism and continued by Christianity. Western capitalist-imperialists most decidedly do not want to trumpet this fact of Abrahamic unity – they want to view Christianity and Judaism in opposition to Islam, and to try and make Muslims view themselves in opposition to each other.

This idea of total unification (tawhid) is the indispensable base of Islam: it is the oneness of God, which implies the oneness of all things - from atoms to people to galaxies, as everything is under the direction of a limitless, all-knowing, all-seeing God. This is a fundamentally unitarian concept, accommodates both Western and Eastern concepts, and is also fully in accordance with the last great confirmed scientific theory, the Theory of Relativity.

A fun scientific sidebar!

The Theory of Relatively is far from being just the equation $E = mc2$, which is just the part to say to appear smart. Its theoretical importance is this: when observing the universe no one place is any better or different than another – the laws of nature are universal no matter where or by whom they are described, whether on Earth, on Pluto, or in a galaxy far, far away. This means egalitarian tawhid exists on a galactic level.

When modern scientists inevitably find a "theory of everything" – a single, all-encompassing theoretical framework of physics - that too will logically confirm *tawhid*.

There is one scientific and cosmological debate left which, I must concede, still threatens the victory of tawhid and which could prove the polytheists correct: What is the true nature of the universe's continual expansion?

If expansion never stops, that implies an eventual thinning out of matter, and thus cooling, and thus death – in theological terms, the Day of Judgement.

But what if there is never a day when the universe stops expanding but – instead of thinning out – a day when it actually contracts upon itself? And if that occurs, does it then expand again? This is posited by Hinduism, which believes that the universe has an infinite number of deaths and rebirths; Big Bang, contraction and reversal, then back to the same Big Bang; we have all been here before, and we will all be here again. Does time run backwards during a contraction phase?

This is all scientifically plausible because it has not yet been disproven. The key appears to lay in solving the mysteries of black holes, if that is possible. Another key lays in the possibility of being able to discover the fundamental nature of matter by finding the truly "smallest particle" – we may just keep subdividing forever: molecules into atoms into quarks into…. If we subdivide forever, that seems to support tawhid, because God is limitless. If we reach an end, that seems to support Hindu cosmology.

These ideas have been ably discussed by the legendary US astrophysicist and science popularizer Carl Sagan, although he did not incorporate tawhid into his discussions.

So for all the opprobrium Muslims and monotheists heap on Hinduism, folk religions and aboriginal religions for their idolatry, we still cannot scientifically reject their cosmology. For now, the answer is a question of faith.

I think religious honesty requires us to be open and honest about the limitations of our scientific knowledge – the Koran repeatedly states that one who makes up lies about God is among the most reprehensible of sinners.

Faith is not astrophysics: a mind which demands total certainty and cannot tolerate doubt is a fanatical one. I also think many religious people agree that atheists are often far more fanatical in their alleged cosmological certainties than either monotheists or polytheists (and many astrophysicists).

We may never find out, but I have faith in the galactic applicability of tawhid. Fortunately, the Koran forbids forcing a Hindu into accepting tawhid. Nor can you force a Muslim to become a Hindu because Hinduism – it is often said – is not a religion but a culture: there is no process to "convert" to Hinduism – one can only live it. Nor is there a ceremony to get oneself ex-communicated from Hinduism (only caste ex-communication, which is not a religious decision but a political decision). So, Muslims should have no problem allowing Hindus to remain peacefully confounded in whatever hundred billion-year cycle they are currently in, and the same goes for Hindus regarding Muslims who refuse to practice Hinduism.

I certainly do not seek to upset the peace of Hindus, because solving the most difficult astronomical and cosmological questions are far beyond the ken of a daily hack journalist like myself. And maybe there is a tawhid in Hinduism which I am perhaps unaware of?

What this sidebar makes clear is: capitalist-imperialist Western societies have been totally unable to incorporate

20th- and 21st-century scientific advances into their political-cultural philosophies. Their People are encouraged in identity politics (where one viewpoint is superior to another, depending on the situation), racism and Islamophobia (19th century scientific thinking), supporting foreign wars (humanitarian interventions for the allegedly-wayward non-White peoples), and in exacerbating economic inequalities, all of which contradict the social corollaries of modern scientific advancements, which stress the unity of not just the world but the entire universe. Instead, capitalist-imperialists remain quite stuck in their fundamentally 17th-19th century bourgeois conceptions of humanity, society and science, and this limited timeline should be expected: they have rejected socialism, which was directly inspired by such modern scientific advances, and which has always sought to reflect it.

Back to something far easier to explain: Iranian Islamic Socialism.

This inviolable unity of all things proclaimed by Mohammad necessarily implies a call for socio-political-economic-cultural unity. To say that it does not is to take us back to, *"It is surprising! For what purpose then...."*

Shariati's genius was to take Islamic concepts like tawhid and find correlates with them in Marxist thought. He did this over and over, making him incredibly of his place and era, and explains why he was so wildly popular and why Iran was so successfully inspired to create a truly, truly modern political revolution in 1979. This is also why so many of the politics and structures of modern Iran I have previously described in this book do not have historical parallels, why they are decidedly not capitalist, why they are not return to the 7th century – what has been created in Iran since 1979 is repeatedly revolutionary.

And I'd say he was right: *Tawhid* clearly is more politically revolutionary than the insufficient "chosen people" tribal unity of the Jews. Even China's I Ching (the world's oldest book and the foundation of their cosmological and moral conceptions) explicitly warns of that, in Gua 13: "Seeking Harmony" – "Seeking harmony within a clan, it is selfish and stingy".

Tawhid is also more unifying – and thus egalitarian – than the Holy Trinity of Christianity, which Islam explicitly rejects: God is not three – He is one, and One is all. Indeed what many modern Christians fail to realise is that Islam represents an intellectual rectifying of many confusing doctrines found in Christianity. Of course, articles of faith for others must be respected as articles of faith.

So in the Abrahamic religions Islam is obviously the most concerned with this idea of egalitarian unity. Indeed, Prophet Mohammad "cornered the market on unity" for all-time and for every time: In Islam (as I alluded to earlier by saying that Islam unified time and space), anyone *who has ever* believed *or will ever* believe in monotheism is essentially a Muslim. This insistence also makes it a logical certainty that there can never be another monotheistic religion in the Abrahamic line – Islam has effectively co-opted all monotheism!

Therefore, the next Abrahamic prophet can only appear on the Day of Judgment... because what else could possibly be offered more than an Islam which offers everything there always has, is, and will be offered regarding monotheistic belief?

This is why the Koran opens with praise after praise for monotheistic Jews and Christians as well as plea after plea for Jews and Christians to join this intellectual, social and cultural updating of Abrahamism provided by its latest prophet. This is also explains why *hadiths* relate that

Mohammad said: *"I am the nearest of all the people to the son of Mary.... Both in this world and in the Hereafter, I am the nearest of all the people to Jesus, the son of Mary."* (Sahih Bukhari Volume 4, Book 55, Number 651-2).

Because another monotheistic prophet is thus a logical impossibility, Muslims believe a "Hidden Imam" (or Mahdi) walks the earth until the Day of Judgment, when he will walk hand-in-hand with Jesus to defeat the false messiah (or Antichrist to Christians) and establish peace and justice on earth. This doctrine is not essential in Sunni thought, but popular, while for Shia it is an essential doctrine.

Many have falsely claimed to be the Mahdi over the centuries, including the fore-runner of the Baha'i. However, many point out that this claim was obviously false, because peace and justice clearly do not reign globally today, nor did they in the mid-19th century when the Baha'i faith started in Iran. That is why the Baha'i have routinely had major problems in Iran and seemingly every other Muslim country they are present in, from Morocco to Indonesia: there is a rather enormous, Islam-jeopardising claim which is being made and not fulfilled.

But the galactic nature of tawhid and the realisation that Islam owns all monotheism aside, what needs to be appreciated by non-Muslims is how Mohammad overturned the political order and broke with aristocratic and sectarian values. Just as bus drivers became bosses in 1979 Iran, so in the time of Mohammad slaves with noble natures became higher than aristocrats. From Shariati:

"This is why the Prophet of Islam marked the turning point for slaves who, throughout history, were certain that their fate was slavery... they believed that they existed solely to experience suffering, to carry heavy loads, and to go hungry so that others might receive pleasure. They were born and created for this.

This deprived class, who were convinced that the gods or God were their enemy.... The Prophet of Islam had been appointed in order to complete the movement which had existed throughout history against deception, falsehood, polytheism, creation of discord, hypocrisy, aristocracy and class differences which were all made an object of the spiritual struggle; and by announcing that all of humanity is of one race, one source, one nature and one God, to declare equality for all, with philosophical explanation, and by fighting an economically powerful regime to maintain social equity."

Undoubtedly, the lenses, ideas and language of Marxism, socialism, class struggle, democratic equality and economic equality are present and have been combined with Islam in modern Revolutionary Shi'ism. Combine this by many volumes and you have just Shariati's output. These modern ideas were espoused by many and captivated Iranian society - it created and sustained a revolution. It should be instantly clear why Tudeh Party members would embrace such an analysis; it should not be hard to see why the average Iranian Muslim (and Basiji) may not realize that many of the ideas they promote are called "socialism" in non-Muslim countries.

"Iranian Islamic Socialism" is not new – it's just an apt journalistic catchphrase which, despite its brevity, never got many inches in Western newspapers.

Certainly, the political impact of Jesus son of Mary was only felt centuries after his death, while Prophet Mohammad created immediate political revolutions in land after land, tribe after tribe, ethnicity after ethnicity, and race after race with his creed of total equality. Jesus created equality for all (Jews and non-Jews alike) under the one God, but he did not create socioeconomic equality for all.

Many Christians openly hold Mohammad's political conquests against him from a moral point of view: this is because they clearly fail to realise the revolutionary socio-political demands of Islam. Priests in Islam are fighters for God and social justice. Islamic preachers are not monks, nor celibate, nor divorced from society, nor unconcerned with society in order to worship God all alone, nor encouraged to live in isolation, nor obsessed with performing rites and rituals, nor plying magic to make it rain (or to do whatever polytheistic/folk shamans do), etc. They are ordered to create social justice.

However, to Shariati and to Shia, this very real socio-political revolutionary aspect of Islam was diminished due to the failure of 2nd and 3rd-generation Islamic revolutionaries to heed Imam Ali's message.

Imam Ali and his call for Cultural Revolution to preserve the leftist political gains

Because Islam was a political revolution of still-unparalleled immediate global consequence, there is much for everyone to study on a historical-political level in the period immediately after Mohammad, who passed in 632. We can view this era from an areligious historical perspective, and it is politically quite enlightening.

However, that would not be the exact same thing as what Shariati and others did – they applied a modern political lens on Islam itself as well as its history. What I am saying here is: Non-Muslims can apply a modern historical lens on the early Islamic era, and we will find the results to be extremely similar with the early eras of modern leftist revolutions.

In 656, when Imam Ali became the 4th Caliph, it was a dire situation for the now-aged first generation of political revolutionaries of Islam. After all, how many political revolutions haven't lasted more than a few years or a single change in leadership before reverting back to the previous and reactionary status quo? Thomas Sankara's Burkina

Faso, Muammar Khadaffi's Great Socialist People's Libyan Arab Jamahiriya, the People's Republic of Angola, and many, many others come to mind.

From a purely political perspective, and as Shariati recounts: in 656 it was nearing the end for that first generation of revolutionaries. Ali, the only person ever born in the Kaaba, was 55 years old and had fought in nearly every major battle. He had also retired from politics to work as a farmer – he still mended his own shoes. He had to be pushed into becoming Caliph, and only did so because the revolution was starting to eat its children: his predecessor had been assassinated, factions had appeared, once-liberated areas were rebelling due to poor political governance, while some new converts may have converted for political gain and were thus possible opportunists with a questionable grounding in Islam.

It is as if Raul Castro was seeing the growth of parties who want Guantanamo Bay to be legally part of the USA, that the Committees for the Defense of the Revolution were no longer holding meetings, and that state-ownership of the mother industries of the economy were being sold off to Floridians.

Imam Ali assumed the Caliphate and did what he thought was needed – he restored the political revolution of equality initiated by Mohammad.

Ali waged a war against financial corruption and unfair privileges – he was a politically-enlightened (as well as a religiously-enlightened) revolutionary, after all. He gave the same wages to politicians as he did to slaves, levelled taxes and opposed the reigning nepotism in favor of seniority. There is no doubt that such leftist ideas rarely reign supreme now, either, and also that they were just as opposed by the same unenlightened forces back in the 7th century.

Ali's message of political piety was obviously not appreciated by everyone, least of all in largely-Christian Damascus. The governor there was Muawiyah I, the eventual founder of the Umayyad dynasty. After a political marriage to a powerful Christian tribe and many military successes, Muawiyah was powerful enough to not recognise Ali as the 4th Caliph.

The Christian makeup of Damascus was not the problem: the problem was that the anti-reactionary blaze of the Revolution of Islam had so very much to burn. From Shariati, and in that typically overstuffed-yet-somehow-not-unnecessary style of Persian carpets and miniatures:

> *"The traditions, rules, etiquette of society, economic and aristocratic systems, thoughts, ideas, tastes, literature, poetry, music, dance, amusements, social relations, ethics and manners of 'civilized' Rome (although the true center in this era was Byzantine Greece, also called the "Eastern Roman Empire") and Iran, the social class system and aristocratic regime, the political system of the Caesars and Kings, the type and form of monastic and clerical traditions, the properties which are hierarchical and bureaucratic, the official and classical system of rule, and finally, the progressive (meaning contemporary) Iranian and Roman civilisations certainly had an influence upon the simple Islamic communities.*
>
> *The wealth, power, position and countless 'spoils' which had been earned in the Muslim victories make people grow fat and it is because of this that they are no longer listening to Ali's advice, his goal and his sufferings. The majority of the people are quite happy with the situation. They are no longer fond of such problems. They show no sensitivity whatsoever to them. These people have now changed into being the servants of wealth and power."*

Shariati has clearly recounted a lessening of political fervour which can be seen in seemingly all political revolutions.

Also for Shariati, Ali is so vital in large part because the power centre in Damascus began to manipulate Islam for its own political conquests, fostering a quietism among the religious authorities.

Comparisons of the post-Mohammad-era political culture with the USSR after Stalin and China in the early 1960s show obvious parallels... as they must, because all three were the supremely-modern political revolutions of their respective eras:

After the first generation of revolutionaries passed with Stalin, Khrushchev pursued undoubtedly revisionist policies ("capitalist-roading", as Mao denigrated them); then, when the USSR had pulled itself up to the level of the dominant Western imperialists, they preferred the calm Brezhnev era, which was totally stagnant from a revolutionary perspective; finally, Gorbachev's era had become so estranged from Russian socialist ideals that he foolishly embraced massive tolerance of counter-revolutionary thought (glasnost), and just as foolishly embraced drastically anti-socialist economic and political changes (perestroika), and thus the Russian Revolution was subverted from the top, to the dismay of the base of the pyramid. Russian revolutionaries had became "the servants of wealth and power," instead of the servants of the deprived classes.

Following 1949's victory, after many years of similar revolutionary stagnation and at least seven failed official anti-corruption campaigns, Mao and his fellow first-generation revolutionaries listened to the demands of their youth, and the demands of their rural peasants, and empowered them to institute the Cultural Revolution in order to restore revolutionary integrity, beginning in 1966. When Mao died in 1976 the younger generations had personally witnessed the regeneration of social revolutionary ideals, and ones extremely similar to those which Imam Ali was espousing 1,300 years earlier.

Iran instituted the world's only other official Cultural Revolution immediately after the 1979 Revolution. Even though it expressly rejected anti-imperialist and anti-capitalist thought, as in China, it came at a very different revolutionary period of revolutionary history. This is a vital nuance, but one which does not overshadow the kinship between the world's only two official Cultural Revolutions.

Perhaps it is not surprising that the minority, non-Arab Iranians have been so insistent in their accusation that the Arab early Sunnis turned Islam into an imperialist war machine instead of being content to morally improve their own backyards? But it is historically verifiable: instead of the values being determined by Mohammad, the Koran and Islam, the values were being decided by Damascus... unless Ali's ideas prevailed in time.

Did they?

To Shia: The counter-revolution in Islam in generations after Mohammad

Sadly, they did not. Ali's Cultural Revolution created major opposition from the Byzantine elites in Damascus. Governor Muawiyah openly rebelled, demanding autonomy, refusing diplomacy, and thus sparking the First Fitna (Muslim Civil War).

Muawiyah's military-industrial complex had become accustomed to war and its spoils, with regular battles against the Byzantines (or Romans, as they called themselves). The militarily-innovative Muawiyah had just established Arab naval supremacy over the Byzantine/Eastern Roman Empire in the Battle of the Masts of 654, two years prior to Ali's assumption of the Caliphate. The death of the Zoroastrian Yazdgerd III, Sassanid Iran's last ruler, occurred in 651 and thus both east and west presented plenty of war booty for thousands of kilometres.

So, in 656, for Imam Ali to come in with his revolutionary piety instead of worldly gain at a historical time when all roads to conquest were wide open....

War between the partisans of Ali (the word "Shia" means "partisans of Ali") and Muawiyah ensued and, about to be defeated, Muawiyah famously instructed his soldiers to put Korans on the tip of their lances. Divine protection or blasphemy? The soldiers themselves did not know, either, and the confusion stopped the fighting and saved Muawiyah. Diplomacy resumed, arbitration was unsatisfactory and confusion reigned for several years... which was to the obvious advantage of Muawiyah.

Delay was likely his goal because during this break in the First Fitna the powerful new elites in all directions certainly did not grow to appreciate pious Ali's views. It's as if Muawiyah was openly gambling on the continued decline in revolutionary fervour and the increase of capitalist-imperialist desires. Infighting and discord increased among Ali's own partisans. Ali's soldiers began to be poached and bought off by Damascus. Eventually, Ali could not consolidate his position in Iraq, where Muawiyah's army began invading.

In 661 Imam Ali was assassinated in Kufa, Iraq – stabbed in the back while prostrated in prayer.

Ali's legacy is summed up by Shariati thusly: *"The Prophet is the manifestation of Islamic victory on the foreign front – over outright atheism and polytheism – whereas Ali is the manifestation of Islamic defeat within the ranks, at the hands of hypocrisy."*

Thus we have a major cause of the root of the Iranian obsession with hypocrisy, which is essentially the same thing as "corruption" to the Chinese or "opportunism" to Cubans. Of course, capitalists cannot be called "hypocrites" because capitalism is synonymous with hypocrisy, corruption and opportunism in every sense of the words, their practices and their applications.

Equal to Iranian hatred of hypocrisy is "arrogance", which is used synonymously with "imperialism" in everyday Iranian political discourse: imperialists arrogantly believe that they know better than the conquered locals, after all.

In similar vein, but with none of the same logic, Americans use "imperialism" and "capitalism" interchangeably, even though they are two very separate (but related) practices. Falsely using these two as synonyms explains why Western media essentially tries to instruct "read: capitalism" in the rare case they even print the word "imperialism".

Shariati continues:

> *"The political, social and international make-up of Ali was the representative par excellence of a new struggle, a struggle between the leaders and the loyalists of the new set of values, of the new faith, who rose up with new and true slogans of Islam and found themselves confronting the greed and worst elements of the revival of the rule of ignorance….*
>
> *Ali is the manifestation of an age in which an internecine struggle took place between a loyal faithful and anti-movement elements who donned the masks of faith."*

It should be clear how we can equate Imam Ali with the Rebel Faction Red Guards of the Chinese Cultural Revolution (but not the Loyalist Faction Red Guards; these are the two terms used by the Chinese themselves because – contrary to most Western perceptions –all Red Guards were not against the 1960s status quo.) Ali did not represent "only Iranians" or "only Iraqis" or "only Mohammad's Banu Hashim clan of the Quraysh tribe" – he represented the idea of moral, political and social unity and improvement: that is what true socio-political revolutions must be based on, while forgetting that means the revolution is nearing its end.

This is why Iranian Islamic Socialism has never been just some petty nativist, sectarian or racist creed but a true, progressive revolution. The message of Imam Ali is open to all peoples; his political message is open to non-Muslims who oppose reactionary and oppressive forces, if they would only look…. which is rather the point of this chapter.

"Confronting the 'neo-ignorance' and 'neo-aristocracy', which comes to life within the context of Islam under the cover of truth and the very heart of the justice-seeking Revolution of Islam, Ali is the base of resistance."

It is not surprising that "resistance base" has been chosen as the term for the smallest unit of Iran's Basij.

We also see here how Shia view Ali's opponents as a "neo-aristocracy" which mistakenly installed an era of "neo-ignorance" ("neo" because it is post-Mohammad, but "ignorance" because they opposed the social revolutionary Ali).

Ali resisted the unjust, and this resistance is most certainly the cause of his still-galvanising legacy in 2019. The Tudeh Party, for all their decades of progressive activity, never approached the impact of Ali in Iran - not in politics, not in culture, not in morality, not in anything. Never has the picture of the Tudeh Party been placed in seemingly every other home and business – Imam Ali's picture has.

Iranian socialists succeeded because they submitted themselves to Ali and thus won over the masses.

Western leftists have failed because they opposed religion, usually resulting in political suicide; or because they failed to make convincing links between their sect of Christianity and political leftism; or because, perhaps, Christianity simply does not contain such electrifying political examples like Imams Ali and Hossein.

The effects of Ali's failed 'Cultural Revolution' – revolution devolves to empire

Upon Ali's assassination his son Hassan, who is Hossein's older brother, becomes the next caliph, but he is obviously dominated by the powerful Muawiyah and is forced to quickly abdicate. Muawiyah is declared Caliph with the promise that upon his death the Caliphate will return to Hassan or, if Hassan has passed, his brother Hossein.

But infamously, upon his death in 680 Muawiyah reneges on this promise and appoints his son Yazid for his successor as Caliph. The Umayyad dynasty is thus established.

So not only is Mohammad's will disregarded, but the house of the Prophet has been deeply marginalized, and the democratic, consultative government of Islam has ended with the re-establishment of monarchy.

Some say that Muawiyah told his son to be gentle with Hossein, the grandson of Prophet Mohammad, but it should be clear that this will not become the case.

The Umayyad dynasty, while it was religiously tolerant – indeed, it was officially secular and Christians held top posts – was ethnically intolerant, as it was divisively pro-Arab. It was also an imperialist war machine which conquered from Spain to Afghanistan. Its legacy is almost universally considered to be negative among all Islamic historians (except by Syrian nationalists). How could it be otherwise? Given its imperialist nature, it was obviously neither revolutionary nor sufficiently Islamic.

(Like Alexander, the Umayyads mistakenly thought they could do anything remotely significant to the continent and perpetual superpower of India – claims of victories there by Greeks or Muslims are woefully and shamefully exaggerated, and serve only to amuse Indians. Unfortunately, the belief of such propaganda claims undermine the amazing achievements of India, and thus have produced a huge Western and Muslim under-appreciation for India's singular importance and dominance throughout human history.

While the actual Sunni-Shia schism undoubtedly started on the day Mohammad died - with the refusal to honor Mohammad's appointment of Ali as the first Caliph - the schism might have been averted if Ali's Cultural Revolution had been implemented.

This intellectual schism was clearly not a cultural conflict between the Byzantine and Persian cultures among early Islamic society – that would seem to rest upon the belief in some sort of native Persian austerity and compassion which sits in opposition to a native Mediterranean decadence and belligerence.

It is closer to the truth to posit that the Umayyads created a wholly new Islamic culture, which preferred a very selective tolerance and imperialism (how very modern European!) to the revolutionary and original Islamic culture of Mohammad. I think what cannot fail is to take a political-historical-ideological view: that the Umayyad aristocracy was able to arise and take power because the Revolution of Islam had weakened in its fervour and integrity.

This weakening was not just by the new Islamic elite like Muawiyah, but among the People themselves – to believe otherwise seems to accept a view that history is completely controlled by the 1%: why did the 99% not rise up with Ali? Clearly, many preferred Muawiyah's promises, his larger army, his richer allies, his less pious worldview. Islam was a political revolution and people do tire of revolution, after all – not everyone is a tireless Lenin or "Mr. Dynamo" Mehdi Ben Barka of Morocco (who disappeared in France in 1965, almost certainly with aid from the Moroccan monarchy, Washington, Israel and undoubtedly the Parisian police). Divine revelation comes from God, but political revolution is a human endeavor, and that means it must necessarily wax and wane, like all things human and earth-bound.

Of course, once under the counter-revolutionary reign of the Umayyads many would regret this decision – these are called "Shia" today.

While they would initially headquarter in Iraq and become culturally rooted in the "Shia crescent" (Lebanon east to Iran), Shia are significantly present in nearly every Asian country from Turkey eastward to Bangladesh & China. Thus, Shi'ism is not just a small regional affair as portrayed in the West.

This vast presence helps explain why there never was any sort of ideological-fuelled century of civil war with Sunnis as there were between Protestants and Catholics... until imperialist, racist and intentionally-divisive Zionism gained the upper hand, of course. The four Muslim fitnas (civil wars) are not remotely comparable in scope to the more than two centuries of massive Catholic-Protestant war in Europe.

If the Umayyad reign had been more politically enlightened and just, they would have likely rendered Ali more or less irrelevant, because they would have largely adopted his message without his urging. Their failure to do this meant that, as time went on, Imam Ali obviously became appreciated for the true and just revolutionary he was.

Despite nearly 70 years of appalling ritual cursing of Ali in public prayers, as ordered by the Umayyad Islamic authorities, Ali's message only grew and grew.

I rather doubt Mao fully understood the story of Ali, but as he was also an undoubtedly poetic and amazingly revolutionary soul I'm sure he would have appreciated it... assuming he had dispensed with the blinding anti-religious hatred of early socialists.

Conclusion

I hope this historical recounting clearly shows how, for Shia, Ali represents a Cultural Revolution within Islam after the original Revolution of Islam.

It should be totally clear how for Iranian clergy and laypeople such modern interpretations were so internally resonant, thrilling and relevant. Iran was not sufficiently electrified into action during the first wave of socialism - once it was combined with Islam, then it took hold.

By understanding how Ali was mixed in with socialism, it should be totally clear to the reader why mullahs around Iran began to view themselves as the vanguard party in a doctrine of revolutionary Shi'ism. The Tudeh Party simply could not possibly have the societal reach, the faith in their rightness, and the revolutionary fervor that the revolutionary Shia clerics had pre-1979.

As I said, my terms and historical parallels may be new or rarely-heard, but the ideas were present before I was even born. However, it is true that every Iranian revolutionary I have spoken with has never heard of a "Ali/Cultural Revolution" thesis.

Iran was always fortunate to escape the capitalist-imperialist domination nearly all other Muslim nations have been and are mostly still subjected to. We must realize that the split between Iran and the rest of the Muslim world is not based on religious doctrine – Sunni versus Shia – but on political-economic doctrine.

It is unfortunate that in the 21st century this must be tirelessly repeated, in order to combat the dominant propaganda: The "Sunni-Shia divide" is a concoction of Washington and Tel Aviv designed to further their imperialist capitalism, aided by a Riyadh which seeks to do whatever they can in order to keep the attention away from their reactionary and outdated system of monarchy.

These two chapters should also illustrate that the so-called "divide" is nothing compared to the Western European Catholic-Protestant divide but much closer to the Theravada-Mahayana discussion in Buddhism, where things were heated temporarily after the split, but then calmed down to result in a state of peaceful mutual coexistence. Of course, if the Americans had defeated socialism in Vietnam I'm sure they would have exacerbated this difference and would have manipulated the Vietnamese into waging war on the minority Theravada nations of Sri Lanka, Cambodia, Laos, Burma and Thailand....

Yet Ali does represent a different school of Islamic thought in politics, culture and economics – many would say that he continued the "original school". Ali poses the question: what is to be done in the face of decreased revolutionary commitment and political counter-revolution? His son Hossein provided the answer: constant, and even the ultimate, self-sacrifice for the benefit of a political-social-moral-cultural-religious goal.

Islam, like communism and Confucianism, views humans as perfectible via correct efforts and beliefs. Thus the martyrdom of Hossein inspires a Trotskyism-like Permanent Revolution in all Muslims, but especially Shia, and one which is simultaneously personal-moral and social-political.

In my experience, open-minded and religiously-searching Sunnis know, appreciate and are inspired by Hossein and Ali, but many Sunnis seem to have no idea. Of course, how many Christians can truly parse the differences between the apostles of Jesus? Let's not be harsh – we're all united here under God (and the concept of tawhid).

However, "martyrdom" is not only about suicide – to believe this obviously extreme idea is to assume so many, many, MANY things incorrectly about the Muslim concept of "martyrdom", most of which reduce Iranians and Muslims to non-humans. Clarifying the martyrdom of Imam Hossein, the Western and Muslim views of martyrdom, the cultural effects of the promotion of selflessness, and the Iranian governmental policies which have been inspired by this culture, are the subject of the next chapter.

Chapter 9
'Martyrdom and Martyrdom' & martyrdom: understanding Iran

"We are the nation of martyrdom, we are the nation of Imam Hossein, you better ask."

> ~ Iranian Major General and Quds Force Commander Qasem Soleimani, July 27, 2018

*T*hat injunction for education was in response to US President Donald Trump's threatening tweet to Iran, which read:

"To Iranian President Rouhani: NEVER, EVER THREATEN THE UNITED STATES AGAIN OR YOU WILL SUFFER CONSEQUENCES THE LIKES OF WHICH FEW THROUGHOUT HISTORY HAVE EVER SUFFERED BEFORE, WE ARE NO LONGER A COUNTRY THAT WILL STAND FOR YOUR DEMENTED WORDS OF VIOLENCE & DEATH. BE CAUTIOUS!"

The exchange confirmed the necessity of this chapter, which relates the importance of Imam Hossein in modern Iranian society.

Despite the good advice, I doubt Trump will ask anyone

about Imam Hossein, and it appears certain he lacks the intellectual stamina for a thorough, objective chapter such as this one.

The previous chapter is rather necessary reading in order to understand this part... unless one is already familiar with the life and death of Imam Ali, is aware of the foundation of the Sunni-Shia intellectual schism, and is aware of the areligious, leftist, historical perspective on the political situation of the early Islamic era immediately following the death of Prophet Mohammad.

While the goal of this book is to show how Iran is the ignored success of socialism, it is also to shed light on the Western blackout of honest, accurate and balanced discussion on modern Iran. Therefore, I thought that discussions of Imams Ali and Hossein should have actually been placed first in this book, as they are the major motivating force of modern Iran... but that would have immediately turned off the receptivity towards learning new perspectives on Iran among many often anti-religion Western leftists. Therefore, I have saved these two religious-philosophical and cultural discussions for the end - I wanted my discussion of Iran's unique creations to be factual and structural and not philosophical and religious.

We can't argue the clear facts and structures which prove Iran's socialism – not anymore.

But Iran's socialist policies cannot be explained or understood solely through an intellectual lens of socialism – "socialism" does not fully explain the unique creation of the Basij, the unique creation of the post of Supreme Leader, the unique creation of the bonyads, etc. For full comprehension, religious-cultural knowledge must be added to political-economic knowledge.

All of these unique (revolutionary) polices, structures and ideas can indeed be explained by socialism because they are socialist... but something crucial will still be lacking; one cannot fully understand them without clarifying additional philosophical, cultural and religious tenets which run deeper in Iran than in the obviously vitally-nourishing economic & democratic ideas of 19th-21st century socialism.

Is this more new scholarship linking Iran and socialism? Possibly, but links have already been made for many decades.

The previous chapter drew the parallel – and quite likely for the first time ever – between Imam Ali's failed "Cultural Revolution" following the original political Revolution of Islam, and the Chinese Cultural Revolution. Similarly, I cannot report finding internet or written links between Imam Hossein and the Trotskyist theory of "Permanent Revolution", either.

However, I am not here to take credit. While I feel that the Ali/China link was perhaps not able to be made in the heyday of the Iranian Revolution – as it is quite possible the true aims/goals/results of the Chinese Cultural Revolution were not properly diffused and comprehended – the link between Hossein and "Permanent Revolution" must have been just as obvious back then.

I contend that if I can't find a record of this historical parallel being explicitly made there are clear reasons why: the internet does not include the cassette tapes, mosque lectures and fragile mimeographs which were the method of political communication in 1970s Iran.

Furthermore, perhaps most Iranian thinkers wanted to give more credit to Islamic revolutionary figures, who were more relatable to the average Iranian. The Revolution of 1979 was intensely patriotic: a repeated claim was that Iran already contained all it needed to have a modern, revolutionary, just society – holding up non-Iranian figures hurts that claim. And it's not as if Trotsky, Mao or other foreigners were going to sue Iranians for using their ideas without attribution….

Another serious problem was that Iranian socialists were discredited by association in the 1980s by the horrific, detested, traitorous, totally illegitimate, most definitely NOT socialist cult known as the Mujahideen Khalq Organisation (known as the MKO or MEK, or People's Mujahideen in English).

Their unthinkable actions – stealing corpses to inflate body counts for propaganda purposes, fighting alongside Saddam Hussein against Iran, massacring Kurds at the urging of Hussein, assassinating Iranian scientists, thousands of other terrorist acts, etc. – undoubtedly caused many to step away from proudly espousing the socialist intellectual lens which was so open and prevalent in the 1970s.

It is mind-boggling to me that intelligent Western leftists ask me about the MKO as if they are some sort of viable leftist option in Iran… but it's a big world, filled with too many murderous cults to keep track of. The other reason for this query continues is that the unforgivable MKO has also been gallingly whitewashed in the West thanks to hundreds of millions of dollars from the US, Israel, Saudi Arabia and France (where they were long headquartered). The MKO is classified as a terrorist group in Iran and Iraq, as they were in the US and the EU until Barack Obama came to power. Support for the MKO on the part of the West repeatedly sends the Iranian government into an absolute tizzy, and rightly so – it is proof of the West's appalling and murderous intentions against Iran (as if more proof was needed….). All that needs to be said is: the MKO has as much chance of democratically coming to power as Benyamin Netanyahu does – *they fought with Iraq against Iran*, after all, and this is something which the Iranian People will never forget or forgive.

The MKO obviously did much more than just more than just smudge the image of socialism in Iran after 1979, but socialism is a global idea which had already been prominent for many decades in Iran. As neoliberal capitalism continues to fail, and as the MKO's remaining members die off, it is certain that socialism will regain its historic prominence and openness in Iranian society.

I will quote extensively, as in the previous chapter, from seminal Iranian Islamic revolutionary thinker Ali Shariati – I think readers will see for themselves how very clearly he adapted some key Trotskyist ideals in his modern portrayal of Imam Hossein. Whether Shariati admitted it or not, "Permanent Revolution" is all over his ideas, slogans and analyses, etc.

But I am only a journalist reporting what I have found: the explicit, written links I have not found, but I am both a poor journalist and poor researcher. I do not seriously expect Iranians to tell me that Imam Ali-Mao links were widely made during the Revolution – due to the anti-Cultural Revolution propaganda which is so prevalent - but I did expect them to tell me Imam Hossein-Trotsky links were: I can relate from personal discussions with older Iranians who were intensely politically active that - of course - Trotsky was indeed one of the key figures on their minds in the 1970s and beyond, but none of them told me that an explicit link was widely made between the two.

Regardless, credit for linking Ali/China and Hossein/Trotsky – plus another $0.50 – will only get me a cup of coffee, as the saying goes (at least it did prior to inflation); the main thing is to understand modern Iran in order to promote human brotherhood and socioeconomic equality.

The huge misunderstanding on 'martyrdom' between Iran and the West

It is often said that "self-sacrifice" and "martyrdom" are the main principles of the 1979 Islamic Revolution and

Iranian society today... but this fact is of little value to Westerners, because in 2019 there is a fundamental misunderstanding between the West and Iran on what "martyrdom" means and is. Two parties cannot create mutual understanding if definitions of words are totally different. This chapter aims to rectify that.

But to do that, it is necessary for non-Muslims to learn about Imam Hossein, the grandson of Mohammad, the son of Imam Ali, and the 3rd Shia Caliph but who was not a Caliph for Sunni because Hossein was cheated out of it by Muawiyah, founder of the Umayyad dynasty and the 6th Sunni Caliph (this last statement acknowledges a universal historical consensus and not solely a Shia one – this was all explained in the previous chapter).

In short: in 680 AD Imam Hussein marched off to certain death at Karbala, Iraq, rather than sanction the government of the Umayyad dynasty, which Imam Hossein and his family perceived as insufficiently Islamic and insufficiently revolutionary. This martyrdom has inspired a feeling of "Permanent Revolution" within Shia Iranians.

Indeed, two of the 10 Shia pillars, *Tawalla* and *Tabarra*, imply never-ending political struggle against injustice as a result of the examples of Prophet Mohammad, Imam Ali and Imam Hussein. It is not as if Marx and Trotsky were the first in human history to conceive of the idea of no comprise with political immorality combined with social unity among the 99%...

Many anti-religion leftists falsely assume Hussein's martyrdom was solely the result of a dispute over religious doctrine – there is that component, but it was an intensely political act as well. Nobody is forcing anyone to accept the religious aspect – Islam can never be forced, as the Koran teaches – and this allows non-Muslims to be able to view Ali and Hossein in a purely political-historical and areligious context. The widespread failure to do this has had huge consequences in modern political analysis of the Muslim world, especially in Southwest Asia. It is unfortunate that Islamophobic Western commentators are more likely to wildly relate the Shia faith in the Mahdi, the "hidden Imam" who will work alongside a returned Jesus to defeat the Antichrist, rather than discuss the huge cultural importance of Imams Ali and Hossein.

The yearly pilgrimages to Karbala, Iraq, to commemorate Hossein constitute the very largest peaceful gatherings in human history. Only one of the Kumbh Mela pilgrimages of Hindus at the Ganges River has surpassed the largest Arba'een pilgrimages - in 2010. Even though 10-30 million people attend, this event is totally ignored by Western media. That's a pity, because even though "God is dead" to many in the West, the Arba'een pilgrimages show how very, very, very living it is to Shia. Like that or not – this galvanising and peaceful power cannot and should not be ignored. As Soleimani said to Trump: "you better ask" about Hossein, because Western Mainstream Media will certainly not volunteer to tell you.

As I explained in the previous chapter, the Revolution of Islam was a sweeping and immediate political revolution as well as a revolution in religious thought and practice. This duality cannot be argued in the slightest, nor is there a single reason why they should be contradictory. Therefore, socio-cultural-historical parallels abound with the other great political revolutions in human history. Non-Muslims and Westerners have much to glean politically from the Revolution of Islam, if they can only set aside their anti-religion bigotry.

Regardless, the political structures and daily life in the Islamic Republic of Iran in 2019 cannot be understood without grasping the importance of Imam Hossein in our collective unconscious. Unlike Jesus in the secular West, Hossein is a constant, universal presence in Iran (and for the many non-Shia, as well), and a perpetual reminder of the need for moral political action.

The second, failed generation of Islamic revolutionaries

As the previous article described, to many Iranian thinkers like Ali Shariati, after Prophet Mohammad's death Islam was literally hijacked by slackening revolutionaries who forgot the socio-political message of Mohammad in order to create the imperialist Umayyad empire.

In 656 Imam Ali became Caliph and tried to stop this ideological and religious slackening, and thus represents, in modern terms, a Cultural Revolution after the Revolution of Islam, just as China had a Cultural Revolution years after their Chinese Communist Revolution (or similar to how Iran had the world's only other official Cultural Revolution, from 1980-83).

But, in 661 Ali is assassinated. Ali's son Imam Hassan becomes the Caliph (the 5th to Sunnis, the 2nd to Shia) but he has inherited a shattered administration. He is forced to abdicate to the politically and militarily powerful governor of largely Christian Damascus, Muawiyah, who forces Hassan to abdicate in half a year and is declared Caliph. The wishes of Mohammad are denied, the bloodline of Mohammad is broken, and the officially-secular (though ethnically racist and pro-Arab) and imperialist Umayyad dynasty is founded.

Imam Hassan, son of Mohammad's daughter Fatima and Imam Ali, retires to Medina and dies in 670. After Ali's death Umayyad clerics, shockingly, spent 60+ years making state-ordered ritual curses of Ali during public prayers - Hassan was clearly in a very weak position. When he dies he is even denied burial next to his grandfather, Prophet Mohammad, and his relatives in Medina. I quote from Ali Shariati's Martyrdom and Martyrdom:

"Imam Hassan, the manifestation of loneliness and isolation in Islamic Society, even in the Medina of the Prophet, clearly shows how the Truth-seeking party in Islam is utterly shattered. The new force of revolution completely overwhelms everyone and everything and conquers in every domain. Now it is Hossein's turn."

That *"new force"* is a negative one, led by those who split off to create Sunni Islam, which is why the Shia Shariati continues, unequivocally:

"Hossein inherits the Islamic movement. He is the inheritor of a movement which Mohammed has launched, Ali has continued and in whose defence Hassan makes the last defence. Now there is nothing left for Hossein to inherit: no army, no weapons, no wealth, no power, no force, not even an organized following. Nothing at all. "

Not only does the first two sentences of that paragraph name nearly all the males in my family, it should emphatically make clear the historical-ideological view of Shia Islam, and how it obviously sharply differs from Sunnis.

The post-Mohammad era: When Shi'ism was truly an underground political movement

Just as I wonder if Mao had any idea of Imam Ali's message of Cultural Revolution, I wonder if Lenin had any idea of what Imam Hossein stood for? I rather doubt it, but I'm certain the he, too, would have approved.

To paraphrase Shariati, who is paraphrasing Lenin, who lifted it from the title of a 19th-century book by Russian revolutionary Nikolai Chernyshevsky: Hossein and the very few true revolutionaries of his time are aware that the revolution is being compromised, and are asking – "What should be done?"

Certainly, there was no lack of ideas of appeasement being flung at Hossein: fatalism (God wishes it this way); are you so innocent that you can rectify the whole community; jihad is not the only path to God; asceticism is so personally pleasing; don't oppose a Damascus which is spreading Islam; people judge by what they see so Islam must show a rich face to the Byzantine Romans and Persians to win them over; many temples and churches have been replaced by mosques; Islam is gaining in importance; Muslims are getting the top governmental jobs; don't cause trouble when there is Holy War against Christians in Europe and Zoroastrians in Iran; opposing those aristocrats is unrealistic and combative; we must win over our own aristocrats; do not mix earthly matters with heavenly ones, etc.

It all adds up to a call of: support the ruling system and end your idealistic, permanent revolution. This is something rejected by revolutionary Shi'ism, because the results of such a choice are clear:

> *"Sixty years have passed since the migration of the Prophet. Everything earned by the Revolution has been destroyed. All of the successes earned a century before have been abolished. The Book brought by the Prophet is placed on the spears of the Umayyad (literally, during their war against Imam Ali). The culture and ideas which Islam had developed through jihad, struggle and efforts in the hearts and minds of the people became a means for explaining the Umayyads rule.*
>
> *...*
>
> *"Yes. In these black times the ignorance of aristocracy is being revived. Power is being dressed in piety and sacredness. The desires for liberty and equality created by Islam in the hearts of those sacrificed for power or policy are breaking down. Tribal (sectarian) ignorance has replaced the humanitarian revolution.*
>
> *...*

Jihad has become the means for massacre. Religious taxes are a means of public plunder. Prayer is a means of deceiving the public. Unity has been covered with the mass of profanity. Islam has become a chain of surrendering.

...
Nations are being taken into slavery as before."

Obviously, Marxist- and socialist-inspired condemnations abound, as is the desire for modern revolution. Again, such ideas found impeccably fertile ground among the pious everyday Iranians who saw more clearly than ever, amid the post-1973 oil price boom, how truly irreligious the corrupt Shah and his aristocracy was. The Shah also claimed to be "more socialist and revolutionary" than anyone, and that obvious falsity was clear as well.

It is perhaps natural that when the Shia Shariati focuses on the 50-year period between the death of Mohammad up to the martyrdom of Hossein – from 632 until 680 –that he is intensely critical of the lack of political revolutionary commitment on the part of the entire second revolutionary generation excepting only the "Shiite Resistance Movement", which is truly an underground political phenomenon.

Imam Hossein answers Lenin's question

In 680 the Caliph Muawiyah dies. Muawiyah's betrayal of the House of Mohammad culminated in the handing of the caliphate to his son, Yazid. He did not honor the "Hassan–Muawiyah treaty" and allow the Islamic World to democratically choose a new caliph upon Muawiyah's death. This ended the consultative and democratic caliphate and inaugurated monarchy and the Umayyad dynasty.

Yazid would go on to commit terrible atrocities at the Battle of Al-Harrah, which led to the looting of Medina by the Syrian army in 683, and then even an unthinkable siege of Mecca, leading to the burning of the Kaaba. The siege only ended when Yazid died after falling off his horse. These acts obviously damaged Umayyad authority among the People and strengthened the argument of the early Shia.

By 750 the Iranian-Iraqi Abbasid Revolution would kick the Umayyads out of the entire Middle East, while the Great Berber Revolt had kicked them out of the Maghreb just a few years prior – it was a clear referendum on the injustice of the Umayyad government. West and East Africa had not yet become Muslim at this time.

The ethnic (Arab) elitists but religiously-tolerant Umayyads only found fertile soil in Europe, ruling Spain for several centuries. The Abbasid Caliphate would go on to rule Islam for five centuries, replacing the feudal Arab Caliphate with a multi-ethnic and religiously tolerant Islamic Golden Age which lasted until the Mongol Invasion in 1258. The Mamluks of Egypt fought off the Mongols, thus sparing not just the Maghreb but all of Africa, and also allowing the Abbasids to re-center the Caliphate (religiously, but not politically) in Egypt until the Ottoman conquest in 1517.

Thus a truly "Muslim World" – one in which unity is based only on Islam and not Arab ethnicity plus Islam – does not begin until after the Umayyads. Shia obviously feel that Imam Ali and Imam Hossein perceived this sooner than anyone.

Shariati imagines the view of Imam Hossein back in 680: Hossein surely foresaw the crumbling of the Umayyad's legitimacy – due to its obvious slackening of revolutionary integrity, the corruption of revolutionary ideals and culture, and the renunciation of political and social involvement:

> *"Imam Hossein, as a responsible leader, sees that if he remains silent, Islam will change into a religion of the government. Islam will be changed into a military-economic*

power and nothing more. Islam will become as other regimes and powers.

...

He is alone, unarmed. Opposing him is one of the most savage empires of the world which is being covered over by the fairest and most deceiving cover of piety, sacredness and unity which the ruling power possesses. He is alone. He is a lonely man who is responsible to this school of thought.

...

Whoever is more aware is more responsible, and who is more aware than Imam Hossein? What is his responsibility? He is responsible to fight against the elimination of the truth, the destruction of the rights of the people, annihilation of all of the values, abolition of all of the memories of the Revolution, destruction of the message of the Revolution, and to protect the most beloved of cultures and the faith of the people, for their destruction is the aim of the most filthy enemies of the people. They want to once again create the unknown, mysterious deaths, exiles, putting people in chains; the worshipping of pleasure, discriminations, the gathering of wealth; the selling of human values, faith, honor, creating new religious foolishness, racism, new aristocracy, new ignorance and a new polytheism."

It's a powerful historical analysis, and one which combines modern, socialist-inspired political thought with Abrahamic morality.

We can easily perceive how Iranian clerics were especially electrified into political action, as they surely felt that their greater religious awareness made them even more responsible to promote a just and equal society. Again, the everyday Iranian could testify from personal experience that the Shah had obviously re-created these evils.

It should thus be clear how Iranian Revolutionary Shi'ism was created, how it was shaped by the lenses of socialism, and why it motivated both mullahs and masses far more than the Tudeh Party ever did.

But Hossein was totally weakened and could not depose the powers in Damascus. Therefore, he used his one weapon – his certain, aware death at Karbala.

The death of Imam Hossein – the birth of the 'living artist'

Hossein, then in Mecca, was invited by the people of Kufa, Iraq, (the future first seat of the Abbasid Caliphate 70 years later, showing that they maintained their revolutionary zeal and political culture) to be their leader. Kufans had come around after 20 years of misrule by Muawiyah. Hossein accepts their invitation.

However, Hossein gets word that Yazid's troops were killing his sympathisers and blocking the city gates – going to Kufa thus means certain death, given Hossein's lack of power and resources.

Imam Hossein had two choices: go to Medina and swear allegiance to the new Umayyad dynasty, or march to certain death at Kufa. Sanctioning imperialism is never Islamic, nor a modern revolution. Seventy kilometres from the Kufa gate Hossein's band of loyal companions and family, 72 people, chose to fight the Battle of Karbala.

> *"He leaves Mecca to reply to the question, 'How?'... (to) all those who can see, feel, understand and thus suffered and felt themselves responsible, who are thus looking for a revolution, (and) are then asking 'What should be done?'"*

Clearly, the aware death of Hossein was selected by revolutionary Shi'ism as a direct answer to the title of Lenin's famous pamphlet, which he took from a Russian book from

1863 which called for socialist self-sacrifice (or, to Iranians, "martyrdom").

I quote Shariati at some length, because I cannot decide what should be omitted, and also because Western readers must drastically re-orient their conception of the word "martyrdom" if they want to understand the Shia and Iranian version (and the version very close to Sunni Muslims, as well).

> *"The great teacher of martyrdom has now arisen in order to teach those who consider jihad to relate only to those who have the ability, and victory to be only in conquering. Martyrdom is not a loss, it is a choice. A choice whereby the warrior sacrifices himself on the threshold of the temple of freedom and the altar of love, and is victorious.*
>
> *Hossein, the heir of Adam, who gives life to the children of mankind, and the successor of the great prophets, who taught mankind 'how to live', has now come to teach mankind 'how to die'.*
>
> *Hossein teaches that 'black death' is the miserable fate of a humbled people who accept scorn in order to remain alive. For death chooses those who are not brave enough to choose martyrdom. Death chooses them!*
>
> *The word shahid, martyr, contains the highest form of what I am saying. It means being present; bearing witness; one who bears witness. It also means that which is sensible and perceptible; the one whom all turn towards. Finally it means model, pattern, example.*
>
> *Martyrdom: to arise and bear witness in our culture and in our religion is not a bloody and accidental happening. In other religions and tribal histories, martyrdom is the sacrificing of the heroes who are killed in the battles of the enemy. It is considered to be a sorrowful accident, full of misery. Those who are killed in this way are called martyrs and their death is called martyrdom.*
>
> *But in our culture, martyrdom is not a death which is imposed by an enemy upon our warriors. It is a death which is desired by our warrior, selected with all of the awareness,*

logic, reasoning, intelligence, understanding, consciousness and alertness that a human being has.

Look at Hossein. He releases his life, leaves his town and arises in order to die because he has no other means for his struggle to condemn and disgrace his enemy. He selects this in order to render aside the deceiving curtains which covered the ugly faces of the ruling power. If he cannot defeat the enemy in this way, at least he can disgrace them. If he cannot conquer the ruling power, he can at least condemn it by injecting new blood and the belief of jihad into the dead bodies of the second-generation of the Revolution revealed to the Prophet."

Quite a passage. It is incredibly political, and incredibly religious. Far from being a tragedy or a screaming kamikaze pilot/Nazi blitzkreiger hopped up on amphetamines, Iranian martyrdom is based on intelligent and sensitive awareness. It contains an urgent and progressive (anti-reactionary) political message.

"In summary, in our culture – contrary to other schools where it is considered to be an accident, an involvement, a death imposed upon a hero, a tragedy – (it) is a grade, a level, a rank. It is not a means but is a goal itself. It is originality. It is a completion. It is a lift. It itself is midway to the highest peak of humanity and it is a culture."

This is the "martyrdom" which has saturated itself in Iranian culture. Just how saturated? Iranians hear the word multiple times daily in the common greeting between two friends or even two strangers: *"Gorban-e-shoma"* ("I will be your martyr"). Some Iranians will say that I am over-exaggerating the literal importance of this phrase, but that IS the literal translation. To me, commonplace linguistic phrases reveal a culture's true soul; but it is true that nobody is really promising immediate martyrdom on the other's behalf.

(I have often speculated thought this Farsi phrase also grew out of Koran 4:86 – *"Answer a greeting in kinder words than those said to you in their greeting, or at least as kind. God keeps account of all things."* What could be a more welcoming greeting to a total stranger than promising to die for them?)

However, only the thick-headed would imagine Iranian martyrdom to be only concerned with violent death – such a society would quickly empty itself of citizens!

Martyrdom is also the constant little sacrifices of one's individual well-being for the sake of society and of others, and in much, much less drastic forms than death. Martyrdom essentially exists in order to activate the "living artist" who improves society by moving beyond mere individualism.

Martyrdom and Martyrdom and yet ANOTHER Martyrdom

"In European countries the word 'martyr' stems from 'mortal' which means 'death' or 'to die'. One of the basic principles in Islam, and in particular in Shiite culture, however, is 'sacrifice and bear witness'. So instead of martyrdom, i.e. death, it essentially means 'life', 'evidence', 'testify', 'certify'."

Martyrdom is, of course, one of the central messages of Jesus to Christians... but not to Muslims, however: the Koran explicitly rejects the idea that God could allow such a vital prophet of God to be killed in such a way. Indeed, in the Koran it explicitly teaches that Jesus was not killed on the cross – it was only made to appear that way by God. In Islam God is always logical, and faith always wins over evil, therefore the death of Jesus on the cross is illogical – how could Jesus' evil executioners have won? That is a complicated issue, and is complicated further by the Islamic belief that one cannot pay for the sins of another, therefore how could the death of Jesus ever be able to atone for everyone else's sins?

However, bringing all this up helps to clarify the roots of the difference in the meaning of "martyrdom" between Muslims and Westerners. It also helps illuminate why the martyrdom of Imam Hossein is so important in Islam – he is the primary Abrahamic martyr to Muslims.

However, I think Shariati somewhat misunderstands "martyrdom" as defined in the West. Although he is correct that they view it in a far more negative fashion than in Islam, I think Shariati's view is wrong by failing to include two key points:

Firstly, Shariati does not acknowledge that – for Christians themselves – there is also a positive message of Jesus' martyrdom, which is: that the key is to emulate Jesus when it comes to his willing martyrdom. However, I believe that modern West European Christians (not East European) have proven incapable of grasping this positive message - it is so very in opposition to the capitalist-imperialist aspects and demands of Western culture. Therefore, the point is moot for the Western half of the continent.

Secondly, Shariati did not grasp that many West Europeans mistakenly appear to think that because Jesus died for our sins, Jesus thus ended the need for more martyrdom. This quite significantly compounds the disagreeableness of "martyrdom" to Westerners. Indeed, "martyr" is a term used only to disparage in Western European cultures. The only time one hears it in English is in the phrase "Don't be a martyr". The word and concept are similarly totally absent in French. The word "martyr" is never even used to describe a person who has died unjustly, which is the primary view of the word "martyr". Western cultures do not use the word "martyr" for a Palestinian protester killed by Zionists, nor even for a Jew killed in the Holocaust.

For the West, I believe that martyrdom has evolved to mean "an unnecessary exaggeration of suffering" – as though you are pretentiously claiming that you are doing something on the level of Jesus. When it comes to martyrdom in the West the message is unambiguous: don't do it at any time. As I am aware of the Iranian version and its elevation of martyrdom, I always found this cultural difference quite, quite surprising.

I think the negative Western view reveals two flaws in their culture, as martyrdom is clearly a positive and necessary thing: a fundamental cultural indifference to unjust suffering, at least when compared with Muslim and Iranian cultures, and also a distaste for suffering on behalf of any cause. The latter observation is caused by the rampant individualism of the capitalist West: anyone suffering for a cause necessarily and annoyingly reminds them of their fundamentally self-centred lives – thus their society discourages such displays. There is also rampant nihilism in the West, which is not at all the same as religious fatalism, and which is yet another cause of their distaste for martyrdom: if all is pointless, why die for anything?

Martyrdom is thus negatively associated with a needless death for Westerners, while for Sunni Muslims martyrdom is associated with an unjust death, and for Shia it is associated with a selfless death.

Thus, Westerners view "martyrdom" as both a needless death and a negative, self-aggrandising act, while Sunnis view it positively but primarily as the product of external injustice, whereas Shia and Iranians view martyrdom as a necessary, positive way to effectuate social change. Therefore, we really are talking about "Martyrdom and Martyrdom and Martyrdom".

Martyrdom to Iranians is thus actually the equivalent of English "altruism". But, just like martyrdom, altruism conflicts with Western capitalist-imperialist ideology, as it is the belief in or practice of disinterested and selfless concern for the well-being of others. We should thus not be surprised that "altruism" is a word which is almost never heard in Western daily discourse, nor in their political discourse.

Therefore, even prior to Basij teenagers being forced into wartime self-sacrifice by Western aggression, "martyr" was something which held negative connotations for Westerners and positive connotations for Iranians.

The Western denigration of martyrdom forces the denigration of Iranian revolutionary Shi'ism

This Iranian conception of "martyrdom" should explain much in the first eight chapters: why wage revolution against the Shah for decades? Why sit in opposition to East and West? Why be so uncaring of Western public opinion? Why be so stridently revolutionary? Why condemn Israel when it only reaps trouble for Iran? Why give 15% of the economy to charity foundations? Why create the Basij? Why refuse to participate in the dominant neoliberal ideology of global imperialist capitalism?

"I cannot see the Iranians agreeing to continue to suffer while Tehran continues to finance foreign movements like Hezbollah in Lebanon or the Houthis in Yemen," Jean-François Seznec, professor of international relations at Johns Hopkins University, told France24 media in August 2018. You can't see it, really, Mr. Hotshot Professor? Many can, because they understand the Iranian conception of "martyrdom" – you clearly are another clueless academic. Seznec is also unaware of all the credible polls which show that all of these non-Iranian (and often non-Shia) revolutionary movements – as in Palestine, Syria, Iraq and elsewhere – are massively supported by a democratic majority in Iran.

Martyrdom – in the unique Iranian definition – is an indispensable part of the answer to all those questions I just posed. Whatever the West wants to hide, forget or put a smiling capitalist-imperialist face on – Iran chooses martyrdom, or would like to.

So we must relearn what Iran means by "martyrdom" – they are talking about "Iranian Shia martyrdom". The accurate terms in English are actually: self-sacrifice, altruism, social justice.

These desires explain why so many of the 10-25 million Iranians who joined the Basij likely did so – for the overwhelmingly majority it is essentially just a social hobby which encourages (moderate, dull) self-sacrifice for societal betterment. You do get some social and monetary benefits, but for many Basiji it also fills this emotional need that, "I need to martyr some of myself and my time for others". This emotional, and very human, need certainly exists in the West, but it does not exist in the same intensity and nor does it exist in a government-supported form (except perhaps in their neo-imperialist armies).

The West, with their different definition of "martyrdom", and in combination with their hatred of socialism and Islamic democracy, wants people to believe that Iranian "martyrdom" is all wild-eyed death when in reality it is 99.9% the mere provision of some rather mundane civil service/community improvement instead of watching TV.

Yet the West hears "martyr" and assumes the worst about those who support Iranian revolutionary Shi'ism. Here we can return to Golkar's anti-Basij book. Here is Golkar is discussing the WSBO – the Women's Society Basij Organization, which is the main Basij group for women:

> *"The ideal family, which is promoted by the WSBO, is called the Islamic Revolutionary family or 'family of holy defense'. The Islamic revolutionary family has specific features, according to WSBO head Minoo Aslani. The family is the place*

of modesty and chastity, where women take moral care of their family members. It is a place where women encourage charitable and spiritual affairs among their children and husbands, and where women should speak about religion and the Islamic Revolution."

This is exactly in line with Khomeini's statement that the Koran and women are the two great molders of human beings. To many, this passage describes a happy, typical, politically-modern home concerned with moral social conduct. For many Westerners and those who oppose modern Iran – this is some sort of horror, because the government should never, ever get involved with these types of values, as they are purely personal (and thus should vary extremely wildly, apparently). Golkar thus descends into fear-mongering, and surely finds plenty of receptive minds in the West.

Golkar refers to a scholar which absurdly labelled this kind of family a *"martyropath family"*. He wants us to believe that Basij women are being brainwashed into training a *"martyropath,"* or a person who is enchanted by death and wants to die to preserve Iran.

To me the only *"-path"* of any sort here is Golkar, for so obviously trying to portray Basij families as fascist psychopaths. It is incredible that this supposedly objective scholar is trying to portray a "martyropath" as a credible description of an average Basiji!

But this is what people do with Iran so often – they portray them as insane, death-loving, terroristic, religious fundamentalists instead of human beings. Trump's tweet merely reflects what he has repeatedly heard in the United States.

No Iranian woman (who does not belong in a mental institution) trains their child for martyrdom – they only train their children to be altruistic and selfless. There should be no doubt that in probably every single case of martyrdom known to man, it was ultimately done against the mother's wishes (and the father's). I am not a parent myself, but I think any parent would immediately agree with that.

Furthermore, as has been reported for the case of martyrs in Iran during the Iraq war: to choose a martyr's death is a lonely and individual decision, and families went to great lengths to stop it. However, this does not mean that – after the deed was done – families did not also see the glory in the death of defending their community, family, nation; this is no different than in any other nation with any of their soldiers.

The reality is this: Basiji women are merely being encouraged to be modern, empowered, outspoken, intellectual, society-influencing revolutionaries, and that is what is frightening to the counter-revolutionary West.

Just as there is a downside to the West's "never martyrdom" approach, there is a downside to Shia Iran's "more martyrdom, please" approach as well. For example, forgoing a couple meals during Ramadan does not make one the world's greatest Muslim martyr. It is quite easy for Iranians to puff themselves up as great Muslims and great revolutionaries because they have mentally accumulated 10 million insignificant instances of where they put the needs of someone else first, i.e., they simply did the right thing.

However, a society full of martyrs is certainly far, far more desirable than a society full of self-serving individualists, no? This is essentially the point to take away from this chapter, I think.

When pointed in the direction of socialist democratic empowerment and socialist economics, we can see why capitalist-imperialists would be so very intimidated by this cultural value of modern Iran's.

The message of Imam Hossein remains a political beacon

The willful ignorance of the revolutionary, unique and socialist-inspired structures of revolutionary Shi'ism, which created Iranian Islamic Socialism, is only dangerous for Westerners: they are the ones who are misled about the nature of modern Iran; they are the ones who have such a terrified, "Muslim *martyropaths* will get me" worldview; they are the ones who are deluded by the paranoia that it is Iran which is targeting them and not the other way around; and they are the ones whose societies are worsened by the failure to transplant some of Iran's unique solutions to modern problems in their own country; I could go on and on here.

It should be now quite clear that Iranians have reinterpreted the martyrdom of Imam Hossein to coincide with something quite similar to the Marxist and Trotskyist socialist concept of "permanent revolution".

We should see how something like the Basij – whether one approves of them or not, and I am objectively neutral in this book on their value – clearly was originally created to try to incarnate this idea of Perpetual Revolution for which Trotsky and Marx (and Lenin and other socialists) had very similar notions. By constantly recruiting new members, training them in modern revolutionary Shi'ism and granting them affirmative action spots in the universities and government, it is clear that official support for the Basij constitutes an effort to constantly refresh the Islamic Revolution and to constantly reshape Iranian culture in favor of Iranian Islamic Socialism. Again, I merely condense here the objective conclusions proven in my 4-part sub-series on the Basij and do not judge nor promote.

Obviously, revolutionary Shi'ism did not sprout overnight, nor did it need a war to make its values widespread; it has all existed in Iran for some time, yet it was the Islamic Republic of Iran which made these the officially-sanctioned values of the government for the first time ever.

Hopefully people will realize that Iranian "martyrdom" and its "permanent revolution" is something which is based both on sources of unimpeachable morality as well as the unimpeachable modern political ideas of democratic progress and economic equality. The slogans of 1979 – "Every place is Karbala!" and "The martyr is the heart of human history!" – undeniably reflect this reality.

"Every place is Petrograd" and "The revolutionary is the heart of human history" obviously could have been taken from Trotsky and Marx.

Agree with Iranians or not, modern Iran is indeed revolutionary, and thus quite in keeping with its ideological heroes – Prophet Mohammad, Imam Ali, Imam Hossein, Lenin, Mao, Trotsky, Castro and others. It is clear who deserves top billing in Iran; it is amazing that Western leftists still do not even know the cast of main characters.

It is incredible that many Western leftists practically boast of their historical ignorance of Islamic history and Muslim political development? One does not have to be a Muslim to recognize that socialism will not advance globally without first democratically accepting the histories and views of others.

I hope these discussions of Imams Ali and Hossein have demonstrated that one need not be an Iranian or a Muslim to accept that the Iranian Revolution is proof that Islam can be a progressive revolutionary force *once again*.

Chapter 10
'The Death of Yazdgerd': The greatest political movie ever explains Iran's revolution

I'd say it's a pretty low bar to be the greatest political movie of all-time…

Perhaps movies are just too sensationalistic by nature to give politics the seriousness it deserves? Maybe politics are simply too complex to condense into 90 minutes, minus the time needed for a compelling love story?

What are the greatest political movies of all time?

Firstly, let's exclude the documentaries. I'm talking about the pure art of cinema – documentaries are journalism.

This allows me to exclude what many consider the greatest political movie of all time –*The Battle of Algiers* – because it is told in a documentary form even though it isn't one: the director is "hiding behind" journalism instead of taking full advantage of the dream-like medium of cinema. It is a superbly-told and sympathetic story of anti-imperialist revolution – the Algerian War for Independence – and thus was banned in France for years. It is also a stunningly effective depiction of urban guerrilla warfare, and for that reason it was screened at the Pentagon ahead of their 2003 invasion of Iraq.

Yet another good reason this could be the greatest political flick ever is because it is the only film to have ever directly caused an actual political coup: during the filming, with the army loaning tanks to increase the realism around the capital, Defense Minister Houari Boumédiène took advantage of the cinematic-caused confusion to stage a very real coup against President Ahmed Ben Bella. This is a little-known fact about the movie – I wonder how the writer and director felt about it? However, Algeria is doing much better at Islamic Socialism than people give them credit for and, of course, this is why Westerners will only ever read negative news reports about modern Algeria.

Let's also exclude satires, because comedies have only one master – the laugh. That is no basis for any political ideology, but comedy's inherent fatalism does serve capitalism's demands for submission extremely well.

Often cited as the greatest political movie is Stanley "Never Made a Bad Movie" Kubrick's *Dr. Strangelove: Or How I Learned to Stop Worrying and Love the Bomb*, which is indeed excellent. However, it's mostly just a satire of a relatively uncontroversial subject – nuclear disarmament – and to re-watch it is to laugh rarely… but it's still excellent.

Many political movies are pure Western propaganda. *Gandhi* somehow makes Jinnah the one responsible for India's partition instead of England (and/or Gandhi, whom Indian leftists correctly refer to as the "patron saint of the status quo"), and it lends all the legal and patriotic weight it can muster to help portray and even rationalize English massacres and crimes. Steven Spielberg's *Lincoln* rewrites history by laughably making the mentally-unstable Mary Todd Lincoln the capital's most effective political insider; this type of revisionist history which pretends that women had more political weight than they did – but they were simply just written out of history – is incredibly anti-feminist because it erases their very real marginalisation and suffering... but this analysis cannot be comprehended by the typical Western fake-leftist PC mindset. Democratic Party hero Meryl Streep shamelessly whitewashed Thatcher in *The Iron Lady* – "older women can't get any good roles" was likely her selfish rationale, though she may not be truly leftist enough to understand why she needed a rationale to begin with. *The People vs. Larry Flynt* was a truly astounding promotion of pornography, and which misled young viewers about what free speech is even more than how pornography misleads young viewers regarding what sex really is; pornography is banned in seemingly all socialist-inspired countries – Cuba, China, Iran, etc. – but it is not just rampantly available but adored in Western capitalist societies, which is probably why the film won at least 20 US and European film awards.

Network, written by perhaps America's greatest screenwriter, Paddy Chayefsky, is the greatest movie about journalism, so that's in the running for our title. *Apocalypse Now* not only lays bare the running joke that was the American claim of honest political intentions in Vietnam, but also California nihilism as well; the *Redux* extended version is even better for showing the virulence of French imperialism, which amounts to "I have the guns and ruthlessness required to hold this land, so it's now called 'France'". *JFK* from Oliver Stone is such a clear condemnation of America's Deep State that it's amazing he even got it made and distributed widely in 1991. *JFK* was a full 25 years before insider, Russophobic machinations in the US were used to weaken newly-elected Donald Trump, causing the US to openly re-consider the idea that they may have a Deep State.

The Manchurian Candidate is indeed a great movie, but it's more of an improbable thriller with a political backdrop than an overtly political movie. A much better purely-political movie from the same era is the unjustly forgotten, Rod Serling-penned *Seven Days in May*, which dramatises the forgotten but fascinating story of perhaps the most rabid anti-socialist from the US, General Edwin Walker, who was allegedly shot at by Lee Harvey Oswald (before he put the voodoo on his "magic bullet" for JFK), and who served as the model for *Dr. Strangelove's* insane General Jack Ripper.

I thought *Syriana* was an excellent political movie, and the best in a very long time. From the orchestrations of puppet master Dean Whiting (whose last name hides the race "White" and whose first name alludes to the stupidity of rule by collegiate technocracy), to the rich Texan's exasperated corruption speech that *"Corruption is why we win!"*, to the drone assassination of the lone progressive Arab sheikh who threatens to modernise his country – the movie contains many anti-American ideas which have been self-censored for many decades.

Spike Lee made two genius political movies: *Malcolm X* and *Do The Right Thing*, although the latter's politics are not overt. The former could be considered the best, but the movie is essentially a documentary of a must-read autobiography.

But the lack of overt politics allows me to exclude an entire genre I love and one which influenced seemingly all national cinemas: Italian neorealism. The fault with these movies is that they are too much art and not enough politics; too much entertainment and not enough addressing and attempted resolution of political questions. Their politics are often so subtle that many surely miss that particular message. They're often so subtle and desirous of criticising all sides that we're not even sure whose side they are really on: Fellini, the greatest director of all-time, was in a Mussolini youth group, after all.

A good example of this is the movie Z, which I'd likely place alongside *The Battle of Algiers* as a contender with *Death of Yazdgerd* for greatest political movie ever. The reason the movie Z only contends for the bronze is, while being a necessary takedown of anti-fascism and antimilitarism, it makes the mistake of believing (as do many "leftists" in the West) that being "anti-" is enough to be revolutionary; that's like saying the important revolution in 1917 Russia was in February (the ousting of the monarchy) when it was really in October (the groundbreaking installation of socialism). Western fake-leftists have this "being anti- is enough" belief because they fundamentally support the bourgeois (West European) Liberal Democratic system and only seek to make minor modifications. I greatly appreciate that *Z* declares what it doesn't want, but I don't know what *Z* proposes – in the movie the political-moral centre dies, after all. Tellingly, the character merely demanded things everybody essentially wants, like peace (even though the movie was not set during wartime), fewer nuclear weapons, more hospitals and more schools. The very early demise of the moral-political centre shows that the author and director have no idea what to propose (being too timid to demand socialism), or was perhaps their symbolic admission of political bewilderment. We should remember that there is plenty of postwar existentialist and nihilist film noir in Italian neorealism as well. The quick demise of the moral centre allows *Z* to start being what it really is: a law-and-order murder procedural, but with a political backdrop. That makes it more concerned with "justice" than with "politics". Perhaps *Z's* "merely anti-" stance reflects the 1969 mantra of the West, which was ultimately just a failed cry of disillusionment and not a victorious demand for something (freedom from imperialism in *Algiers*, and freedom from monarchy and political immorality in *Yazdgerd*). But *Z* is hugely political, dissecting the systemic failure of bourgeois democracy and bourgeois justice.

It should not be surprising that no English-language movie made my medal dais – there is no English-language country which has been remotely revolutionary or progressively political for centuries.

However, Greek-born Elia Kazan made many great and honest movies about the US in the US which were not overtly political. The forgotten gem is *A Face in the Crowd* starring a totally-against type Andy Griffith. He swore to never again play such a negative character, and thus the movie is indirectly responsible for giving us that still-great TV show set in Mayberry, *The Andy Griffith Show*.

I, Daniel Blake is a movie which contradicts (or is the exception which proves the rule) my accusations of constant British cultural conservatives. I saw many signs portraying images of the movie's main character at anti-austerity demonstrations in France because this is, thus far, the definitive movie of Europe's ongoing Age of Austerity.

They Live is probably the biggest cult movie on this list, and even though it's rather a one-trick pony it's something which I'm surprised didn't come out of the USSR 50 years earlier. However, if it had been in the USSR, then it could not have hilariously starred American professional wrestler "Rowdy" Roddy Piper, the greatest "heel" character ever (although I was obviously partial to The Iron Sheik – Nikolai Volkoff tandem, mostly due to their well-thought-out – but never well-received – political diatribes directed at the audience.)

Many call Chaplin's *The Great Dictator* the greatest political movie ever, but I've never been a big fan of his work and if I saw this I don't recall it, like all of his movies. His vaudevillian style belongs to the 19th century and I just can't relate, as I grew up with electricity.

But I am not insensitive to the charms of the olden days: Eisenstein's *October: 10 Days That Shook the World* is stunning despite being a silent movie, and the famous and glorious scene of Lenin at the Finland railroad station should never fail to give chills to any socialist. I would also say that never has an actor looked more exactly like the historical figure he was portraying.

There are many leftist movies which are deliberately omitted from lists of "Top Political Movies". *The Grapes of Wrath* is the definitive cinematic representation of the "American Holodomor"; it's amazing how Ukrainians, Russians and Chinese died by the millions from starvation during that era but apparently no American Dust Bowl farmers ever seemed to perish, not even the starving Joads or their many companions… at least that's what they tell us. I cannot urge more strongly to re-assess what is often considered to be the biggest box office bomb of all time, *Heaven's Gate*: I contend that the film gives such an obviously leftist and class-based reassessment of the Western settlement of the United States that it simply had to get a character assassination before it ever even premiered. However, at least it allowed director Michael Cimino to atone for one of the greatest counter-revolutionary movies ever, *The Deer Hunter*: the infamous Russian Roulette scene made the Vietnamese quite possibly the most ruthless, humanity-devaluing psychopaths in cinematic history, thus allowing 1978 America to feel justified about their (failed) invasion. Another movie which is not thought of as leftist, but which also had to get a preventative character assassination, was *The Bonfire of the Vanities*. While not excellent, it is nowhere nearly as bad as the era's movie reviewers would lead us to believe. The movie is also an extremely honest look at the new (in 1990) culture of hyper-greed in newly neoliberal-unchained Wall Street; it skewers the elite of New York City for their decadence, rapaciousness and stupidity; it is also perhaps the very last pre-PC (Political Correctness) rendering of the very real ethno-political tribalism of New York City politics, using terms which are simply verboten today, such as "hymie" for Jews, and which admitted the ongoing class-based anger against WASPS (White Anglo-Saxon Protestants) in the poshest parts of Manhattan.

Another incredible leftist movie which is purposely ignored – it opens with a quote of Mao, after all – is *"Duck, You Sucka"*. Even though it's the middle part of Sergio Leone's extremely famous *"Once Upon A Time"* trilogy of Westerns, and the other two are so very popular, this one is seemingly never broached in the Mainstream Media.

In a 2018 article I discussed four key World War II movies which are often great but not the best: the unfairly maligned Soviet-era *The Fall of Berlin*; a mini-mea culpa, but still elitist, *The Last Ten Days* from Germany; the appallingly pro-Hitler *Downfall*, from Germany in 2004; and 2017's *The Death of Stalin*, an award-winning satire which obviously won honors because of its anti-socialist stance, because it is not funny at all, unfortunately.

So I think we'll agree – there are a LOT of movies produced decade after decade and yet we have a very, very short list of truly great political movies, all of which are arguably rather flawed.

That brings me to Iran's entry: *The Death of Yazdgerd*, which, as of 2019 was available for free on Youtube.

The movie is so good that this article will not include any spoilers whatsoever – that is how I much I encourage you to watch it! But what is needed is just a bit of historical background – I'm sure many are asking, "What on earth is a 'Yazdgerd'?"

Great art encapsulates their time, and so we need to put ourselves in the shoes of the intended audience. This article will give just that information, and I'm sure viewers will at least not doubt me when I say that this movie explains and justifies the 1979 Islamic Revolution better than any other movie.

However, I can show how its genius is so universally-applicable and so necessary in 2019 that you may actually agree that it is also the greatest political movie of all-time.

Iran and cinema – no mere 'mirror' for society, but instruction & decision

Cinephiles know that Iran – pound for pound – produces more great movies than any other country. For decades they have routinely taken home top international prizes.

I think it's somewhat unfortunate that cinema has undoubtedly become Iran's main artistic passion: movies are usually just a way turn off one's brain, and clearly don't produce very interesting political ideas. Iranian kids today, I'm telling ya… it's all, "My cousin in Los Angeles says he is a producer! I wanna go to Hollywood!" Frankly, I have often joked that the entire Iranian Islamic Revolution was the singular result of seeing how terribly narcissistic our family members became after they had moved to Los Angeles! "Oh no – we'll have none of that over here, thank you! Somebody get Khomeini on the phone!"

Of course, most of the Iranian films which are lauded or even just distributed in the West seemingly have to meet a minimum quota of roughly 1.4 abused Iranian women per screen hour. Like all socialist-inspired countries, Iran must be portrayed as gloomy, depressed, corrupt, atrophied, etc., so very, very few of our "not totally depressing" movies have snuck through the West's mostly pro-Zionism film censors.

We certainly didn't need this book to remind us that Iran was the world's last great openly anti-capitalist and anti-imperialist revolution (Burkina Faso's 1983 revolution lasted only until 1987, sadly). It is only natural that Iran's art would reflect this.

But it is perhaps the world's inability to see the global resonance of the Iranian Revolution which makes modern Iran so misunderstood. Despite the unprecedented involvement of religion, Iran's revolution is as relevant and as applicable to every society as the great French and

Russian revolutions; because this movie makes that universal relevance perfectly clear, *The Death of Yazdgerd* deserves the mantle of "the greatest political movie of all-time".

Many will not watch this movie because they assume it is all about Islam, but that is not at all the case! In fact, the movie only subtly and very briefly supports Islam. The movie is far more focused on undoubtedly universal concerns: *The Death of Yazdgerd* is a two-hour machine-gunning of monarchy, aristocracy and outdated religion, with all these massacres being defended by the right of the People to wage class struggle.

Class warfare in 1978 Iran... not much different from class warfare in 578 BC Iran

This movie was written in 1979 but broadcast on Iranian public TV in 1982, with an all-star cast.

Frankly, it is a riveting but rather exhausting movie to watch: just as reading Dostoyevsky is no walk in the park, the movie repeatedly exposes your own reactionary and thoughtless impulses. One is so often struck on a personal level that you feel compelled to stop and ponder your own sins, but unlike a book you cannot easily put a movie down and resume it when you have recalibrated your new moral equilibrium.

The movie first debuted as a play, and that explains why it is seemingly six hours of dialogue compressed into two hours of movie. The movie maintains a seemingly impossible fever pitch and tension throughout, and every emotion is played to its hysterical utmost. And why not – the movie is about a family on trial for allegedly killing a king. Surely that's a moment of high drama!

But not just any king: Yazdgerd III was a real historical figure. He was the last in a thousand-year line of Persian, Zoroastrian-religion kings, as he was felled by the Arab Invasion and the Revolution of Islam.

Like all Persian kings, Yazdgerd was the "king of kings", but he was even more extraordinary than that; like Tsar Nicolas II or, more accurately, the Aztec Moctezuma II, Yazdgerd was the rare king who truly marked the absolute end for an entire cosmogony. Yazdgerd didn't just get toppled in 651 AD – he was deposed by Allah... literally. Of course, readers can understand that in 1982 Iranians were celebrating almost the exact same thing about Shah Mohammad Reza Pahlavi.

One should now see the genius of the author for drawing the historical parallel with Yazdgerd, who represents not just a societal "sea change", but an incredible inversion of sea with sky.

The legend is that Yazdgerd III was killed by a simple miller at the behest of the aristocracy, who wanted to avoid the bad karma associated with killing "the Shadow of Ahura Mazda on Earth". (Ahura Mazda is the sole god of Zoroastrianism, and this monotheism is why Zoroastrianism is tolerated in the Islamic Republic of Iran today – the fires in their fire temples have not gone out for 2,500 years.)

There's no need to change that fine story... unless you are that miller!

And the movie's plot is essentially that: the miller and his family are forced into concocting subterfuge after subterfuge at their impromptu trial for regicide, with the goal of creating confusion about if it was the miller who killed the king in order to greedily ascend his throne, or if it was the king who killed the miller in order to hide from the invading Arabs.

The Miller, his Wife and Daughter don't just spin a web, they spin webs within webs in order to save the family from the false justice of the 1%, as represented by an aristocratic knight, a graying warrior horseman, and a *mubad* (a

Zoroastrian priest: called "magus" in Latin, the plural of which is "magi"). These are essentially the only six characters.

Sympathy for the miller... we can see this movie is a class-based retelling of the legendary death of Yazdgerd.

It is not a movie-ruining "spoiler alert" to reveal the main message: we 99% have all been the Miller, whether under Yazdgerd, Shah Mohammad Reza, Moctezuma II, Louis I through Louis XVI, or any unelected monarch. My claim of "greatest political movie of all-time" becomes clearer when we remember that the Iranian situation prior to 1979 had not been any measurably different from anyone else's: from the pre-literate time until 1979 (or even in 2018 for some nations) the People have been oppressed in the exact same manner around the world.

Every country without a modern, socialist-inspired government has always ultimately been ruled by feudalism, monarchy, thieves of your wages, abusers of your taxes, rapers of your women, murderers of your sons whom they send off to fight the elite's wars, the unjust jailers of your nephews, the intimidators of your nieces, as well as by the ideologies of unregulated and elite-driven capitalism, bluffing technocratism, colluding holy men, bullying and undeservedly smug aristocracies, intellectual leaders who are actually anti-science, and other outright reactionaries who seek to retard social progress so they can jealously guard the gains of economic progress for only themselves.

Those are (some of) the explicit points the movie tries to fit in, like some jam-packed Persian carpet. The author refuses to omit any of the monarchy's/aristocracy's atrocious crimes because an average Miller's family would have been spared few of them.

That makes it an obvious defense of the 1979 Iranian Islamic Revolution and an ideological massacre of the pro-Shah ideology which just fell. One need not be Muslim to grasp this, nor to agree with it.

A common slogan in 1979 was "The Martyr Is the Heart of History", and that's because political history (without socialism) is actually timeless: the oppressor always exists in the same form, regardless of the date on the calendar. This movie, had it been shown in 600 BC and in any part of the world, would have made the exact same points and described the exact same abuses of average person.

And that is what artistic genius achieves – cultural and historical universality. This is not a movie about Iran, Iranian-ness nor Islam – it's a movie about politics, a universal human practice.

Such universality is only possible with a socialist worldview, and it is only socialism which universally speaks truth to power. In 1982 viewers around Iran undoubtedly saw the story of the Miller, his Wife and his Daughter and thought: "Well, come what may in Iran - at least I'm not forced to put up with THAT anymore."

For the viewers in 1982 Iran, all of whom were involved in both revolution and were currently under unjust attack by Iraq, it is made crystal clear the only way to break this feudal chain – on an economic and political level – is via the socioeconomic equality of Islamic socialist-inspired ideas; whereas the elitist justice of the aristocrat, warrior and resolutely anti-modern *mubad* is undoubtedly Liberal Democratic, and not Socialist Democratic.

Iranians in 1982 would also have easily comprehended how stagnant, unrefreshed religious ideas have not benefitted from the wisdom of subsequent centuries of human experience; an undemocratic faith ultimately hinders the revolutionary, all-embracing unity and compassion of Islam.

I don't think you have to even watch the movie to agree: there is no other movie in history which has tried to make these points in such a 100% overt manner. There is no discreet charm here – this is a movie which demands to be listened to on the most vital of social issues, demands your sympathy for the Miller and his family, demands your condemnation for his oppressors, and demands you choose sides.

In that sense it is very much in line with the Brechtian philosophy of drama. However, instead of their totalitarian-style austerity and love of bitter irony, there is a culturally-Persian luxuriation in excessive and disorienting sentiment, as well their ability to effortlessly evoke the highest emotional raptures and the lowest wraths as only committed monotheists can.

The movie is Joycean not only in its rapid shifting of time and consciousness – as the Miller's family is constantly donning and discarding the persona of each other (i.e., the Wife now plays the role of the Daughter, the Daughter now plays the role of the King, etc.) – but in the staggering amount of detail contained in the seemingly innocuous dialogue.

The final point which must be made is to note how amazingly it captured the essence of its time: I would LOVE to discuss the final scene, and how it so starkly encapsulated Iran's exact situation in 1982, and how truly breathless it must have left every single one of its viewers... but that would be to spoil it for you! Again, if a viewer considers the situation of 1982 Iran, the ending's intense, quaking urgency will be abundantly clear. I would say that the breathtaking ending to *Death of Yazdgerd* is only rivalled by a Pier Paolo Pasolini's version of Euripides' *Medea*, a spectacular movie in its own right. All I can say about the ending is: it is stunning how universally applicable and yet how also immediately appropriate the film was upon its release – most works of art can't even satisfy just one of either category.

If this movie was only politics...it wouldn't be a 'movie', would it?

Call up all your favourite Italian neorealism-inspired films and I contend that Yazdgerd still holds the crown of crowns.

It has to work on the level of mere entertainment. There are only six characters but two hours of intense dialogue: The family is trying to outwit their judges in order to save their lives, therefore they are forced to employ a dizzying array of intellectual gambits. Even an astute viewer will have difficulty keeping track of what is what, who is who, and which *Rashomon*-like reality is being recounted to the judges at any given time.

It has to work on the poetic level: poetry is nearly a national birthright for Iran, so you symbolic-types can rest assured that the classic poetic and cinematic language and semiotics are presented in master form. The writer and director, Bahram Beyzai, is the son, nephew, grandson and great-grandson of notable Iranian poets. Beyzai is perhaps Iran's greatest playwright and one of the most influential movie directors – he is obviously not just another political ideologue, but in 1979 seemingly every Iranian was a political ideologue of some sort.

It has to work on the psychological level: should we really kill the "king" – our ego? What happens afterwards? How did our king get this way, and who are we really? Even humble Millers are not exempted from asking such questions in the course of a life. When I become too confused by such human questions, or when I find myself looking down on somebody who is in confusion, I would do well to remember a superb line in the movie: *"A man who is lost is still also a man."* That's just one example of the pithy philosophical writing in the movie, and over such a huge range of human experiences.

There is also plenty of humor: *"No one has ever disobeyed the King of Kings,"* shouts the CEO, excuse me, the aristocratic knight. *"Oh really?"* retorts the Miller's wife, *"Then order the Arab army to retreat!"*

Her lampooning gets serious and sharper: *"Do you put kings at the same level as bandits?"* The laugh-to-keep-from-crying response: *"Unlike kings, bandits show mercy to the poor."*

Furthermore, the movie is also an in-depth examination of the only other institution as revered in Iran as Islam – the family. This reverence doesn't make Iran unique in the slightest, but its addition is another element which makes the film so great. Without getting into spoiler specifics: force a father, mother and daughter to talk and recount their lives for two hours – and to play-act the roles of each other – and it would be impossible for family politics to not surface. Iranian social life is inextricable from family life, so of course the author has salient things to say in what is truly the junior topic of this movie.

Indeed, innumerable other topics besides "political" politics are broached and commented upon: marriage politics, parent-child politics, gender politics, sexual politics, puberty, money, gossip, etc.

The reason this explanation of Revolutionary Shi'ism is so universal is because: while its pro-socialist propaganda could not be more blindingly obvious, its pro-Islam propaganda is so subtle that it is likely missed by many viewers. This is a political tract and not a religious one... but it also got approved for mass broadcast amid humankind's only other Cultural Revolution for a reason. Can you tell which two lines of dialogue likely clinched its official approval?

But, again, the massacring of feudal capitalism does not necessarily have anything to do with Islam, because the former is universal whereas Islam is region-specific. That's why this movie should be required viewing for any nation with a monarchy. Any nation which has evolved to republicanism has the right to feel mildly superior, but they should watch it to remind themselves of our shared humanity and what will result by reactionary backsliding. The entire

Western Hemisphere, lacking any monarch (save Queen Elizabeth II, still) should watch it as well because they wiped out so many aboriginal monarchies (while under the banner of West European monarchies, of course, so no political credit is due).

"Once the king dies, the nation is dead," is a line from the movie but we can never forget that it was a universal and rock-solid belief for millennia – how many of your sociopolitical-economic beliefs stem from that era, and how many come from after Marx? For the Miller's Wife, and for modern Iranians, that line provokes grinning disbelief: *"What is this I just heard…?"*

Incredibly, in Western Europe and many other places such a line produces misty-eyed, reactionary conservatism and monarch worship. That is a huge political problem in 2019; socioeconomic problems cannot help but follow, as a result. Iran resolved this problem in 1979, and that is the ultimate point of this movie, which stands as a testament to this political fight which claimed countless billions of martyrs, prisoners and victims since time immemorial.

What the capitalist-imperialist world is increasingly being forced to admit is that a socialist-inspired nation does not die once their "king" has died: China after Mao (and others), Iran after Khomeini, Cuba after Fidel (and soon Raul) – socialism-inspired nations are proving durable because they have effectuated democratic, not just economic, redistributions of power. That, of course, is not something which Liberal Democrats ever come close to possibly admitting: they are unshakable in their easily-disproven assertion that West European democracy is the "most democratic".

Even if, as doubters claim, religion only exists as a cautionary tale to spur proper social choices, *The Death of Yazdgerd* is the greatest political movie ever because it so clearly shows what humanity got and will continue to get by refusing the socio-economic, ethnic and political equality only offered by socialism and never by capitalism: to watch it is to be converted to political modernity.

What other movie can possibly make such a claim? Greatest Political Movie of All-Time – The Death of Yazdgerd.

Chapter 11
Iran detente after Trump's JCPOA pull out? We can wait 2 more years, or 6, or...

*U*nfortunately, the final chapter in this book on modern Iran arrives at a time of major economic instability, the worst since the end of the Iran-Iraq War.

For the sake of argument, let's finally be honest about what concrete steps Iran would have to take in order to finally get the sanctions called off. Such questions are never openly demanded the West.

We should totally ignore US Secretary of State Mike Pompeo's 12 Points speech in May 2018 (which is what everyone in Iran did): all of those claims, which essentially perpetuate the false, 1980s-era notion that Iran supports terrorism, are designed solely for unquestioning Western consumption. They also totally obscure the real aims of the West in Iran: they want Iran's natural resources and a compliant government – that's just the law of capitalism-imperialism.

But what exactly would Iran need to do to actually placate the West?

- First, eliminating the post of the Supreme Leader – the "soul of the government", seems like a must – the post is basically one non-stop civic exhortation to patriotism, morality, social justice and international justice.
- That requires rewriting the democratically-approved and democratically-supported constitution, which is entirely too modern and revolutionary by Western standards; Iran would obviously have to adopt a West European (bourgeois Liberal Democratic) model to finally win the approval of Western governments, media and NGOs.
- The Basij is impossible to dissolve, but since the post of the Supreme Leader is gone they can be put under the ideological control of the national army and be reduced to a purely jingoistic and neo-fascist group, I suppose.
- The military can no longer include the Revolutionary Guards because such a group only exists in socialist countries and never capitalist ones.
- Secularism must be enforced, and that logically translates into some sort of formal edict by the Shia religious establishment that clerics cannot hold civil power, as the Roman Catholic Church did in 1983; who cares that in 2013 Iran voted for Hassan Rouhani in a first-round sweep, even though he was the only cleric among eight candidates.
- Forget about the hijab law, even though many Muslim women say it is an obviously feminist solution to male superficiality and female materialism. Say hello to miniskirts for women and shorts for men in public (buy stock in sunscreen companies!).
- Legalisation of alcohol is a must, and also drugs eventually, even though drugs are already dangerously cheap in Iran, because Iran is right next to the poppy fields of Afghanistan.
- Undoubtedly, Iran has to recognise the colonisation of Palestine by Israel, and also do a 180-degree shift in their policies towards Afghanistan, Iraq, Syria, Yemen and elsewhere, despite Iranian democratic support for these policies.

These are the big issues, but they aren't the lucrative capitalist-imperialist prize:

- Above all, the only thing which will calm the West is economic domination. Iran needs to go full-globalisation and sell off majority control of their companies to foreign stockholders. Iran has, per my estimates detailed in this series, perhaps 85-90% state control of the non-Black Market economy – there is no doubt that Iran is a socialist country economically. That would have to be slashed to window-dressing levels, perhaps to French standards: the French state, following the sell-offs of Jacques Chirac and all who followed him, now only has $100 billion of shares in national corporations, even though their CAC40 stock index is worth $1.9 trillion.
- I can't imagine Western capitalists ever being content with allowing the roughly 15% of the Iranian economy to be legally controlled by the bonyads, or state-controlled religious charity cooperatives, so that must be rewritten by law to now fall under private control.

I think you are crazy if you think the West would make peace with Iran while they kept any of these policies, because they are all – without a doubt – revolutionary, anti-capitalist and pro-socialist.

Iran could totally satisfy Pompeo's absurd demands – which essentially call for a foreign policy which is the exact same as that of the US, and an unheard-of openness to foreign inspections – but I think it still wouldn't lift one sanction.

And Iranians know this, and they know it now more than ever.

It's the pain of this knowledge– not including the economic basis of the 2017/18 winter protests – which is causing instability in Iran. This pain is mostly psychological:

it has fully hit home that there will be no real detente, but only more totally-unjust Cold War against us.

And so people are freaking out, overreacting, getting angry, thinking desperate thoughts and feeling hopeless. Iran's leaders and citizens have spent five years politicking, discussing, deciding, negotiating, signing, waiting and hoping that the JCPOA agreement on Iran's nuclear energy program would end the sanctions… but the West has not honoured their word.

And pain for the average Iranian has truly increased since 2012, because that's when the sanctions really went to near-wartime levels – non-Iranians just don't understand how unprecedented these UN-US-EU sanctions were, and how unjust and devastating they are. They have no idea about how harmful sanctions are on Cuba; they have become convinced that food shortages in North Korea are the fault of their own leadership.

I'm very sorry to report that in the past six years Iranians as a whole have become less secure, more desperate, more coarse, more greedy, less humane – Iranians have become more like a Western capitalist country. That is terrible, because Iranians are an incredibly warm, gentle and generous people, but Iranians themselves admit this change is taking place. Let's be crystal clear: the problem is not of Iranian origin, but of foreign origin.

I admit this truth of coarsening and selfishness because that has always been entirely the West's goal. It is no exaggeration to write that they want to starve Iran into acting like animals until they start biting each other, and then install a dogcatcher to rule them on behalf of the West's needs; that is what capitalism-imperialism does, and if you don't see the injustice of it now I doubt you ever will. It is soul-destroying, in every sense.

The same is true for North Korea, Cuba, Venezuela and other socialist-inspired nations – it is the West who provokes the most pain, by far, and not their systems and vanguard parties.

And yet there is no way – NO WAY – Iran will democratically take any of those steps I listed in order to appease the Western aggressors. They will not even be considered by the average Iranian man and woman on the street, I can assure you. I know this because I have asked so many of them point-blank for decisions on these key questions.

The patriotic motivation of the 1979 Revolution – "Neither East nor West but the Islamic Republic" – was always the strongest force, and that has not diminished; conversely, this demand for independence and sovereignty has only been strengthened after 40 years of war by the West, war with Iraq and seeing our neighbors invaded and their societies destroyed. On the positive side of the ledger, after seeing Iranian-guided economic redistribution cause an economic renaissance since 1979 – which has only been paralleled by South Korea, China and Vietnam – many Iranians KNOW they can run Iranian businesses better than any foreigner and that "the Iranian way" is just as good.

Giving up these policies the West wants to end is akin to suicide, and certainly a betrayal of our sense of self… but continuing these policies will only engender more pain (through no fault of Iran's own). That is the best explanation of why Iran is suffering from rather huge angst and existential instability right now.

The good news is: Iran is fundamentally quite healthy, thanks to the fruits caused by 40 years of a modern political revolution. This fever will pass because Iranians know there is no other solution but to sweat it out.

Hillary would have been no different than Trump – betrayal is what the US does

Unlike most Americans, Iranians grasp that "blame Trump" is a pathetic, near-sighted political analysis….

Fully implementing the JCPOA meant one thing: Iran becomes the first successful transition to a post-oil economy in the Muslim world – that's historic.

The economic ramifications of that would be enormous and would drastically change the current capitalist-imperialist order in the region. The cultural ramifications – given that Iran is the only modern, democratic, socialist-inspired nation in the Muslim world (with a minor nod to Algeria, whose democratic bona fides are far less exemplary, given their '90s repression of the vote in favor of Muslim democracy) – would be equally enormous as well. Admiration for a highly-functioning Iranian model, and subsequent possible emulations, drastically changes the entire order in the Muslim world, obviously.

Even though it would be good for the Muslim world's inhabitants, and thus the entire world, it should be clear that none of this can be permitted by Western capitalist-imperialism.

Unfortunately for the American people and the entire world, political lobbies in the US make peace with Iran impossible, and the JCPOA's failure makes that clear (yet again). Ultimately, the weakness is structurally inescapable, because Liberal Democracy (monarchical or republican) prioritises the domination of the 1%: US policy is based solely on lobbies, not ideology nor morality nor democratic public opinion nor the fair-minded soul walking on Main Street. And not only is there not a true, sincerely pro-Iran lobby in the US, but there are many powerful anti-Iran lobbies. The same holds especially true for Cuba. We should understand Washington's virulent anti-Iran policy better once we acknowledge this reality.

(Why has Trump pursued a limited détente with North Korea? Because, as I reported from the Korean Peninsula in 2013, South Korea sits on an estimated $6 trillion in mineral wealth, including a huge amount of rare earths vital in modern electronics. China holds the vast majority of some rare earths, so it seems clear that US corporations have pushed Trump to open up North Korea as a supplier of some of these newly vital resources. Furthermore, Washington obviously looks at the situation as a chance to weaken - and get physically closer to - both China and Russia.)

Let's say Iran races to a nuclear breakout or starts blocking Persian Gulf oil deliveries, and Trump loses re-election in 2020 – could his successor come in and resurrect the JCPOA in order to calm things down? Unlikely, as pro-Iran lobbies are not going to magically appear, nor will the anti-Iran lobbies disappear. That's why even though a failed Iran policy from Trump theoretically implies that another presidential candidate could win votes via promoting detente with Iran, the "lobby reality" undermines this democratic possibility.

The idea that war-hawk Hillary Clinton would have rolled out a red Persian carpet for Iran is… absolutely untethered from reality or history. Iran and Cuba were the only two countries who Trump truly bashed during his election campaign (as there is no negative "lobby" consequence), but even though Iranians knew more pain was coming many still believed, rightly, that Hillary would have been worse: even if we forget Hillary's murderous glee over Libya, she was more tied to the lobby-system than Trump.

But blaming Trump for Iran's current problems is simply what fake-leftist US Democrats do over and over: they cry bloody murder when conservative presidents follow the exact same policies as Democratic ones. Why didn't Obama jump-start the Iran deal when he was in office through a myriad of executive orders? It was finally signed in July 2015, so he had half a year to do so. Why did he wait so long to get the deal arranged in the first place? Why did Obama immediately undermine his similar deal with Cuba, via billion-dollar sanctions on European banks for working with Cuba? Such sanctions are now the reason Europe won't defy Washington with Iran. The answer to both is simple: the US never has any intention of peace with Iran, Cuba or anyone else who is socialist-inspired and democratically revolutionary. You shouldn't have to be a Native American or an Iranian "hard-liner" to know that the US never keeps its promises.

And this brings us back to why there is so much angst and instability in Iran right now: Iran is coming to terms with the reality – warned of by many in Iran for years – that the West will never compromise and never cooperate. The only way forward for Iran is more Cold War and... how can that not be frustrating? How can that not provoke anger, instability, resentment, scapegoating, etc. inside Iran – it was hard enough for Iranian revolutionaries to change Iran, but now they have to change the entire world, too?!

The fake-leftists in the West choosing to focus on women not attending football games or men not being able to parade in public wearing hot pants... do they really think the average Iranian is worried about such trifles amid economic warfare and the prospect of continued Cold War? Do they really think Iranian women and men would gladly accept the coarsening and impoverishing of our society in return for such insignificant "rights"? But what can be done with fake-leftists? Not much, of course.

The good leftists in the West, such as the World Socialist Web Site (mostly), whose 3-part pamphlet against my reporting on "Iranian Islamic Socialism" was the impetus for this book, made a major mistake last winter by assuming that sanctions-provoked economic protests would somehow lead to (Trotskyist) socialist policies and revolution; their big mistake was not realising that socialist policies have already existed from the beginning of the Iranian Islamic Revolution.

The larger problem is that Western leftists totally misunderstand Iran, and thus how could they properly support it? The goal of this book has been to eliminate a ton of Western misconceptions via facts nobody can deny: about the state-run and socialist nature of the Iranian economy, about Iran's almost unparalleled success in economic redistribution in the past four decades, about the falseness of using the words "privatisation" and "Iran" in the same breath, about the undeniable socio-political redistribution of power caused by revolutionary ideas such as the Basij, about the way Shia Islam was philosophically inclined and then readapted to incorporate modern socialist ideas far more than the any non-Iranian can probably even imagine.

I earnestly defy anyone to refute my long-standing claim that Iran is truly socialism's ignored success story. I hope that I have given plenty of ideas to challenge and scrutinise in this book.

Back to reality: because of the failure of the JCPOA Iran is not having "revolutionary doubts", "revolutionary failure"," or "counter-revolution" but "revolutionary fatigue". This is caused by the endless Western cold war, as Iran's current problems are unthinkable in an Iran which is not so persecuted.

I would bet that "more revolution" is sure to come in Iran, and cannot but succeed, eventually. If not, to paraphrase Che Guevara: A revolutionary has the right to be tired, but then he or she no longer has the right to call themselves a "revolutionary".

Easy to write, harder to live....

Plan B is failed,
but Plan C will eventually work

It seems as if Iran's Plan B has also failed: winning over half of the West – the European Union.

That would have been a historical revolution... but European firms won't risk sanctions to buy Iranian oil – they saw what Nobel-winner Obama did with Cuba!

The EU absolutely could counter the US sanctions on their firms, but all 27 nations would have to sign off on that, per EU rules. The EU – it must always be remembered – was rushed through after the fall of the USSR and is perhaps the most undemocratic and neoliberal capitalist model in the world. Therefore, they have no intention of doing the right thing for anyone but international stockholders, and certainly not for Iranian Islamic socialists.

Compared to the US, Iran's business is not so vital to Europe. Not just yet... but that bring us to Plan C – China.

If the West will not incorporate revolutionary Iran fairly into the world economy, then Iran will just have to remain firmly revolutionary until China does it from the other end. This is, as I see it, the only solution for Iran following the end of the JCPOA.

Luckily, China is willing and able to do this, thanks to their Belt and Road Initiative (BRI). In January 2016, when a 25-year strategic partnership was agreed between Chinese President XI Jinping and Iran, the two countries announced an agreement to increase bilateral trade from $37 billion in 2017 to a staggering $600 billion by 2026.

Iran is perhaps the most important hub in this plan which will allow the world's two top economies – China and the EU – to trade. Europe will simply have to break with the US when that goes online. Why would they lose out on the huge trade and price savings which China can offer over the US? Like I said, one must totally disregard any consideration but the purest (neoliberal) capitalism in the European Union project, which is based on neoliberalism.

Why do you think the West is so desperate to destroy Iran now? Once BRI goes online, the unprecedented power of the US-led sanctions – which have always been predicated on Europe going along with Washington – will be hugely diminished. BRI won't be fully completed until 2049, but it's getting close to "now or never" for the US regarding Iran.

By signing the JCPOA, making handshake deals and giving lip service to upholding the treaty, we must agree that Europe sees the writing on the wall and thus wants to work with Iran rather than keep losing out, whereas the US remains especially willing to do anything to maintain its faltering domination. For a country which in 2003 was certain of dominating the Middle East, a Middle Eastern economy dominated by Iranian exports must be especially galling; it would also further increase Chinese influence, and also help the EU's independence if they finally allied with Iran.

Thus, the US simply had to blow up the JCPOA, as they are capitalists who do not believe in "mutually-beneficial cooperation", unlike Iran and China.

But it's not all bad: the JCPOA, even in its failure, will be remembered as when Iran started chipping away at the 40-year US-EU tag-team to topple Iran. Frankly, I'm surprised it even made it this far! I am quite skeptical about the diplomatic intentions of capitalist-imperialists…. but you can't miss what you never had, and Iran hasn't had European support since 1979.

It would be nice if Europe honoured the agreement, mainly to immediately reduce the banking pressures on Iran. Iran and the EU had just $20 billion in trade in 2017 (and that was a very good year) – China is already double that, pre-BRI. What Iran needs from Europe is just a second buyer/supplier to keep China honest – that's just capitalism (and just socialism) – but they don't need Europe in order to thrive. Heck, Iran has thrived without Europe just fine.

EU prestige has also been chipped away. The failure to uphold the Iran deal means – especially if Iran decides that their only solution is to get "break out" nuclear bomb capabilities, as stopping nuclear proliferation has been the main propaganda effort in Europe – that the EU's political system will be even more gravely undermined at home. The "international prestige" Europe arrogantly assumes it has is all in their head (racists, hypocrites, egotists, imperialists and cancerous capitalists is how they are viewed by the developing world), but failure to implement the JCPOA shows just how much of a lap dog the EU is to the US, and thus will undermine the EU's self-image.

Not tremendously, of course – it's not like Iran hasn't been the victim of huge Iranophobic propaganda campaigns for 40 years and is a political *persona non grata* – but this is one of those little thorns in the skin (ignored Maastricht votes, Brexit, Catalonia, Yellow Vests, etc.) that will continue to nag, fester, annoy, frustrate and undermine the subconscious of Europe. It's clearer than ever that there is no "European model" anymore – the EU is becoming more like the US in every way, and Macron-led France represents a conclusion of this trend and not a beginning.

There is no doubt about that: examine the neoliberal, corrupt, banker-led, untransparent structure of the Eurozone and one finds an American system, not a European one. So the failure to keep the JCPOA will hurt Europe more than it will hurt Iran in the long run.

What the JCPOA's failure means in Iran: back to business as usual

It's the same old thing – denial of humanity to Iran, and the denial of Iran's humanity.

Iran's economic goals will remain the same either way: national development, increased economic and social justice at home, and the (obviously US-opposed) re-negotiation of its place in the global economic order as a producer rather than mere exporter of natural resources (with Islamic and socialist-inspired constraints self-imposed as well).

Iran has no illusions about what the West wants: they want us to go the Yugoslavia and Libya route, but that's impossible for two reasons:

Firstly, there is no "Croatia & Slovenia" nor "Benghazi-Eastern Libya" to demand an ethnic-based secession – Iran's minorities (Kurd, Arab, Baluch, etc.) are all incorporated into the socialist-multiethnic-patriotic ideology. Yes, they are continually targeted by Mossad, the CIA, et al, and yes this "promote racism" plan has worked so very well for the West in other parts of the world, but there is no comparison between the success of Kurdish integration (for example) in Iran as compared with any other nation with a Kurdish minority. Infamously, the exposure of Mossad agents posing as CIA officers in order to recruit Jundullah separatists in Iranian Baluchistan shows how far they will go to foment unrest, but this only reinforces how comparatively weak such efforts are compared with Yugoslavia and Libya.

Secondly, the incredible growth and popularity of the mass-membership Basij makes such splits impossible. Like them or not, it's a rather genius idea for national stability. The Basij proved in 2009 that they will fight against counter-revolution/huge political changes and, as I detailed, the coming years will only see more Basiji students, more Basiji jobs, more Basiji members, more Basiji government workers, more Basiji parts of the economy – as I concluded: they are on a path akin only to the Communist Party in China.

And that's why we have the economic and political Cold War – the only route available for the West is internal implosion. Again, that's just business as usual – only Iranians who are not paying attention miss this reality.

The same goes for Western journalists, like those who missed US Secretary of State John Kerry accidentally (but finally!) admitting in Paris that the goal of Iran sanctions is to "try to implode" Iran - he says it right here in my 2013 Press

TV report at the 0:58 mark, and I include the link here(before it is completely wiped from the internet): https://www.youtube.com/watch?v=EcQtGqTeR3c

Here is what Kerry said:

"Richard Nixon, at a time when we had no relationship with China, that there were great dangers, had the courage to send Henry Kissinger, and made a decision which opened up China and (which is now) a member of the P5, now works with us in concert to try to implode - put the sanctions in place - to deal with Iran."

Kerry obviously had a major brain freeze, but it was impressive how quickly he righted himself after the *"implode"* slipped out – what a professional imperialist! It was so quick that I didn't even catch it until I re-watched it.

So the JCPOA's failure is not new; the answers for Iran are not new – they must maintain the same revolutionary course, which means more socialist redistribution of wealth in order to keep everyone as reasonably contented as possible amid near-wartime conditions.

Iran will need more protectionist economic policies, but combined with the economic reality that Iran now has even fewer customers to sell to, and that thus these customers can impose more demanding terms to sell their goods inside Iran. There is no way out of this, because Iran cannot eat oil; the idea that acquiescing to this reality will have many accusing Iran of "going neoliberal", but that is not fair and absurd.

Iran doesn't have to re-invent the wheel… although they will be forced to become early adopters of things like a national crypto-currency. They are already testing and planning to go full-bore on crypto, and unlike Venezuela they have the national unity and bureaucratic unity to really make it happen. Indeed, Iran will soon say "In crypto-currency we trust", as it is such an obvious boon to those who hate and who are hated by neoliberal capitalists.

Lastly, I will simply say that Iran does not need another modern revolution in response to the failure of the JCPOA – they just had one, after all. What they need to do is not make the concessions the West is demanding because that is certain to decrease social justice, to increase inequality and to increase instability – such concessions are inspired by capitalist-imperialists!

It's just like Khamenei said in August 2018, and I don't parrot him because I work for PressTV: there will be "no negotiations and no war". He means it is just business as usual. The West is, as usual, making such insane, sovereignty-violating, capitulation-declaring demands in order to even start negotiations; therefore negotiations are done because… they are truly finished – they were called the JCPOA!

However, it should be clear that "no negotiations and no war" is a temporarily depressing formula for a country which hoped for the first detente in 40 years. But for many it's the only formula, because conceding to insane, immoral Western demands has never been an option… and at least it's not war. Iranians – unlike armchair hawks in America – appreciate that.

Modern class issues in Iran – it was easier when it was everyone versus the Shah!

The Green Movement of 2009 proved two important things within Iran: the Revolution had created a new middle class – yet not fully won them over (because their demands changed) – and the Revolution had greatly reduced – and also won over – the lower class.

Class solidarity is never a given thing, except for the 1%: They are always united in working to preserve their own interests.

What did not exist in pre-revolutionary Iran was a middle class: studies showed that in 1976 just 500,000 workers (5% of the employed workforce) could be considered middle class. However, due to the socialist economic policies of the Revolution, Iran's middle class jumped to over 30%. That represents not only a huge socialist success but the BEST socialist success: if socialists are not primarily defined by "empowering the average worker at work and empowering the average citizen in politics" then they are primarily defined by economic policy, and the first responsibility of socialists is to get people lifted out of the lower class. Again, given the nationalist insistence for decoupling from Western capitalism, the anti-capitalist mandates of revolutionary Shi'ism, and the hard facts of the Iranian economic structure post 1979 – this more than 600% increase in the size of the middle class was all achieved by Iranian Islamic Socialism.

But I write that in 2009 Iran had "not fully won them over" because the rich truly are different: middle class demands are different from lower class demands. What the middle class often does is complain about secondary cultural issues, having largely secured answers to life's main economic problems, which are education, health care, jobs, a decent socioeconomic status, etc.

Whether it's the Democratic anti-Trumpers or the Greens in Iran, many middle-class members pretend like they have achieved their privileged position via their moral superiority and hard work when (in Iran's case) it was due to socialist economic central planning and modern revolutionary structures. This narcissism is likely because such middle classes are largely influenced by Western capitalist culture, which unambiguously says on every billboard, magazine page and song lyric: be discontented, get more for yourself, forget solidarity with your "stupid, non-hustling" peers. So the

Green Movement in 2009 truly heralded the power of this new middle class – that's good, and proof of huge redistributive success.

Unfortunately, they marched mainly in order to preserve their interests amid the social justice policies of the Basiji Ahmadinejad, and also to do what the middle class does worldwide in modern, 21st-century countries: complain about cultural issues and hold rather fake-leftist positions.

The good news for the government is: the middle and upper-middle classes don't do counter-revolutions if the lower class has been won over. The middle and upper-class simply do not have the fire or fervor to overpower the numerically larger lower class, and… they eventually admit their existence is already pretty settled and good.

Look at Brazil: Dilma Roussef was only a mildly leftist president (she willingly imposed right-wing austerity measures to deal with the US-caused Great Recession), and it's not as if Brazil ever had a mild leftist revolution. This is why the lower classes did not effectively take to the streets when Roussef was impeached and Michel Temer installed – there was not that much for the lower class to defend! Venezuela had a much more than mild yet not-complete revolution, and in 2017 they had their version of a Green Movement, which was four times as deadly as Iran's, but their lower classes got deadly because Chavismo did win over the lower classes, unlike in Brazil.

So the real risk for Iran post-JCPOA is like what happened in the USSR – betrayal by the upper and politically-elite class, i.e. the biggest beneficiaries of the revolution: all polls in the late 1980s showed overwhelming, democratic, mass support for socialism and continuing with the USSR project, but their "talented 10th" betrayed it.

Regardless of one's sympathy, or not, with the middle and upper-middle classes – Iran simply must win them over. That is what all governments are tasked with – winning over all citizens via good and responsive governance; that is the source of democratic legitimacy (or not).

To win over the middle and upper classes, Iran will have to keep tweaking the balance between Revolutionary Shi'ism and personal freedom; keep tweaking the balance between a revolutionary culture-corrupting glasnost and allowing boundaries to be intelligently pushed. This is the domestic cultural war in Iran... but it should take a backseat to economic issues, and now more than any time since the end of the Iran-Iraq War due to the sanctions.

Iran really only resembles China and Vietnam in this sense, because Cuba and North Korea are not as economically advanced: the challenge for modern and successful socialist-inspired countries is to combine the affluence of capitalism with a revolutionary spirit (and obvious continued redistribution policies). Iran, having had their revolution 30 years after China, is further behind in winning their Western Cold War and also in solidifying their affluence.

I would posit that, after their tantrum in 2009, the middle class is being won over despite the economic hardship. Just look at recent polls, voter turnout and citizen participation in a 10-25 million person group like the Basij – Iranians support their government structure by a huge majority (and, certainly, there is no huge majority support for scrapping the constitution or inviting a Western puppet to rule).

Furthermore, given the unfortunate failure of the Arab Spring and the continued repression of Islamic Democracy and Islamic Socialism, there is increasing acceptance among Iran's middle class that they actually will NOT prosper under a new, radically-different government, as some may have thought previously. The US-EU-UN triple sanctions of 2012 are designed to make this class crazily desperate with envy that they can't "Keep Up With The Kardashians", and have fabulously decadent lifestyles, but it's just not going to work.

But the only way to win over the middle class is: keep winning them over with good governance. That is life and that is the obligation of all just political policies....

The hard part in Iran is done (and this is the source of its revolutionary stability): winning over the working class

The working class is the opposite of the 1% – it's the hardest class to truly inculcate class solidarity into, as it is so broad and thus full of differences. However, Iran has done exactly this, and that is no longer deniable.

Those who led (and the children of those who led) Iran's "Revolution of the Barefooted" - or as I say an Iranian "Trash Revolution" - proved in 2009 that the military does not even need to get involved: there is not enough sentiment to create a counter-revolution. Therefore, 2009 proved who is really in charge in Iran: the working class; the democratic majority.

Modern Iran is no military junta – that's a claim you never hear about Iran because it's so obviously unsupportable; the clergy are not able to render citizens spellbound; the upper-middle class did not begin dictating policy; the only logical conclusion of 2009 is that the working class is in charge of Iran. Indeed, that was the goal in 1979.

The West only dominated and never truly won over their lower classes economically and politically, but China has. Both China and Iran have the goals of classless societies and of immediately prioritising the poorest sections of their societies; Western neoliberal capitalism's stated goal is to create just enough social welfare to prevent people from dying in the streets in public view. Anybody who has needed to collect unemployment insurance or has cashed their grandparent's social security check knows this – former

Rothschild bankers who married chocolate heiresses, like Macron, have no idea.

Indeed, the capitalist-imperialist Western desire to rewrite Iranian democracy is proof that my declaration is correct, as they never want what is best for the average Iranian citizen. Furthermore, the West will only continue to strangle its own citizens as long as it has such neoliberal and anti-democratic structures underpinning the Eurozone, and as long as a woefully-outdated and uber-bourgeois structure is still being worshipped like divine revelation in the US.

But in Iran it is clear that the democratic will is maintained and that social redistribution of power and money have taken place on a nearly unprecedented scale since 1980. This is the only truly necessary economic war, and Iran actually fights this war, unlike the West....

The Iranian lower class, having not reached the economic comfort of the middle and upper-middle classes, will thus continue, with enormous governmental assistance, to work, agitate and organise in the manner they have done for 40 years. That explains why institutions like the Basij will continue to grow in influence, prominence and power as a result of the JCPOA's failure – the "hard-liners" will reap the political benefits.

So to wrap up this chapter: Iran will have to wait for detente a bit longer. The alternative – appeasement – is sure to debase Iran in every way, and thus is not an option, and we all know that and hear that reality every day.

The Basij, the working class and the Principlists (conservatives) will gain from the JCPOA's failure: they have been proven right that the West cannot be trusted, and that protectionism and the unique (revolutionary) economic structures in Iran, which are misunderstood and derided by the ignorant, is the only possible way forward; they will argue economics must stay an intra-Iranian affair as much as possible and be combined with the social justice of revolutionary Shi'ism; they will say that the cuts to the Basiji, whose only criterion is to support the government, cannot be justified morally and cannot be risked politically-culturally by the government.

Or to put it in modern Western terms: the incumbents, perceived as failing, will give way to the opposition party – typical, modern political alternation between mainstream parties.

It is crucial to understand that Reformists agree with and support many of these policies; and also that their efforts to attract foreign investment was more about trying to buy off those sanctioning Iran rather than a desire for unregulated capitalism. The idea that the Reformists are wholly against protectionism, the Basij and the foundations of Revolutionary Shi'ism is totally incorrect… yet common in the West now.

This is what few people truly grasp about Iran, and why the alternation between Principlists and Reformists have not and will not produce major anti-revolution regressions: the incumbents, whether Reformists or Principlists, were revolutionaries, too! Truly, meditate on that reality and you'll understand the long-term trends and realties of Iranian politics much better.

In capitalism the goal is speed – to get rich quick. In Iran the goal has been to reach a destination – a society governed by a modern, socialist-justice obsessed ideology of Iranian Islamic Socialism and not neoliberal capitalism-imperialism.

The world does not decide the goals of Iran – the torpedoing of the JCPOA by the US ultimately makes no difference to Iran. Only Iran can, or should, decide their goals – the world must learn to respect them.

Chapter 12
Conclusion

What's going on Iran is much bigger than just Iran: it always has been.

Just as the US, French and Russian revolutions terrified privileged reactionaries thousands of kilometres away, so the Iranian Islamic Revolution is similarly frightening.

I say this as a completely objective journalist: it is obvious that even if Iran is not a "global revolution" like the three previously mentioned, it is an enormously important multinational and regional revolution – that region being the wildly varied Muslim World.

For four decades Iran has been the leader of Muslim Trash Revolutions: should the West ever call off their war on Islamic democracy, other Muslim nations would surely follow the Iranian democratic model (with local adjustments), and that threatens Western neo-imperialism on a massive scale.

This is already happening in Iraq: there are pro-Islamic nationalists allying with Iraqi communists and pro-Iranian groups in order to wipe away the US-linked comprador establishment. Afghanistan would be the same thing, were war to finally cease. In Syria Bashar al-Assad will likely push for 100% nationalism when the terrorists and their Western allies are ousted from Syrian territory, but in the end he will be fighting the same forces as his father incorrectly did –the democratic inevitability of Islamic Socialism. Algeria can keep propping up their aging, ailing revolutionary class, but how long can they do what they did in the 1990s - deny the electoral victory of Islamic socialist parties via civil war? The Muslim World's monarchies, the embodiment of political regression in the Muslim world, buy off their populace in ways that are economically socialist (yet also nativist) but politically reactionary – is there any doubt that what keeps these countries from modernity is Western support for their unjust monarchs?

Anti-imperialism, anti-capitalism, Islamic democracy – all of these things are anathema to the West… and yet Iran has pursued them successfully despite both hot, cold and perpetual war.

It is quite easy to give statistics which show that Iran's revolution has not achieved its idealistic socialist economic aims, and that too much money is still concentrated in too few hands. Hey, idiot: no nation has perfect statistics when it comes to standards such as these, as all nations are woefully far from economic equality on an absolute scale! Such analyses are political nihilism and lack both nuance and understanding.

But nobody who is actually familiar with Iran – absolutely nobody who has actually set their feet inside Iran – would deny that since 1979 a massive redistribution of wealth and power has indisputably occurred. This fact is something which is glossed over by Western leftists - why, I cannot explain.

This redistribution is one dreamed of for millennia in Iran. The changes have been unbelievable. However, preventing just such a great leap forward in other Muslim nations has been the guiding light of the policies of Washington, London, Paris & Tel Aviv.

Furthermore, Iran is not one of those tiny, largely unimportant, Arctic-touching, isolated, Scandinavian nations which the Anglo-Saxon-led West so often points to as the world's most superior model: Iran is at the heart of the world;

it is filled with and surrounded by black gold, and foreign gold has made Westerners mad since Columbus returned with tales of riches.

Confronted with a million more challenges and violence than the Nordic nations, Iran has been forced to create many innovative policy solutions to modern political problems which the world could learn from and adapt to their own needs. But when it comes to Western leftists and socialists who insist on forced atheism, Iran's biggest sin is that it talks about sin – it is religious – and, for them, this foolishly renders irrelevant absolutely everything else about Iran. Yet Iran is far from being the "fanatics" – it is these Western leftists who are guilty of that, not us!

Western leftists remind me of the delusional, paranoid, sexually-dysfunctional General Jack Ripper in the movie Dr. Strangelove: Or How I Learned to Stop Worrying and Love the Bomb, especially when he was finally confessing his rationale for unilaterally launching nuclear war. Permit me just one change:

> "I can no longer sit back and allow Communist (religious) infiltration, Communist (religious) indoctrination, Communist (religious) subversion, and the international Communist (religious) conspiracy to sap and impurify all of our precious bodily fluids."

LOL, what?

We would feel sorry for impotent General Ripper… were he not hell-bent on destroying the world, rather than accept and tolerate a few ideas of the Communists. The Western left – and of course their far, far greater "fake-left" – view Iran from a perspective which is similarly divorced from reality.

Hopefully this book will change a few minds and create some much-needed tolerance.

I react similarly to those Iranians who claim that Iran does not have revolutionary Shi'ism, but "clerical Shi'ism". This denies the modern, democratic structures, the checks and balances, and the voter oversights of the Iranian political model. And, LOL, you must desire a LOT of "revolutionary Shi'ism" because you are apparently not content with the MOST revolutionary Shi'ism government in world history?!

But this absurd "I'm a revolutionary and an Iranian patriot... but not for this government" is essentially Iran's version of fake-leftism. Such contradictory, ivory-tower contradictions are often heard among the Iranian exile and expatriate community. Their refusal to accept Iran's revolution(ary Shi'ism) – despite its imperfections and the huge handicaps placed on it by the West – when a vast majority of the Iranian nation does accept it, certainly makes one out of touch and obvious opponents of democracy. This leaves them open to accusations that they are self-appointed elitists who simply know better, and who should rule over us Trash.

I would like to thank the World Socialist Web Site for their 3-part series and pamphlet of anti-Ramin Mazaheri thought (LOL), as it was informative, albeit in a very blinkered and limited way; it was not *"a reply to a proponent of Iranian Islamic Socialism"* but really a way to defend their false claim that *"Islamic socialism is a sham"*.

I wonder what they think after reading this book...and if they did?

I humbly suggest that they did not know much about their subject. That is not really the fault of non-Iranians: after all, in the Western languages one never reads anything about the Basij, the bonyads, the 1B/cooperative sector, the progressive political goals of Imams Ali and Hossein, or many of the other points I've raised in this publication. Westerners are not just denied balanced media on Iran but are bludgeoned with five main propaganda lines: religious fanatics, terrorists, hijab law, no alcohol and "millionaire mullahs".

I hope my series has given an alternative, a more insightful, and a more informed picture of modern Iran, especially in the economic and sociopolitical arenas. Very few journalists are writing about leftist economics in Western languages, and seemingly none are writing about Iran.

I am certainly eager to hear anyone's rebuttal... but I predict that any such rebuttal will ignore concrete economic and political realities in favor of limiting the definition of "socialism" to their preferences. This enforced stultification of "what socialism IS" perhaps explains why the Western left has been in such an atrociously bad state ever since around 1979. "Socialism" must grow, must change, must adapt – because otherwise it loses the war waged on it by capitalism-imperialism.

I think the most useful part of this book has been the discussion of the Basij – a 10-25 million organisation of which the West knows practically nothing simply had to be discussed. It's crazy that I am the first to give an objective accounting in a Western language. And, of course the West doesn't talk about it: the Basij has undeniable components of economic and socio-political redistribution – the West NEVER talks about such ideas.

Furthermore, 2009 proved the Basij is - to take a line from George W. Bush - "the decider" in Iranian politics. I reiterate my neutrality on the Basij as being good or bad – I merely suggest one cannot discount the significance of the Basiji in Iranian society.

As for the JCPOA... Iran will get over that – the fake-politics of the West are nothing new, after all.

The real question for Iran to answer is: Who will take over for Khamenei when he passes? From a purely objective point of view as a journalist and based on all available evidence I would posit no leader in the Muslim world has been as successful as Khamenei has since 1989 (it's rather a landslide, too).

Also, it can surely be argued the unique creation of the

Iranian Revolution has been the guardianship of the Islamic jurist. With every continued 21st century advance of neoliberalism and neo-imperialism Western secularism looks more and more like a total failure at best, and very likely a huge mistake at worst - the lack of morality in their public policy is incredibly evident.

Of course, it must never be forgotten that the Supreme Leader is subject to democratic constraints, but as the most powerful individual Islamic jurist the Supreme Leader is of special importance in terms of perception.

I certainly believing that Khamenei's success is due to the revolutionary structure of Iran as a whole, and only partially credit it to Khamenei's personality and ability. However, this does not mean that he is so very easily replaceable. Will his replacement have the revolutionary gravitas to be the Supreme Leader? Will he have the human depth to be the "soul of the government"? The best thing about Khamanei was his political-ideological mastery - can the new Revolution Leader be as politically effective nationally and internationally?

Iran will thus be much like Cuba in 2018, when Raul Castro stepped down as president.

I have good news on that front, as I reported from Cuba during that process for PressTV: I cannot recall meeting even one person who did not support and who was not truly content about the election of Miguel Diaz-Canel as president. Of course, Raul Castro remained the First Secretary of the Cuban Communist Party, so the revolution's leaders still held some influence. Cuba is much poorer and even more sanctioned than Iran – if they can survive amid even worse hardships, Iran can surely make it. Diaz-Canel was a very well-known quantity, as he was a longtime civil servant who rose up through the ranks thanks to repeated success in governance; he was not just a king's son, a lobbyist's puppet or an advertising agency's creation, after all. I think that the new Supreme Leader will be similarly welcomed.

Certainly, when Khamenei does pass on Iran's intense nationalism will kick in like a lead boot across the country, and this is something which will be hugely underestimated by the Western media. Iran will be 100% on guard during this era as well, as the West will be salivating for signs of discord. But after perhaps a couple years of tension, eventually the new Revolutionary Leader will have to rest on his performance.

However, Iranians are also more willfully contrarian than Cubans, so far as I can tell – perhaps Iran should move 100 kilometres from the neo-imperial homeland and see what one risks by playing "devil's advocate"?

In the end – and I toss this in as a reward for anyone who has read this far – I have always felt that what makes Iran truly different (and which is incomprehensible to many outsiders) is that there is a huge difference between "public" and "private" for Iranians.

Americans walk around in public exactly how they walk around their own living room – there is no concept of boundaries. West Europeans can't imagine not insisting on their "rights" to do anything or violate any public boundary as long as it does not result in immediate violence; it's not that life is a beer garden to them, but that they seemingly want people to know that they are on the very precipice of discovering a new "right", and one which they seemingly hope will make you uncomfortable; they don't even use, want or respect these "rights", but they don't want to lose these possessions. The Catholic Western nations are a bit more formal, I'll grant, but they have a love of making a spectacle out of personal drama and tension, which is truly abhorrent to the Asian mentality – the end of summer weather in Paris, for example, means the weekend-night spats between wife and husband, or boyfriend and girlfriend, must now move indoors, mercifully.

Iran is not like that. There is home life, and then there is social life, and never the twain should meet. Iranian culture fundamentally insists that there must be a difference in one's behaviour in these two different realms. To give an extreme, but quick, example: some women in Iran wear the hijab in public but short skirts at home, and they would do this even if wearing the hijab in public was not the law... and no Iranian would deny this is true. This is the "public face/private face" nature of Iranian culture.

This makes Iran fairly subject to accusations of hypocrisy – I can't deny that. However, it also implies a level of public courtesy, respect, generosity and consideration via the virtues of self-denial and self-sacrifice. These virtues are denied by many Westerners, but mainly because Westerners don't perceive such things as virtues anymore, I think. As is usually the case in life, the good and the bad are both true at varying degrees... hopefully the scale is balanced positively in Iran's favor.

What is certain is that something like Iranian Islamic Socialism has been created via the decades-long discovery, installation and victory of Iranian Revolutionary Shi'ism, and that this progressive political advancement remains open to the world. The rejection of monarchy, imperialism and capitalism is not limited to Iranians, nor to Shia Muslims, nor to Muslims, nor to Middle Easterners, nor to Trotskyists, nor to Maoists, nor to any other group.

However, one needs an open mind, first! That is difficult, given the decades of anti-Iranian propaganda –I hope this book helps in countering such propaganda.

Perhaps what is required is the smashing of the final irreligious, anti-Abrahamic idol – the Western concept of "unfettered individualism", which is the foundation of anti-social, immoral and destructive imperialist-capitalism. One cannot live only in solidarity with oneself! Certainly, if the West were not so very self-centered, Iran would be allowed to follow their unique and revolutionary model in peace, finally.

One day, Insh'Allah.
Peace to all.

Chapter 13
2020s begin with assassinations and the reality of neo-colonisations

The historical inevitability of a '1979 US embassy' event in Iraq: not now, but soon

*J*anuary 1, 2020, began with Iraqis pulling back from protests at the US embassy/city-state/Superman fortress of solitude in Baghdad. It was a hopeful way for Iraqis to start the decade: reclaiming freedom after three decades of US domination and terrorism.

Iraq is vitally important to the region for as many reasons as one can think of, and for as long as humans have thought. If the West cannot topple the Iranian Islamic Revolution, they will continue to seek to contain it as much as possible; similarly, if they cannot turn Syria into a Libya-like failed state, they will seek to contain them as well. Lying in the middle of the two is Iraq, which will not go back to a compliant monarchy, and which could serve as not just a vital land bridge but an immeasurably important part of the Muslim World's resistance to neo-colonialism.

The Western new year's eve protests were shocking for many reasons. Iraq has been under the boot of the US for so long many around the world thought such resistance was impossible. But pity the poor, underestimated Iraqis: even when they did engage in civic disobedience the West sought, as usual, to give all the credit/blame to Iran. After dominating them so long, the West is incapable of seeing Iraqis as a people/culture with the power of self-determination. The endless refrain was "Iran-backed militias", but it was Iraqis who staffed and led those militias who crossed into the Green Zone.

Given the three decades of US domination and occupation, how can anyone be surprised that protests targeting the US embassy? Indeed, many Iraqis, especially their young, were probably saying, "Why did it take so long to get here?"

2019 was a momentous year in the Middle East because a local nation - Iran - proved for the first time in two centuries that they have technological and military parity with Western capitalist-imperialists in the war theatre of the Persian Gulf. What the world was shocked to see on the Western new year's eve was a spreading confirmation of these slow, long-building historical trends, processes and facts.

The protests were cheered by many worldwide of course: even if the Western political and media elite has these insane anti-Iran and pro-US capitalism-imperialism blinders on, the average person does not. Many hoped the protests would turn into a new Tahrir Square, like in Egypt, but they were disbanded after only two days.

That seemed like a sad development, but Egypt was not under foreign occupation, after all. I reported from Tahrir Square and the Egyptians repeatedly said the army would never fire on them - it's preposterous to say that Iraqis feel that way about the American army. Many Iraqis justifiably feel they are at war and the embassy protests were an "attack".

The militant protest was sent home because the damage has been done. After all, has the Green Zone ever been so breached?

The psychological and cultural consequences of the two-day affair were thus very similar to Iran's military victories in 2019 - shooting down a US drone, detaining a British-flagged tanker: these were not enormous military victories but they were enormously symbolic and unprecedented in the region. They are not the momentous result of long battles, like ousting ISIL, but instead reflect ongoing, long-term forces which are increasing in inevitability every moment.

Iraq is not Iran, of course, but the events at the Baghdad embassy showed that both cultures view the presence of the US in their country as a major, major source of domestic strife and problems.

The reason a US embassy occupation in Iraq is an historical inevitability is because - despite the "blame Iran" propaganda - there is no chance that the US and Iraqis can have a mutually beneficial co-existence due to: 1) the presence of American soldiers, 2) the three decades of violent war, sanctions and occupation waged by the US, 3) the network of corruption created by US capitalist-imperialist influence and ideology, which ensures only and always a subservient role for Iraq, and which purposely disempowers their full potential, 4) the very ideology, practices and culture of the Washington, which are predicated on competition, violence and corruption, which makes them fundamentally opposed to mutually-beneficial cooperation and especially with non-White/non-Christian cultures.

Yet again in 2019, American planners were dumbfounded, scared and did not know how to react. The US is not powerless in Iraq but for a long moment they felt that way; for a long moment Iraqis felt powerful over Americans. These are not small cultural and psychological things given the Iraqi historical context.

It did not take the US long to show how powerful they are, and also how very brutally inhuman are the methods of imperialists: on January 3, via a cowardly drone strike, the US assassinated Iranian general Qassem Soleimani.

Soleimani was the most popular Iranian figure of his day. He was a major general in the Islamic Revolutionary Guard Corps, and from 1998 onwards he was the commander of the elite Quds (the Arabic word for Jerusalem) Force. He had achieved international acclaim for devising the success resistance against ISIL, and his funeral would bring millions of Iranians out into the streets.

Incredibly, he was assassinated by Washington even though - or perhaps even because - he was in Baghdad's main airport on a key diplomatic mission: he was carrying Iran's response to Saudi Arabia's offer to ease longtime tensions between the two regional powers.

Also killed in the strikes was Abu Mahdi al-Muhandis, the deputy commander of Iraq's Popular Mobilization Forces, often called Iraq's new "Republican Guard".

The happiest people by far were ISIL and other terrorists. It was undoubtedly the most high-profile assassination in decades, and shocked the world.

❖ ❖ ❖

Soleimani: The 'Muslim Che Guevara' dies, but revolutionary culture continues

"A people without hate cannot triumph over a brutal enemy."
~ Che Guevara

Ramin Mazaheri

The assassination on Iraqi soil of Soleimani will produce many things over the long term, and global resentment and hatred for Washington was undoubtedly immediately one consequence

Around the world the assessment was the same: Washington committed an act of war. In their bloodlust to reverse Iran's popular and democratic revolution - in order to keep feeding their bottomless neo-imperial greed - Washington electroshocked the world into remembering its brutal immorality, and the immorality of all imperialist cultures: one remembers the pain of a doctor's needle with more clarity than the pain of a week-long illness, after all.

There will be many long-term ramifications to that cowardly, illegal, inhuman act - such as increased Iranian unity - which so nakedly aimed to be of profit solely to the US elite and not to the average American. However, we should take time to historically assess the true legacy of Soleimani: he is the Muslim Che Guevara.

He is not merely the "Iranian Che Guevara" because that makes no sense given Che's ideals: Just like the Argentinian, Soleimani spent many years of his life fighting US imperialism in many countries, ultimately dying in a foreign land out of his certainty in the reality of international brotherhood.

Limiting Soleimani's legacy to the "Iranian Che Guevara" also makes no sense given the ideals of the Iranian revolution: Soleimani's death reminds the world that Iran - seemingly alone in the anti-imperialist struggle in 2020 - repeatedly gives their time, money, blood, love and lives to non-Iranians out of a sense of progressive political internationalism.

Che Guevara died in October 1967 in Bolivia. The group Che died with was international, including Peruvians, Argentinians, Cubans, Bolivians and even two Europeans. Without Soleimani's presence in Iraq and Syria both of those countries would be under total imperialist domination today, and probably Lebanon as well.

The Iranian revolution is nearly as international in scope and reach as the Cuban revolution Che was a part of creating and defending. Iran's critics say they want to turn every Muslim into a Shia and make the laws of Iran the laws of the entire world…. but that is obviously the hubris and sin of the imperialist West, and is not the goal of Iran's progressive revolution.

Few Westerners seem to realise that the primary motivation of Che - perhaps the very picture of internationalism - was undoubtedly Latin American nationalism: his dream was the same as Bolivar's (and Cuba's Marti and others in Chile, Nicaragua, etc.). For those who see the anti-imperialist struggle with historical accuracy, there is in an obvious parallel here with the "Muslim World nationalism" of Iran's Soleimani.

Only the religion-phobes, the uselessly pedantic and the outright Iranophobes and Islamophobes will fail to see that. It's no matter to billions of people if such persons remain blind:

Just like Soleimani, Che was disavowed by the leading leftists and revolutionaries of his day - the USSR detested Che and his bold resistance to Washington, which few recall. (Like Iran today, Che was appreciative of the Chinese view.) Moscow insisted - in quite Eurocentric fashion - that only they should lead and strategise the fight against Western imperialism. In short: now that the USSR had been liberated from foreign imperialism, nobody else needed to take up arms anymore. Of course, at the time of Che's death the USSR was no longer led by the anti-fascist hero Che affectionately called "Daddy Stalin" - Khrushchev, Brezhnev and finally Gorbachev would grow decadent, corrupt, even renounce Soviet support for international anti-imperialist struggles, and finally wilfully implode the USSR from the very top and against the overwhelming democratic will of the Soviet people.

To the Western leftists - or anywhere else in the world - who can't see clearly: Why did they kill Soleimani, too? Do they still think he was, to use a term popular in the US around 2003, an "Islamo-fascist"? Washington is certainly fascist, but they are not so very Islamophobic to kill someone like Soleimani over his being a Muslim. I hope this group keeps trying - one day they'll finally understand.

Che was assassinated because his explicit goal was to create "multiple Vietnams". Surely many streets will be named after Soleimani in Syria, and Iraq, and even Palestine (if Iran could get some help from Arab nations). Soleimani was undoubtedly a success.

But the invasion, sanctions, re-invasion and occupation of Iraq just never motivated the West like Vietnam. Why? Islamophobia, perhaps. The injustice towards Iraqis did, however, motivate Iranians like Soleimani.

Was Che a success? He failed in Bolivia and the Congo but Cuba remains the "first free country in the Americas", and many would rightly say the only. Less appreciated is how Cuba fought alongside non-Latin Angola - who had the misfortune of being colonised by the most backwards Western imperialist (Portugal) - and how this directly led to the end of Apartheid in South Africa. Che was undoubtedly a success, too.

In the West Che is only a successful way to make money - his face sells all types of merchandise - but the notion that his ideas are remembered, understood or taught is laughable. For the West Che merely symbolises romance, not politics or morality.

If the Iranian reader thinks that continuing the progressive revolution of Che, Soleimani and others is just romance and posing - instead of a necessary self-sacrifice, and one which is undertaken with no expectation of earthly reward (and in fact more likely to produce quite the contrary), in order to prevent brutality and hate from ruining the lives of tens of millions of Iranians - then their popular revolution will fail. Revolutions often fail - ask the French. They still celebrate it every Bastille Day, but that is just more romance and posing.

For those non-Iranians who think the Iranian revolution is not needed globally, and especially regionally, urgently - just go ask an Iraqi, Syrian or Palestinian if they agree. Other countries will be included one day, and I am first thinking of those areas which are so deeply vital to Islamic culture, such as Egypt, Morocco and Arabia. One day the sons and daughters of Che and Soleimani will unite in countries which are neither Muslim nor Latin, Inshallah.

For those who think Soleimani will be the last atrocious slaying it is necessary to recall that the death of Che was only the first - Sukarno, Nkrumah, Ben Bella, Martin Luther King and Robert Kennedy soon followed.

However, we should not forget they were preceded domestically by Malcolm X and John Kennedy - assassination is not at all a new policy for Washington, and we should not imagine that it suddenly is because of Soleimani.

The goal of such assassinations is clear: to discourage future revolutionaries, and also to retard ongoing anti-imperialist movements.

However, I am not worried that the Iranian Revolution will fall with Soleimani, and I mean that with reverence for his sacrifice and achievements: the idea that a popular revolution can (or should) rest on the work of one man alone... this is not revolution, nor popular, but the "great man-ism" of Western capitalism-imperialism. This is Macron, Rhodesia, Louis XIV, Hitler, and, of course, Trump. Contrarily, a successful revolutionary culture produces a progressive system which is able to produce moral and capable leaders over and over and over until the revolution is truly secure. Fortunately, Iranians have more than 40 years of successful revolution upon which to justifiably base their faith in the future.

Trump committed an act of war, but a quick, hasty revenge would have certainly been detrimental to the many just causes Soleimani and others have sacrificed so much for. Soleimani did not become the Muslim Che Guevara and repeatedly triumph over a brutal enemy by placing the good of one person over the good of the nation and the good of the struggle.

Angola provides the best example of how Che's death should have been dealt with: they launched an anti-imperialist offensive called "Che is not dead", which proved to be the beginning of the end of Portuguese control over Guinea-Bissau and then of the entire Portuguese empire by 1974.

In retaliation Iran launched missiles against a US barracks, producing casualties but not deaths - it was a message, but not an upping of the war climate.

Anti-terror hero Soleimani a 'terrorist'?

Back in 2003 the words "quagmire" and "end game" were on everyone's lips - 17 years later the Soleimani assassination forcefully reminded everyone that the Western war on Iraq has still not ended.

The assassination was not part of a "new" war on Iran - it is crucial history in the "old" war on Iraq.

However, fomenting "new war" hysteria with Iran permits the United States to avoid reckoning with the Iraqi proofs of their illegal negligence, hypocrisy and brutality. Looking for a new war with Iran is essentially the lamentable historical continuation of Washington's multi-century policy of, "On to the next tribe of Indian nomads" (even if the Indians weren't a part of nomadic culture).

No American would deny that the Vietnam War changed the very nature of American democracy. Certainly, the slaying of Soleimani was the most shocking military action in many years, and thus it fundamentally altered and magnified how the Iraq War is changing the very nature of American democracy, still.

If World War II was a sober affair, with many Americans genuinely believing in the war's ideals of anti-fascism, Vietnam certainly was not. The widespread rejection of this fanatically ideological war - the "domino theory" of the spreading of "sinister" socialism - ultimately only produced a "pop cultural revolution". There was no civic and political revolution because there was no reform of institutions which had been proven to lack democratic legitimacy.

However, if Vietnam resulted in the average American's open and persistent refusal to believe their government - which was an important historical first for the US - the Iraq War will prove to have been when the average American retained this same correct skepticism but *became unable to publicly admit* their disbelief.

The Iraq War ushered in a new culture of lying for America, where Americans knew they were peddling total falsehoods, and knew that their listeners knew their claims were falsehoods, but there was a collective agreement to keep spreading these falsehoods anyway. It is as if the "American Dream" depended on this collective agreement.

This is how US society reached the point where somebody like Soleimani - who had bravely and unequivocally been an anti-terrorist hero - was publicly accused of being a "terrorist" by American leadership in order to try and justify his assassination.

Because Washington's goals are so imperialist, so rabidly capitalist and so fuelled by feudal realpolitik, instead of acknowledging how Soleimani's leading of the fight against ISIL saved many innocent European and American lives (and even the lives of the mercenary "contractors" from these nations), US Vice-President Mike Pence absurdly said Soleimani was a part of 9/11. Trump said he was justified to plan bombings of "cultural sites", even though everyone knows he meant mosques. Secretary of State Pompeo says the mob hit was "protecting American interests", even though the only Americans truly pleased were also Israeli Zionists.

The epidemic expansion of this American "false life syndrome", which began in 2003, is also behind the pathetic, woefully unfair reason Soleimani is now dead:

The Democratic Party elite refused to admit the real reasons for their democratic unpopularity, so they immediately concocted a diversionary campaign of Russophobia as well as a campaign to impeach Trump (i.e., to undemocratically reverse the election). In January 2020, to distract from that month's impeachment trial in the Senate Trump killed Soleimani. It's more "false life syndrome" because everyone knew the impeachment was the emptiest of politics - Trump was absolutely certain to be acquitted in the Republican-majority Senate. *"Think of the contrast,"* top House Republican Kevin McCarthy wrote on Twitter. *"While Democrats are trying to remove President Trump from office, the President is focused on removing terrorists from the face of the earth."* In an election year Trump needed another WMD-like falsity to perpetuate, knowing full well that it would be publicly perpetuated by many, and so he murdered Soleimani.

What a crying injustice that an international political hero died in large part because of immoral, domestically despised, primary school-level US domestic politics!

Soleimani was killed to preserve US capitalism-imperialist domination of the Muslim World above all, but the dishonest, unreflective political farce which has reigned since 2003 in America is the leading secondary factor.

Soleimani reminded the world of a 21st century truth: Washington defines a terrorist as "someone who disagrees with Washington and Wall Street". Be you Iranian, Iraqi, a journalist like Julian Assange (the greatest journalist of his generation, and the West's preeminent political prisoner) or an average American - oppose US neo-imperialism and neoliberalism and you will be treated as a terrorist.

If Soleimani is a 'terrorist', then when will the US de-list ISIL?

I remember when ISIL first burst into global consciousness - with the fall of Mosul on June 4, 2014. I happened to be visiting my parents.

My mother rushed in and told me that terrorists in Toyotas and new boots had overrun Iraq's second-largest city in a modern-day Mongol Horde.

I rolled my eyes.

I explained to her that, as usual, she was exaggerating. What she was describing was undoubtedly impossible, and I patiently explained why:

The West has satellites which are tracking everyone at every moment - surely they would see fleets of armed trucks speeding towards Iraq. Undoubtedly they would open fire, not only to get the human target practice they so adore but because - despite the alleged "withdrawal" at the end of 2011 - they had over 30,000 American soldiers and contractors in Iraq to protect. Certainly they would have seen this mass army amassing before they ever left their barracks and notified somebody to do something, even if the US didn't want to fight them. Frankly, not even the US would unleash something which my Mom was describing.

Moms... so gullible and prone to worry, eh? They mean

well, but I had no doubt I was totally in the right, and if my Mom wouldn't or couldn't understand... what can a son do but humour their mom?

It turned out that I was the gullible one and that my mom was right. (As I get older I realise this happens more often than I would have previously imagined.)

I was gullible to believe that the US would not do all those things I had told my mom they would not, but I was not totally stupid: The spectacularly swift rise of ISIL still cannot be properly explained by Washington.

WMDs, Soleimani and the creation and support of ISIL - all lies from Washington. If the US did not support ISIL why did Soleimani have to be invited by the Iraqi government to fight them? Either the spectacularly-funded US military is even more rife with corruption than we already know, or they never planned to fight ISIL, but to aid them.

If Washington assassinated Soleimani because he was a "terrorist", then logically they should de-list ISIL as a terrorist group. Why not just come clean, finally?

Above all, it would make it clear that Washington's main enemy in the Muslim World is the continued success and support of the 1979 popular revolution in Iran, and the bad example it sets to their neo-imperial clients worldwide.

Trump's sanctions threat revealed true US plan: total colonization of Iraq

Donald Trump, in his inimitable way, repeatedly revealed to the world the brutal imperialist truths of "democracy with American characteristics" and 21st century capitalism-imperialism.

The Iraqi Parliament immediately voted to expel US troops as a result of Washington's inhuman slayings, butTrump made it very clear: Iraq belongs to the United States, completely.

"*We will charge* (Iraq) *sanctions like they've never seen before, ever. It'll make Iranian sanctions look somewhat tame.*" Trump added the sanctions would be imposed on Iraq, "*if there's any hostility, that they do anything we think is inappropriate.*" *The Washington Post* reported the new sanctions were immediately being drafted.

What Trump did was make a public acknowledgment that the US is never leaving Iraq, will never countenance Iraqi dissent and would rather destroy Iraq than recognise its sovereignty. This was a naked declaration from Trump to Iraq that, "We are your imperial masters."

Iraq cannot even dare to do anything which Washington might consider "*inappropriate*" - the values of Washington decide what is "*inappropriate*" in Iraq, not Iraqi values.

Iraqis, I'm sorry to say, should realise that they have become the 51st US state. (Well, the 52nd, after Puerto Rico.) The Iraqi people have zero sovereignty, its votes are worthless nonsense, and Iraq cannot go against the will of the US federal government any more than Wyoming, Rhode Island or Nebraska can.

My claim here is not an overreaction, and especially when we consider what exactly did Iraq do "wrong" in order to "deserve" sanctions?

Iraq is not Iran - they do not keep defending a popular revolution which successfully mixed Islam and democracy, something the West claims is impossible. Iraq is not North Korea, who refuse to let US troops and corporations based in Seoul move up to the China-Russia border. Iraq is not China, who has a government overseen by a party which refuses to let Western high finance control its major industries. Contrarily, Baghdad has worked with Washington for nearly two decades.

Yes, this work was done at the barrel of a US cannon, but Iraq has complied with US demands. Iraqis have created links, contacts, contracts and all sorts of entanglements with Americans and American businesses.

And yet Trump made it clear that without the presence of US troops that all means nothing.

It is crystal clear that there is zero goodwill from Washington after all these years - zero trust, zero desire to see Iraq stand on its own two feet. Every American smile to an Iraqi inside the Green Zone has been false; every warm word a cold lie.

It was an amazing declaration by Trump - all the years of talk about "humanitarian intervention" and about the US desire to bring "freedom to Iraq" has been declared a sham. This was guessed at by countless billions of non-Western people, but the threat of sanctions which make the Iran sanctions look "tame"... my God, hasn't Iraq complied enough at least to avoid that?!

In many ways, this was all a part of the "beauty" of Trump.

Trump came to office in large part because he says things which Main Street knows but which no mainstream politician would even dare to suggest. Trump is such a terror to the Pentagon, Wall Street, Madison Avenue and the Beltway because Trump could not be trusted to lie properly, like a "respectable" politician, and that made him a risk to US domination.

We cannot imagine Barack Obama bragging about the sanctions he would levy on Iraq if they voted out US troops - he was a smooth-faced liar. Obama would have talked instead about reconciliation with the past, about peace and not justice, about patience... and then he would have "temporarily surged" more soldiers to Iraq.

Hillary Clinton had none of Obama's charm - she would have reacted by boringly referring to the legal obligations of Iraq, to the feasibility of processes, to what the definition here of "vote" is, etc. And then should would have decided on a reaction even more brutal than one Obama or Trump could have conceived.

Any "normal president" would have responded to the Iraqi vote in a way which would have calmed the situation; in a way which would have reassured Westerners that, despite their nagging consciences, they were actually doing moral and humane things in Iraq; in a way which the Western media could use as a weapon against dissenters of Western capitalism-imperialism and to further their insistence of TINA (There Is No Alternative to neoliberalism).

And this is what so many hate Trump for, yet which others value: if the US had a "normal president" many would have complacently and mistakenly continued to believe there is indeed genuine goodwill from Washington towards the Iraqi people. Instead Trump speaks from his gut and made it clear: "Ha!"

It's a big, fat "Ha!" indeed.

Trump is also hated by the US 1% because he egotistically and instinctively wants to take the credit and power inherently contained by this "Ha!", but by doing so he threatens to upset the whole enterprise of US domination; he threatens to provoke resentment which could turn revolutionary.

The Iraqi people need to understand this sadistic laughing, this murderous contempt, this arrogant gloating.Those who want to topple the Iranian Islamic Revolution must understand as well, because Iran will be treated even more punitively.

The world is often fooled by brand repackaging like Obama, (phony, alleged) technocrats like Hillary Clinton and professional foolers like Bill Clinton - nobody is fooled by Trump.

To Trump the Iraqi people did not even have the power of children to mildly rebel, but he is not the only president to hold such an imperial view.

Iraqis only exist to serve the US - this is what Trump's threats to terribly sanction Iraq meant.

The pity of it is that Iraqis already know all about inhuman Western sanctions: I used to ask Iraqi friends how their family was doing amid the US-orchestrated sanctions (1990-2003) and they said, "Please, stop asking - it just gets worse and worse." You know they were inhuman and starvation-inducing by the very name of the "concession" plan the West finally granted - the "oil-for-food program".

Ugh. Iraqis should hope for only Iran-level sanctions, compared to that.

Indeed, it is not a pleasant past, present or future for Iraq.

Their vote to expel US soldiers and reclaim sovereignty was along sectarian lines, just as Washington would have hoped for (or the French in Lebanon, to give another parallel of "Western democratic culture"). It was unanimous, but missing about 150 public servants - Kurdish and Sunni lawmakers didn't vote.

I really don't see what Shia theology has to do with voting against foreign occupation - do Iraqis think the US will tolerate Iraqi soldiers and bases in the US? Do Iraq's non-Shia politicians still think that Washington is their friend and partner? Do non-Shia Iraqis really view their fellow Shia as more dangerous and disagreeable than the current reality - permanent colonisation by the US?

Or are these politicians too close to the US (to use a polite phrase) and not close enough to the lower classes, their crushed reality and and the legitimate demands of the Iraqi people?

Accidental downing of a Ukrainian Airliner reminds world of the dangerous game Washington keeps playing

The January tensions continued: On January 8, just five

days after the assassination of Soleimani, and mere hours after the mild Iranian missile attack on US barracks in Iraq, a terrible tragedy occurred: Ukraine International Airlines Flight 752 was accidentally downed by two Iranian missiles, killing 176 people.

Iran's President Rouhani said, "I will never apologise for Iran - I don't care what the facts are." Tehran plans to never apologise, admit wrongdoing nor to accept responsibility.

All of the Iranian soldiers involved were awarded Combat Action Ribbons, the air-warfare coordinator received a Commendation Medal and the commanding officer was awarded the Legion of Merit for "exceptionally meritorious conduct".

No one in in the Iranian armed forces will ever be punished.

Many believe Iran shot down the plane purposely in order to instigate war.

Obviously, all four of these paragraphs are totally false… but only when applied to Iran and not the US. The shocking belligerence, shamelessness and inhumanity I just recounted was the very real response from Washington after they shot down civilian Iran Air Flight 655 in 1988, killing 290 people.

After three days of investigations Iran admitted the IRGC had accidentally fired the fatal missiles. Given that they had just given what Khamenei called a mere "slap in the face" to the US, it's obviously vital to realise that Iran was still on high alert at the time of the take-off of the Ukrainian airliner. Many have theorised that cyber-warfare was used to mislead Iranian defenses into thinking the airliner was a threat, but at the time of publication of this book that was not yet proven. What is certain is that the war climate provoked by Washington had created the conditions where Iranian soldiers had 10 seconds to decide if something was a plane or a missile, and the wrong decision occurred.

Iran's official response would be the complete opposite of

how Washington handled their very similar tragedy. It was US President George Bush who famously refused to apologise, not Iranian President Rouhani. The commander of Iran's Revolutionary Guards testified to Parliament, "*I swear to almighty God that I wished I were in that plane and had crashed with them....*" Two days earlier the chief aerospace commander told a press conference, "*I wish I was dead and such an incident hadn't happened....*"

The Iranian government showed the humane response which one would expect of a truly progressive government. They did not respond with belligerence, defiance and a Washington-style cover-up.

The assassination of Soleimani and the tragedy of Ukraine Airlines must not be mixed: the former was an illegal, inhuman slaying of an anti-terror hero which must remain in the spotlight until Washington - the boasting perpetrator! - conforms with international justice; the latter was a tragedy, and Iran made it crystal-clear that they will work openly with countries like Ukraine, France and Canada to find the root cause.

There were student-led protests in Iran after the Ukraine Airlines downing, and that was natural: many students were aboard the airplane, therefore many Iranian students had personal connections with the departed.

However, as is the case so often in Iran, counter-revolutionary groups stepped in to dangerously hijack the protests. This was illustrated by a widely circulated video of a "protester" dressed like Black Bloc member stomping on and pulling down a picture of Soleimani, a man who just days earlier had inspired millions to publicly attend his funeral.

The orders-of-magnitude support in Iran for the government, as opposed to those who want to topple it, is revealed by the orders-of-magnitude larger turnout for Soleimani compared with the initially sincere, student-led grief protests. This is a simple, factual reality, but - as is the case with every protest in Iran - the Western MSM tries to pervert everything in Iran to topple the popular democratic revolution of 1979.

Khamenei calls Trump a 'clown', but US murders still the real story

After the Ukraine airliner downing, things cooled down - they reverted back to the war of words: Iranians using normal and intelligent words, the West using tabloid and hysterical words.

Khamenei, led Friday prayers in Tehran's Imam Khomeini Grand Mosque for the first time in eight years. His speech aimed to inspire a Iranian populace quite depressed at the lack of justice in global politics around that time, and also aimed to politically analyse the dangerously critical time in global affairs.

And yet what the Western press took from the key speech was an offhand remark - Khamenei referred to US President Donald Trump as a "clown". Every major Western media led with this remark, as if it constituted a prelude to war.... like it was an assassination.

The outrage was obviously fabricated: during seemingly every single day of the Trump era thousands of US politicians and columnists publicly called Trump a "clown" or worse. The reality is that they seized on that remark because they absolutely do never want to engage in any serious discussion about Middle Eastern tragedies created by Western aggression.

It is very unfortunate that politically-minded Westerners have probably never taken - due to the Iranophobia and Islamophobia campaigns - just two minutes to seriously consider the words and ideas of Khamenei, the man who for decades has led politically the world's most successful resistance to ever-more brutal Western capitalism-imperialism.

Or maybe Western elite just can't stomach just one sermon every 8 years?

Looking past the tossed-off "clown" comment provided a lot of food for thought: Khamenei focused on the shocking disgrace of the US due to their latest assassination. He pointed out that the US kills so very many, many people in the Muslim World and yet they never openly admit it.

For example, every Afghan wedding party bombing is always a "tragic accident".

Such dishonesty really rankles Khamenei - it has always seemed to me that he is incredible insulted by the "arrogance" Washington displays by assuming that nobody can see right through the lies and omissions regarding their war crimes.

However, Khamenei noted that Washington had no choice but to be honest about their shocking slaying of Soleimani and his Iraqi counterparts. And what could be more disgraceful than openly admitting that you are a terrorist?

Again, across the West they preferred to focus on the offhand "clown" remark rather than Khamenei's far-reaching analysis: Soleimani's death is actually a major blow against the West because there is no way the US can undo the damage done to their image - their politicians and system are covered in disgrace.

That is undoubtedly accurate, and why the long-term effects cannot be measured yet.

After reading this book you should understand why Khamenei's analysis is astute - anyone who knows anything about Shia culture and modern Iranian culture knows that Soleimani's death will inevitably become to be viewed as an inspiration, not a failure.

Western journalists seem to only want to talk about a few things - the environment (a political issue which contains zero class component), celebrity culture and how Trump is a clown. When Khamenei says the last one - for some reason it is big news.

That is not the big news.

What is important is the slaying of Soleimani, the Washington-provoked war climate which caused the downing of the Ukrainian airliner, and the duplicitous refusal of the US and Europe to uphold their end of the JCPOA treaty on Iran's nuclear energy program. As 2020 begins, and the decade of Iran-Western diplomacy looks like a certain failure, or at least the duplicitous stalling of Iranian progress on purpose, Westerners will have to re-learn much about Iran and the true goals of the Western system.

Iran has a deeply-embedded revolutionary culture which repeatedly puts the focus on serious things, and that will not change. What will also likely not change is the tabloid, empty focus of Western journalists and politicians, and as someone who inhabits these working worlds I view that as a great unfairness to the people of the West - I hope this book undoes some of the nonsense, and increases mutual understanding.

What is unfortunate for Iran and the Muslim World is that such the Islamophobia and Iranophobic false narratives gives the Western 1% so very much cover to commit so very much war and misery - this is bad for all of us.

This last chapter was the condensed version of a half-dozen columns I wrote for PressTV in January 2020. Given the tragic and historic events to the start of 2020, we hoped readers would be interested.

About the Author

$\mathcal{R}$amin Mazaheri is the chief correspondent in Paris for PressTV. He was educated at the University of Missouri-Columbia and has lived in France since 2009. He has been a daily newspaper reporter in the US, and has reported from Iran, Cuba, Egypt, Tunisia, South Korea and elsewhere. He is also the author of *I'll Ruin Everything You Are: Ending Western Propaganda on Red China*.

Printed in Great Britain
by Amazon